People, Personal Expression, and Social Relations
in Late Antiquity, Volume I

People, Personal Expression, and Social Relations in Late Antiquity, Volume I

With Translated Texts from Gaul and Western Europe

Ralph W. Mathisen

The University of Michigan Press
Ann Arbor

2006   2005   2004   2003   4   3   2   1

A CIP catalog record for this book is available from the British Library.

Library of Congress Cataloging-in-Publication Data

Mathisen, Ralph W., 1947–
    People, personal expression, and social relations in late
antiquity / Ralph W. Mathisen.
    2 v. cm.
    Includes bibliographical references and index.
    ISBN 0-472-11245-7 (v. 1 : alk. paper) — ISBN 0-472-11246-5
(v. 2 : alk. paper)
    1. Rome—Social life and customs.   2. Social classes—Rome.
3. Social status—Rome.   4. Rome—History—Empire, 284–476.
5. Church history—Primitive and early church, ca. 30–600.
I. Title.   II. Series.
DG78.M378   2002
937'.09—dc21   2002009068

To my students:
past, present, and future

Acknowledgments

Grateful acknowledgment is made to the Penguin Group (UK) for permission to reprint translations from *Gregory of Tours. The History of the Franks,* translated by Lewis Thorpe (Harmondsworth: Penguin Books, 1974).

Preface

Recent years have seen a tremendous explosion of interest in the literature of Late Antiquity, which has been manifested in the publication of both Latin texts and English (not to mention other language) translations. Large numbers of editions of late antique authors have appeared in collections such as the *Corpus christianorum (CCL)*, the *Corpus scriptorum ecclesiasticorum Latinorum (CSEL)*, the *Sources chrétiennes (SC)*, and the Budé, Loeb, and Teubner series. Many Latin source collections, such as the *Acta sanctorum, CCL*, the *Monumenta Germaniae historica,* and the *Patrologia Latina* also are now available in electronic format.

If the Latin texts appeal primarily to specialists, the appearance of many translated works relating in a greater or lesser way to Late Antiquity have made this literature available to a vastly expanded audience. In particular, one notes the many late antique authors and works that have recently appeared in the University of Liverpool's "Translated Texts for Historians" series, including Avitus of Vienne, Cassiodorus, "Chroniclers of Early Medieval Spain," the *Chronicon paschale,* Eutropius, Gregory of Tours's hagiographical works, Hilary of Poitiers, the *Liber pontificalis,* "The Lives of the Visigothic Fathers," Optatus, Ruricius of Limoges, Vegetius, Venantius Fortunatus, and Victor of Vita, to name a few. Many other translated works also have been published, such as C. E. V. Nixon and Barbara Saylor Rodgers, trans., *In Praise of Later Roman Emperors* (Berkeley: University of California Press, 1994). And these are all in addition to the massive number of authors translated in the "Fathers of the Church" and "Ancient Christian Writers" series, not to mention the translation series of the University of Pennsylvania Press and Columbia University Press, many of which are cited in the bibliography.

Along with the works that have been translated in toto, there also have appeared a large number of collected sources in translation. Particularly noteworthy are A. D. Lee, *Pagans and Christians in Late Antiquity: A Sourcebook* (London: Routledge, 2000); M. Maas, *Readings in Late Antiquity: A Sourcebook* (London: Routledge, 2000); and A. C. Murray, *From Roman to Merovingian Gaul: A Reader* (Peterborough, Ont.: Broadview, 2000). Also worth noting is Patrick J. Geary, ed., *Readings in Medieval History* (Peterborough, Ont.: Broadview, 1989), not to mention earlier collections such as J. N. Hillgarth, ed., *The Conversion of Western Europe, 350–750* (Englewood Cliffs, N.J.: Prentice-Hall, 1969); and C. D. Gordon, *The Age of Attila: Fifth-Century Byzantium and the Barbarians* (Ann Arbor: University of Michigan Press, 1966). Yet other collections of translations focus on specific genres, such as hagiography: one notes Jo Ann McNamara, John E. Halborg, E. Gordon Whatley, trans., *Sainted Women of the Dark Ages* (Durham, N.C.: Duke University Press, 1992), a useful adjunct to the earlier F. R. Hoare, trans., *The Western Fathers: Being the Lives of Martin of Tours, Ambrose, Augustine of Hippo, Honoratus of Arles, and Germanus of Auxerre* (New York: Sheed and Ward, 1954) and William C. McDermott, ed., *Monks, Bishops and Pagans: Christian Culture in Gaul and Italy, 500–700* (Philadelphia: University of Pennsylvania Press, 1975).

Some of these collections, such as those of Lee and Murray, introduce new translations done by their editors, but most of them recycle existing translations. In all cases, the compilers have diligently ferreted out selections (rarely more than a few pages in length, and often just a few lines) relating to assorted topics such as "The Roman Empire," "The Roman Army," "Christianity," "Law," "Barbarians," and so on. All of these source collections are useful as adjuncts to historical narratives. But none has any real connective tissue.

It was in the context of a growing number of translations lacking in extended historical, cultural, and literary contexts that Jim O'Donnell suggested in 1991 that I think about using texts and translations to create a book "that is *not* 'just' a textbook or a reader or a sourcebook-in-translation, but a work of scholarship too." My task, working with Ellen Bauerle of the University of Michigan Press, was to put a collection of texts into a scholarly context, to present the texts not only as texts-qua-texts, but also as an integral part of a scholarly discussion, that is, to use them to show something. What I proposed doing was to use extended source citations to provide some in-depth insight into the people of Late Antiquity by focusing on their human sides: their personal interactions, their prejudices, their ambitions, their faults, their kindnesses, their successes, and their failures. Such a study would of necessity be largely anecdotal, for it would use personal experiences that often appear only as obiter dicta to illustrate in a microcosm the kinds of situations that people confronted on a global scale.

It soon became clear that incorporating the Latin texts into the same volume as the translations was not going to work. Not only would the resultant volume have been hopelessly cumbersome, but the translations and the Latin also largely had two different audiences, that for the first being predominately historians and the general public, whereas that for the latter would be primarily advanced Latin students. This difficulty was solved by creating two parallel volumes, one of which wove the translations into a coherent narrative, and the other of which presented a collection of Latin texts that could be either read in tandem with the volume of translations, or used alone as a late antique Latin reader.

What the first volume proposes to do, therefore, is to use translated passages to present a fleshed-out and integrated view of late antique society. Rather than offering a glut of disjecta membra ("here's one brief excerpt, and here's another, and another"), much longer passages are selected that are used to create a connected account that portrays, "up close and personal," how the people of Late Antiquity lived their lives and interacted with each other. The second volume, on the other hand, focuses on the Latin words and texts in which these people expressed themselves. Further discussions of the nature of each volume appear in their respective introductions.

These two volumes have gestated for a long time. Completed versions were delivered to the Press in 1997, and, following editorial review, updated versions was delivered in May of 2000. A number of people have contributed their thoughts, comments, and criticism along the way. Along with Jim, Ellen, and James Laforest of the Press, Hagith Sivan of the University of Kansas made valuable comments on an early draft. After Ellen's departure from the Press, the manuscript benefitted from the helpful shepherding of Colin Day, Collin Ganio, Jennifer Wisinski, Erin Snoddy, and Christina Milton. Along the way, Danuta Shanzer of Cornell University provided innumerable helpful hints regarding late Latin usage. But it is my students who have provided the most important ideas and insights relating to how these volumes could have the greatest impact, and it is to them that they are dedicated.

Contents

Abbreviations

Anderson, *Sidonius*	Sidonius Apollinaris. *Poems and Letters.* Trans. W. B. Anderson. 2 vols. London: Loeb, 1936, 1965.
Avit.	Alcimus Ecdicius Avitus, bishop of Vienne.
Carm.	*Carmina* (Poems).
CCL	*Corpus Christianorum, series Latina.*
CIL 12	O. Hirschfeld, ed. *Corpus inscriptionum Latinarum.* Vol. 12: *Inscriptiones Galliae Narbonensis Latinae.* Berlin, 1888.
CIL 13	O. Hirschfeld, C. Zangenmeister, A. von Domaszewski, O. Bohn, and E. Stein, eds. *Corpus inscriptionum Latinarum.* Vol. 13: *Inscriptiones Trium Galliarum et Germaniarum Latinae.* Berlin, 1899–1943.
CLRE	R. S. Bagnall, A. Cameron, S. R. Schwartz, and K. A. Worp. *Consuls of the Later Roman Empire.* Atlanta: Scholar's Press, 1987.
CSEL	*Corpus scriptorum ecclesiasticorum Latinorum.*
CTh	*Codex Theodosianus* (Theodosian Code).
Dalton, *Gregory*	*The History of the Franks by Gregory of Tours.* Trans. O. M. Dalton. Vol. 2. Oxford: Clarendon, 1927.
Dalton, *Sidonius*	*The Letters of Sidonius.* Trans. O. M. Dalton. 2 vols. Oxford: Clarendon, 1915.
Duchesne, *Fastes*	L. Duchesne. *Fastes épiscopaux de l'ancienne Gaule.* 2d ed. 3 vols. Paris, 1907–15.

Epist.	*Epistulae* (Letters).
Faust.	Faustus, bishop of Riez.
Gennad. *Vir.ill.*	Gennadius of Marseille. *De viris inlustribus* (On illustrious men).
Greg.Tur. *Glor.conf.*	Gregory of Tours. *Gloria confessorum* (Glory of the confessors).
Greg.Tur. *Glor.mart.*	Gregory of Tours. *Gloria martyrum* (Glory of the martyrs).
Greg.Tur. *Hist.*	Gregory of Tours. *Historiae* (Histories); also known as the *Historia Francorum* (History of the Franks) or the *Decem libri historiarum* (Ten books of histories).
Greg.Tur. *Vit.pat.*	Gregory of Tours. *Vita patrum* (Life of the Fathers).
Mathisen, *Ruricius*	Ralph W. Mathisen. *Ruricius of Limoges and Friends: A Collection of Letters from Visigothic Aquitania.* Liverpool: University of Liverpool Press, 1999.
MGH AA	*Monumenta Germaniae historica, Auctores antiquissimi.*
MGH Epist. 3	W. Gundlach, ed. *Monumenta Germaniae historica, Epistulae.* Vol. 3. Berlin, 1892.
MGH Leg.	*Monumenta Germaniae historica, Leges.*
MGH SRM	Bruno Krusch and (for vol. 1, pt. 1) Wilhelm Levison, eds. *Monumenta Germaniae historica, Scriptores rerum Merovingicarum.* 7 vols. Hannover: Hahn, 1884–1979.
Pharr, *Theodosian Code*	Clyde Pharr. *The Theodosian Code and Novels and the Sirmondian Constitutions.* Princeton: Princeton University Press, 1952.
PL	J.-P. Migne, ed. *Patrologia Latina.*
PLRE	*The Prosopography of the Later Roman Empire.* Vol. 1: A.D. *260–395,* ed. A. H. M. Jones, J. R. Martindale, and J. Morris. Vol. 2: A.D. *395–527* and Vol. 3: A.D. *527–640,* ed. J. R. Martindale. Cambridge: Cambridge University Press, 1971, 1980, 1993.
PLS	*Patrologia Latina, supplementum.*

Ruric.	Ruricius, bishop of Limoges.
Salv.	Salvian of Marseille.
SC	*Sources chrétiennes.*
Sid.Apoll.	Sidonius Apollinaris, bishop of Clermont.
Thorpe, *Gregory*	*Gregory of Tours. The History of the Franks.* Trans. Lewis Thorpe. New York: Penguin, 1974.

Introduction: Historical
Background and Sources

As a period, Late Antiquity falls between classical antiquity on the one hand and the Middle Ages on the other. It generally is considered to have spanned the years from A.D. 260, the beginning of the reign of the Roman emperor Gallienus, until 641, the death of the Byzantine emperor Heraclius. But the dates are flexible and often are extended a century or more on either end.[1] Segments of Late Antiquity also go by several other names. In western Europe, one encounters the Later Roman Empire (ca. 284–480) and the Early Middle Ages (from as early as ca. A.D. 480, if not before).[2] In the east, there are the East Roman Empire or the Early Byzantine Empire (beginning as early as A.D. 284), and the early Islamic period (after ca. A.D. 600). These kinds of periodicization imply that Late Antiquity was either the end of (i.e., "Late") something or the beginning of (i.e., "Early") something. But, in reality, Late Antiquity was something in its own right.[3]

In the west, Late Antiquity saw the gradual withering of classical society, government, and religion, and the formation of a strictly western European, Christian society that eventually would culminate in the

---

1. Some would expand the dates and include the period, for example, from Marcus Aurelius (161–80) to the ninth century. For an overview, see G. W. Bowersock, Peter Brown, and Oleg Grabar, eds., *Late Antiquity: A Guide to the Postclassical World* (Cambridge, Mass.: Harvard University Press, 1999), where a period of A.D. 250–800 is suggested.

2. Some medievialists, however, consider the Early Middle Ages to have begun circa the ninth century.

3. A point made by many recent studies, but perhaps most influentially by Peter Brown, *The World of Late Antiquity* (New York: Harcourt Brace Jovanovich, 1974); see also Ralph W. Mathisen and Hagith S. Sivan, eds., *Shifting Frontiers in Late Antiquity* (Aldershot: Ashgate: 1996).

modern-day western European nations. As for eastern Late Antiquity, the Roman Empire continued and evolved as the "Byzantine Empire," and the seventh century saw the birth of another major world religion, Islam, along with the Islamic caliphate.

This volume will be concerned with two factors that hitherto have interfered with our ability to appreciate the full significance of Late Antiquity in western Europe.[4] They involve, on the one hand, our perceptions of society, and, on the other, our uses of the source material.

Perceptions of Society

The first consideration relates to people. All too often, in both the ancient and the modern sources, one sees only "official" personalities: individual aspirations and activities are portrayed primarily as they related to politics (both secular and ecclesiastical), official duties, military encounters, or formal-cum-public social interactions. On top of that, these depictions deal almost exclusively with the male, aristocratic elite.

The following presentation will provide insights into personalities by highlighting the individual, nonpublic, and nonelite sides of society.[5] Attention will focus upon personal concerns and desires, private interactions, and family life, including detailed consideration of the roles of women and children, who often do not appear in a natural manner in the traditional sources. It will be seen that the communities of Late Antiquity were comprised of real people who lived in real places and who had real hopes, interests, and apprehensions. The development of late antique society will be portrayed from the perspective of the people who experienced it and made it happen. Even if they were unaware that they were part of pivotal historical processes,

---

4. It also is intended to underscore the role played by western Europe in establishing the character of Late Antiquity, in contrast to the easternizing perspective of other volumes, such as Bowersock, Brown, and Grabar, *Late Antiquity.*

5. Since 1990, increased and welcome attention has been given not only to the role of nonelites, but in particular to the role of women in Late Antiquity; see G. Clark, *Women in Late Antiquity: Pagan and Christian Lifestyles* (Oxford: Clarendon, 1993); and A. Arjava, *Women and Law in Late Antiquity* (Oxford: Clarendon, 1996); note also Jo Ann McNamara and John E. Halborg with E. Gordon Whatley, eds. and trans., *Sainted Women of the Dark Ages* (Durham, N.C.: Duke University Press, 1982). There also have been many studies since the 1980s on the role of women later in the Middle Ages; see, *inter alios,* D. Herlihy, *Opera muliebra: Women and Work in Medieval Europe* (Philadelphia: Temple University Press, 1989).

their individual stories illustrate in a microcosm the global changes that were occurring.

This was a period of social disruption. The old paternalistic Roman social system, of course, still endured, with male aristocrats monopolizing the social prestige and political authority. But the survival of this regime was threatened by three momentous developments: the rise of the Christian church, the disintegration of the Roman Empire in the west, and the establishment of the barbarian kingdoms.[6] The old Roman secular male elite became infiltrated by a new ecclesiastical and barbarian male elite. Furthermore, previously nonelite groups, be they the less socially privileged, the economically disadvantaged, or those marginalized because of their ethnicity or gender, were able to find niches of opportunity provided by the changing times.

The ostensibly rigid social hierarchy, with its great gulf between the privileged and the unprivileged, was tempered by "safety valves" that allowed persons from disadvantaged groups to enjoy types of self-expression that normally were monopolized by the more privileged. By examining the activities of these individuals one can gain a more nuanced appreciation of the significance that Late Antiquity had for society as a whole. The resulting picture will be more representative of the entire population, less a reflection of a few famous men.

In such a context, traditional references to "members" of "upper" and "lower" classes cannot accurately describe the social realities of Late Antiquity. In the model presented below, individuals participate simultaneously in social circles based upon gender, religion, ethnicity, legal and economic status, and family relationship. In each instance, their degree of privilege and their status relative to others are determined not only by societal perceptions of them but also by their own idiosyncratic abilities to pursue their personal ambitions, aspirations, and interests.

---

6. Throughout antiquity, the term *barbarian* was used to signify otherness, that is, "them" as opposed to "us." It did not uniformly denote a particular ethnic background. It was used by Greeks to describe Romans, by Romans to describe Germans, and even by Germans to describe other Germans. By ca. A.D. 600, it ceased to have any effective meaning even as a generic ethnic indicator. Here, it is used as a convenient nonpejorative term to describe all of the new arrivals in the Roman world in the late fourth century and afterward: See Ralph W. Mathisen, *Roman Aristocrats in Barbarian Gaul: Strategies for Survival in an Age of Transition* (Austin: University of Texas Press, 1993), 1–5; and Walter Pohl and Helmut Reimitz, eds., *Strategies of Distinction: The Construction of Ethnic Communities, 300–800* (Brill: Leiden, 1998).

The Source Material

The second purpose of this book is to focus on the sources qua sources. Much of the literature of Late Antiquity has not been adequately studied. Some works have not yet even been placed in their proper chronological, geographical, or historical context. Several different kinds of sources will be cited, translated, and examined below. But this volume is not intended simply to be a "late antique reader" that spans centuries and continents. Its primary focus will be upon a relatively homogeneous group of Latin sources from Gaul, with occasional forays for comparative purposes into Britain, Spain, and Italy. Doing so will provide coherence in time and space. There will be no assumption, for example, that the people of the eastern Mediterranean had the same perceptions and values as those of continental Europe.

Moreover, in order to investigate the topic of "personal expression" as thoroughly as possible, it will be necessary to seek out other material over and above such commonly cited sources as Sidonius Apollinaris and Gregory of Tours.[7] Late Antiquity was a very productive period in a literary sense, and other, less trodden, ground can yield invaluable insights. Particularly priceless in this regard are personal correspondence (such as the letters of Ruricius of Limoges), secular official documents (such as *formulae*), records of church councils, saints' lives, the stray drama, and inscriptions. Several rarely cited documents by and about women are particularly instructive.

This volume also will employ extended quotation of sources. All too often, it seems, the literary remains of Late Antiquity have been used as a mine from which nuggets of information—single words or phrases—have been gleaned for this or that purpose. This practice is not always conducive to interpreting a piece of literature in its proper historical, cultural, religious, or literary context.

One particular consideration is that the literature of Late Antiquity cannot be assessed, as if often is, in terms of the familiar literature of classical antiquity. It is not simply an insipid, debased, or repetitive version of Cicero or Vergil. The cultural and intellectual environment of the year A.D. 450 was vastly different from that of, say, 50 B.C. or A.D. 50. Society had evolved. Culture had become more eclectic. Literary style had been transformed. Religious issues in particular came to

---

7. Ten letters of Sidonius are included below; there are more citations from Gregory, primarily in the last two chapters.

monopolize the attention of the most talented and influential writers. One need not assume, as many have done, that the literature of Late Antiquity was somehow worse than that of the Augustan era; it was merely different.[8] The conventions and themes of late antique literature reflected the preferred style of the age.[9] Every bit as much as the literature of classical antiquity, the literature of Late Antiquity needs to be interpreted and appreciated in the context of its own times.

Late Antiquity is represented by a multitude of authors, many of whose works are still extant. Even contemporaries had a hard time keeping track of them all. Several writers, including Jerome (ca. A.D. 400), Gennadius of Marseille (ca. 495), and Isidore of Seville (ca. 630), compiled literary dictionaries entitled *De viris illustribus* (On illustrious men) that probably represented the contents of their personal libraries.[10] Gennadius's collection, also known as *De scriptoribus ecclesiasticis* (On ecclesiastical writers), contained brief biographical sketches highlighting the literary accomplishments of some one hundred authors. Most of the entries are jejunc lists of compositions, such as the entry on Gennadius himself:

.1[11]   I, Gennadius, a priest of Marseille, wrote eight books *Against All Heresies,* also six books *Against Nestorius* and six books *Against Eutyches,*

---

8. Even students of Late Antiquity have disparaged the quality of the literary remains. See Ramsay MacMullen, *Corruption and the Decline of Rome* (New Haven: Yale University Press, 1988), 2 ("Literature declined"); André Loyen, *Sidoine Apollinaire et l'esprit précieux en Gaule aux derniers jours de l'Empire* (Paris: Les Belles Lettres, 1943), 166 ("escapist," "puerile," "pedantic," and "superficial"); T. R. Glover, *Life and Letters in the Fourth Century* (Cambridge, 1901; rpt. New York: G. E. Stechert, 1968), 11 (a "sterile age"); C. E. Stevens, *Sidonius Apollinaris and His Age* (Oxford, 1933), 81 ("continual cultural decay"); Samuel Dill, *Roman Society in the Last Century of the Western Empire* (London, 1899; rpt. New York: Meridian, 1958), 438–39 ("a rapid movement of decline" and "a failure of mental energy").

9. See, e.g., Michael Roberts, *The Jeweled Style: Poetry and Poetics in Late Antiquity* (Ithaca, N.Y.: Cornell University Press, 1989), countering the claims, e.g., of Erich Auerbach, *Literary Language and Its Public in Late Latin Antiquity and in the Middle Ages,* trans. Ralph Manheim (New York: Pantheon Books, 1965), 258, that late antique writers were "hopelessly cut off from reality."

10. Jerome and Gennadius: G. Herding, *Hieronymi De viris inlustribus liber* (Leipzig, 1879, 67–112; E. C. Richardson, ed., *De viris inlustribus,* Texte und Untersuchungen zur Geschichte der altchristlichen Literatur 14.1 (Leipzig, 1896), 1–56; Isidore: *PL* 83:1081–1106.

11. Gennad. *Vir.ill.* 99: E. C. Richardson, ed., *Jerome and Gennadius, Lives of Illustrious Men* (New York, 1892), 112; *PL* 58:1120 (no. 100). For Gennadius's *Liber ecclesiasticorum dogmatum* (Book of ecclesiastical teachings), see *PL* 58:970–1054. The other works are not extant.

and three books *Against Pelagius,* and the tracts *On the Thousand Years* and *On the Apocalypse of the Blessed John,* and this work; and I sent a letter *On My Faith* to the blessed Gelasius, bishop of the city of Rome.

Occasionally, Gennadius's compilation included more detailed biographical information, as in the entry on the Gallic blue blood Gaius Sollius Sidonius Apollinaris (ca. 432–485). Sidonius was the son-in-law of the emperor Eparchius Avitus (455–456), served as prefect of Rome in 468, and then, like many Gallic aristocrats, finished his career in the church, becoming bishop of Clermont circa 469. His letters are one of the best, and most cited, sources for Gallic history and personalities. According to Gennadius,

I.2[12]   Sidonius, bishop of Clermont, wrote works that are varied, pleasing, and doctrinally sound. He was a man of piercing intellect, fully cultivated in matters both religious and secular; he wrote a noteworthy volume of letters to diverse individuals, composed in diverse meters and prose, in which he demonstrated his literary ability. Truly strong in Christian vigor, even in the midst of the harshness of the barbarian ferocity that then oppressed Gaul, he is considered to be a catholic father and a distinguished scholar. He flourished at the time when Leo and Zeno[13] ruled the Romans.

A few words now might be said about the different genres of literary material. An important category for the study of personalities is epistolography, or letter writing. A greater number of letters and collections of letters survives from Late Antiquity than from any previous period. Correspondence served as a means by which increasingly isolated senators, and in particular ecclesiastics, could maintain their social, intellectual, and political ties with each other.

In the early fifth century, collections of the letters of the pagan senator Symmachus of Rome, and of the bishops Paulinus of Nola and

---

12. Gennad. *Vir.ill.* 92: Richardson, *Jerome and Gennadius,* 109; *PL* 58:1114–15. This chapter appears in only three of the manuscripts and like six other entries, including those on Gelasius and Gennadius himself, may have been an early posthumous addition.

13. Leo ruled 457–74, and Zeno 474–91. Sidonius seems to have died ca. 485.

Ambrose of Milan, were compiled and circulated.[14] Shortly thereafter the letters of Jerome (a priest of Bethlehem also known by his Latin name, Hieronymus) and Augustine (bishop of Hippo in North Africa) appeared, followed toward the end of the century by the Gallic collection of Sidonius Apollinaris.[15] At the beginning of the sixth century, in Gaul, the collections of Ruricius of Limoges (ca. 485–510), Magnus Felix Ennodius of Pavia (ca. 514–521), and Alcimus Ecdicius Avitus of Vienne (ca. 490–518) were compiled.[16] Smaller groups of Gallic letters survive for the monk Sulpicius Severus (ca. 400), the priest Salvian of Marseilles (ca. 425–490), and the bishops Eucherius of Lyons (ca. 432–451), Faustus of Riez (ca. 462–490), Remigius of Reims (ca. 480–533), and Caesarius of Arles (502–540).[17] Many other writers are represented by but a single letter.[18] And it should be noted that women as well as men participated in the exchanges of letters, even if theirs seldom survive.[19]

These letters provide evidence for the continued pleasure taken in classical scholarship. They gave their writers, most of whom were

---

14. Symmachus: O. Seeck, ed., *MGH AA* 6.1 (Berlin, 1883); Ambrose: O. Faller, ed., *CSEL* 82 (Vienna, 1968); *PL* 16:913–1342; Paulinus of Nola: G. de Hartel, ed., *CSEL* 29 (Vienna, 1894).

15. Jerome: *Lettres,* ed. and trans. Jérôme Labourt, 8 vols. (Paris: Budé, 1949–63); I. Hilberg, ed., *CSEL* 54–56 (Vienna, 1910–18); Augustine: A. Goldberger, ed., *CSEL* 34, 44, 57–58 (Vienna, 1895–1925); J. Divjak, ed., *CSEL* 88 (Vienna, 1981); Sidonius: Anderson, *Sidonius; Sidoine Appollinaire,* ed. and trans. André Loyen, vols. 2–3 (Paris: Les Belles lettres, 1970); P. Mohr, ed. (Leipzig: Teubner, 1895); C. Leutjohann, ed., *MGH AA* 8 (Berlin, 1887); Dalton, *Sidonius.*

16. Ruricius: A. Engelbrecht, ed., *CSEL* 21 (Vienna, 1891), 349–450; B. Krusch, ed., *MGH AA* 8 (Berlin, 1887), 299–350; R. Demeulenaere, *CCL* 64 (Turnholt, 1985); Ennodius: F. Vogel, ed., *MGH AA* 7 (Berlin, 1885); G. de Hartel, ed., *CSEL* 6 (Vienna, 1882); Avitus: R. Peiper, ed., *MGH AA* 6.2 (Berlin, 1883). Such collections often were not "standardized" and were of a private nature.

17. Sulpicius Severus: C. Halm, ed., *CSEL* 1 (Vienna, 1866); Salvian: G. Lagarriguc, ed., *SC* 176, 220 (Paris, 1971, 1975); F. Pauly, ed., *CSEL* 7 (Vienna, 1883); C. Halm, ed., *MGH AA* 1.1 (Berlin, 1877); Eucherius: C. Wotke, ed., *CSEL* 31.1 (Vienna, 1894), *PL* 50:701–26; Faustus: *CSEL* 21; *MGH AA* 8:265–98; Remigius: *MGH Epist.* 3; Caesarius: G. Morin, ed., *Sancti Caesarii Arelatensis opera* (Maretioli, 1942).

18. See R. Mathisen, "Epistolography, Literary Circles, and Family Ties in Late Roman Gaul," *Transactions of the American Philological Association* 111 (1981): 95–109.

19. We usually know of women's correspondence through the surviving replies of their male correspondents: Sidonius, for example, includes a letter to his wife Papianilla, Ruricius several to his friend Ceraunia, and Ennodius quite a few to a number of women. Jerome's and Augustine's earlier correspondence with women is well known.

ecclesiastics, an opportunity to exercise their rhetorical ingenuity, and thus can make for some difficult reading. Moreover, because letters could be a very private kind of literary expression—although one always must be aware that published letters were intended for public consumption, and the writers sometimes had an ax to grind—they also are an excellent source of personal expression and anecdote.

Hagiography, the composition of saints' lives *(vitae),* was another popular literary genre, and different regions competed to promote the merits of their favorite sons and daughters.[20] Hagiography, moreover, was not merely an equivalent of biography.[21] In a saint's *vita,* the message was much more important than the minutiae. The author wished to show how the saint exemplified Christian virtues, not to write a history.[22] Nonetheless, many historical events, and in particular many examples of social activities, were incorporated as a matter of course. And because hagiographers were not trying to interpret history, they also were not trying to distort it. Therefore, one usually has little reason to question a writer's good faith as to what is reported in a reasonably contemporary *vita,* even if the author's historical judgment and critical acumen might be defective, and the facts faulty. Saints' lives written centuries after the fact, however, were naturally much more subject to embroidery if not outright fabrication.

As for history, few fifth- and sixth-century authors turned their attention in this direction. Sidonius, for example, declined to write a history of his own times because to do so would have meant that "either falsehood be spoken with disgrace or the truth with peril."[23] The works of most of those who did write contemporary history do not survive.[24] The most significant extant narrative of these times was writ-

---

20. See H. Delehaye, *Les passions des martyrs et les genres littéraires,* 2d ed. (Brussels: Société des Bollandistes, 1966); McNamara, Halborg, and Whatley, *Sainted Women;* and Thomas F. X. Noble and Thomas Head, eds., *Soldiers of Christ: Saints and Saints Lives from Late Antiquity and the Early Middle Ages* (University Park: Pennsylvania State University Press, 1995).

21. See P. Cox, *Biography in Late Antiquity: A Quest for the Holy Man* (Berkeley and Los Angeles: University of California Press, 1983).

22. See Peter Brown, "The Rise and Function of the Holy Man in Late Antiquity," *Journal of Roman Studies* 61 (1971): 80–101, and *Society and the Holy in Late Antiquity* (Berkeley and Los Angeles: University of California Press, 1982); and Raymond Van Dam, *Saints and Their Miracles in Late Antique Gaul* (Princeton: Princeton University Press, 1993).

23. "Turpiter falsa periculose vera dicuntur" *(Epist.* 4.22.5). See Ralph W. Mathisen, "Sidonius on the Reign of Avitus: A Study in Political Prudence," *Transactions of the American Philological Society* 109 (1979): 165–71.

24. Such as Sulpicius Alexander and Renatus Profuturus Frigeridus (Greg.Tur. *Hist.* 2.9).

ten by a native of Clermont, Georgius Florentius Gregorius, more commonly known as Gregory of Tours, who served as bishop of Tours from 573 until 594. Among other works, mostly brief biographies of saints and martyrs, Gregory wrote the *Histories,* better known as the *History of the Franks,* in ten books.[25] One of his main themes was to show how the will of God always prevailed, usually on the side of a bishop. His history often is anecdotal and reflective of his personal experiences—and for these reasons is invaluable for a study of late antique society.

Otherwise, in default of traditional histories, one must turn to several jejune chronicles for a temporal framework.[26] The chronicle of the Gaul Sulpicius Severus covers the period from the Creation to A.D. 397, the death of St. Martin of Tours.[27] Later chronicles, however, tended to be modeled upon, and to provide continuations for, the chronicle of Jerome, which went from the Creation to A.D. 378. These include, from Gaul, the *Chronicle* of Prosper Tiro (A.D. 379–455), the *Gallic Chronicle of 452* (A.D. 379–452), and the *Gallic Chronicle of 511* (A.D. 450–511); from Spain, the *Chronicle* of Hydatius (A.D. 379–469); from Italy, the *Chronicle* of Cassiodorus (Creation to A.D. 519); and from the Balkans, the *Chronicle* of Count Marcellinus (A.D. 379 to 534).[28] Even briefer chronicles include those of Marius of Avenches (A.D. 455–538), Victor of Tonnena (Creation to A.D. 566) and its continuator John of Biclara (567–590), and an anonymous collection from Caesaraugusta (Saragossa) (A.D. 450–568). From the seventh century comes another anonymous chronicle, called that of "Fredegarius," covering Frankish history A.D. 584–652.[29]

Finally, one of the most ubiquitous documents surviving from Late Antiquity, representing the genre of epigraphy, is the inscription, a text inscribed on stone.[30] Most extant inscriptions are epitaphs, but one also finds dedications of buildings or statues, imperial decrees, mile-

---

25. For the texts, see *MGH SRM* 1; for translations, see the bibliography.

26. For chronicle texts, see *MGH AA* 9, 11.

27. See G. K. Van Andel, *The Christian Concept of History in the Chronicle of Sulpicius Severus* (Amsterdam: Hakkert, 1976).

28. Note Richard W. Burgess, *The Chronicle of Hydatius and the Consularia Constantinopolitana* (Oxford: Clarendon, 1993); and S. Muhlberger, *The Fifth-Century Chroniclers: Prosper, Hydatius, and the Gallic Chronicler of 452* (Leeds: F. Cairns, 1990).

29. *MGH SRM* 2. See John M. Wallace-Hadrill, "Fredegar and the History of France," *Bulletin of the John Rylands Library* 40 (1958): 71–94.

30. See L. Keppie, *Understanding Roman Inscriptions* (Baltimore: Johns Hopkins University Press, 1991). Other materials included pottery, metal, and glass.

stones, and so on. In spite of their prevalence, inscriptions are not cited as often as they might be in source collections or used in discussions of contemporary society. Nonetheless, they can provide some precious insights into the most personal forms of expression.

Many different kinds of sources, therefore, will be used to paint a picture of people, personalities, and personal expression in Late Antiquity. The following chapters begin by describing the different kinds of social groupings that existed during Late Antiquity and the ways in which people interacted; they then proceed to look at factors that worked to disrupt and restructure the established social order. At the same time that the texts illustrate the different kinds of literary sources available for Late Antiquity, they also portray a society experiencing change and establishing its own identity during a crucial period of human history.

In order to get as close as possible to the individuals themselves, the *ipsissima verba* (exact words) of the sources will be cited. Wherever possible, either complete sources (such as letters and inscriptions) or protracted excerpts from lengthy sources (such as histories or saints' lives) will be used.[31] Over 140 translated selections from over seventy different sources are included below. Over half of these passages, and fifty of these sources, never before have been translated into English, and many of these never have been been translated into any language. Most translations are my own; some passages that have been translated previously are retranslated to place them more effectively in context and make them consistent with the other translations.[32] The complete Latin texts, along with discussions of manuscript traditions, variant readings, and stylistic considerations, are provided in the companion volume.[33] Additional texts not included in this volume also are incorporated there. Corresponding passages in each volume can be identified by the selection numbers in the left margin of the text.

---

31. In the case of some brief passages, the Latin text is cited in the notes; otherwise only the translations are given in this volume with the Latin presented in volume 2.

32. In general, existing translations are used for the works of Gregory of Tours and Sidonius Apollinaris, which have been translated several times in the past. For previously translated texts, see the bibliography.

33. *People, Personal Expression, and Social Relations in Late Antiquity,* vol. 2: *Selected Latin Texts from Gaul and Western Europe* (Ann Arbor: University of Michigan Press, 2002).

CHAPTER 1

The Aristocratic-Literary World

In some regards, Late Roman society had the appearance of being rigidly stratified.[1] Its most privileged members made up the senatorial class. By the fourth century A.D., "senators" were no longer solely those who were actually members of the Senate in Rome; they had come to comprise an empirewide aristocracy whose members had any number of claims to belong.[2] Anyone who was the descendent of someone who had been a senator could be called a "senator." Furthermore, many offices in the imperial administration bestowed senatorial status upon their holders, either while in office or upon retirement. Beginning in the fourth century, the most important ecclesiastical offices, *episcopus* (bishop) and, sometimes, *presbyter* (priest), also placed one in the aristocracy.[3] Furthermore, by the fifth and sixth centuries, even ambitious

---

1. See P. Charanis, "On the Social Structure of the Later Roman Empire," *Byzantion* 17 (1944–45): 39–57; Samuel Dill, *Roman Society in Gaul in the Merovingian Age* (London: MacMillan, 1926; rpt. New York: Barnes and Noble, 1970), and *Roman Society in the Last Century of the Western Empire,* 2d ed. (London, 1921; rpt. New York: Meridian, 1958); and, in particular, Arnold H. M. Jones, *The Later Roman Empire, A.D. 284–640: A Social, Economic, and Administrative Survey* (Norman: University of Oklahoma Press, 1964).

2. See M. T. W. Arnheim, *The Senatorial Aristocracy in the Later Roman Empire* (Oxford: Clarendon, 1972); John F. Matthews, *Western Aristocracies and Imperial Court, A.D. 364–425* (Oxford: Clarendon, 1975); and G. Ostrogorsky, "Observations on the Aristocracy in Byzantium," *Dumbarton Oaks Papers* 25 (1971): 1–32. For Gaul, see K. F. Stroheker, *Der senatorische Adel im spätantiken Gallien* (Tübingen: Alma Mater, 1948; rpt. Darmstadt: Wissenschaftlichen Buchgesellschaft, 1970).

3. See E. Chrysos, "Die angebliche 'Nobilitierung' des Klerus durch Kaiser Konstantin den Grossen," *Historia* 18 (1969): 119–29; Th. Klauser, *Der Ursprung der bischöflichen Insignien und Ehrenrechte* (Bonn, 1949); and F. Lotter, "Zu den Anredeformen und ehrenden Epitheta der Bischöfe in Spätantike und frühem Mittelalter," *Deutsches Archiv für Erforschung des Mittelalters* 27 (1971): 514–17.

members of town councils (known variously as *decuriones, curiales,* and *municipales*) came to describe themselves as "senators."[4]

The Aristocratic Elite

Senators were the most status-conscious members of society. Within the senatorial aristocracy there were fine distinctions in rank. Those with the highest status bore the title *vir inlustris* (illustrious gentleman), and there were further gradations within the *inlustres,* such as *vir gloriosissimus* (most glorious gentleman), or *patricius* (patrician). Senators of the second grade had the rank *vir spectabilis* (respectable gentleman), while those of the lowest tier, to which the vast majority belonged, had the entry-level title *vir clarissimus* (most distinguished gentleman).[5]

Senators neglected no opportunity to promote themselves. For example, those who had the good fortune to be named "ordinary consul" (only two were appointed annually, and they gave their names to the year), circulated to their friends folding ivory plaques called diptychs that had engraved on them scenes of the consul performing his duties along with a list of his titles.[6] For example, the diptych of the consul Astyrius, who assumed the office in Arles on 1 January 449, read:

1.1[7] Flavius Astyrius, most distinguished and illustrious, count, former master of both services, ordinary consul.[8]

The senator Turcius Rufius Apronianus Asterius of Rome, perhaps a relative of the preceding, itemized his *cursus honorum* (career) in a

---

4. See F. Gilliard, "Who Were the Senators of Sixth-Century Gaul?" *Speculum* 54 (1979): 685–97.

5. See Otto Hirschfield, "Die Rangtitel der römischen Kaiserzeit," *Sitzungsberichte der königlichen-preussischen Akademie der Wissenschaft* 25 (1901): 579ff.; P. Koch, *Die byzantinischen Beamtentitel von 400 bis 700* (Jena, 1903); and H. Löhken, *Ordines dignitatum: Untersuchungen zur formalen Konstituierung der spätantiken Führungsschicht* (Cologne: Bohlau, 1982).

6. See R. S. Bagnall, A. Cameron, S. R. Schwartz, and K.A. Worp, *Consuls of the Later Roman Empire* (Atlanta: Scholar's Press, 1987); and R. Delbruck, *Die Consulardiptychen und verwandte Denkmäler* (Berlin, 1926–29).

7. *CIL* 13:10032.2; see *PLRE* 2:174–75.

8. The master of both services (that is, the infantry and the cavalry) was the top-ranking imperial general.

subscription to his personal copy of a manuscript of Vergil copied in A.D. 494, the year of his consulship:

2[9]   I, Turcius Rufius Apronianus Asterius, a gentleman most distinguished and illustrious, ex-count of the domestics and protectors,[10] ex-count of the private largesses, ex-prefect of the city, patrician and ordinary consul, read and emended this codex of my brother Macharius,[11] a most distinguished gentleman, not with my own ability but by the will of Him[12] to whom I am devoted even in all things.

Not only does Asterius express his Christian devotion, he also demonstrates how Roman aristocrats portrayed their *militia* (official duties) and *otium* (leisure activities) as part of a unified package.

Senatorial women were accorded status in the same manner as the men whose rank they shared. For example, Proba, the daughter of Q. Clodius Hermogenianus Olybrius (consul in 379) and wife of Sextus Petronius Probus (consul in 371), was lauded in an inscription put up circa 400 by two of her sons, Probinus (consul in 395), and Probus (subsequently consul in 406):[13]

3[14]   For Anicia Faltonia Proba, who adorns the Amnii, Pincii, and Anicii,[15] wife of a consul, daughter of a consul, mother of consuls: her sons Anicius Probinus, most distinguished ordinary consul, and Anicius Probus, most distinguished quaestor elect, dedicated this, bound by her maternal merits.

This passage also demonstrates the extent to which Roman aristocrats prided themselves on their names, a conceit that was satirized by the late-fourth-century historian Ammianus Marcellinus: "Some men, dis-

---

9. Otto Jahn, "Die Subscriptionen in den Handschriften römischer Classiker," *Königlichen-sachsischen Gesellschaft der Wissenschaft zu Leipzig. Berichte* 3 (1851): 348–51.

10. The "domestics and protectors" were the imperial bodyguard.

11. A friend of Asterius, not his brother by blood.

12. I.e., God.

13. *PLRE* 1:732–33. One wonders why a third son, Olybrius, also consul in 395, was not named in the inscription.

14. *CIL* 6:1754 = H. Dessau, ed., *Inscriptiones Latinae selectae,* 5 vols. (Berlin: Weidmann, 1954–55), no. 1269.

15. The names Amnius, Pincius, and Anicius had a long distinguished history, although by the fourth century only the family of the Anicii really amounted to anything anymore.

tinguished (as they think) by famous fore-names, pride themselves beyond measure in being called Reburri, Flavonii, Pagonii, Gereones, and Dalii, along with Tarracii and Pherrasii, and many other equally fine-sounding indications of eminent ancestry."[16] Ammianus's names, it might be noted, are all fictitious.[17]

Aristocrats regularly used their rank and influence to their own advantage. The degree to which they could do so was determined by the extent of their *potentia* (power), that is, their ability to compel others to fulfil their wishes.[18] Indeed, *potentia* was the most prized possession of both secular and ecclesiastical aristocrats.[19] It also was feared. The anonymous Gallic author of the *Poem on the Providence of God* opined in the early fifth century that high status and bad behavior went hand in hand:

1.4[20]   The greatest status in the world is found among the unjust; the good, however, who have been suppressed, have almost no share in it. Whoever is violent, cruel, crafty, and greedy, whose heart lacks faith and whose tongue lacks modesty, such a one is admired, loved, revered, and honored by all; upon him the highest offices and wealth are bestowed . . . Falsity prevails in judgments and the truth falters; punishment attends the innocent, and salvation the guilty.

---

16. Ammianus Marcellinus, *Histories* 28.4.6; for translation, see J. C. Rolfe, *Ammianus Marcellinus,* vol. 3 (London: Loeb, 1972), 141.

17. In concocting fictitious names of senators he was doing no more than the unknown author of the *Augustan History,* which also was written in Rome at about this time.

18. Cicero, *De inventione* (On invention), 2.56.168, observed, "potentia est ad sua conservanda et alterius attenuenda idonearum rerum facultas" [*potentia* is a power over useful things used for preserving one's own and for diminishing those of another]; see also Peter Brown, *Power and Persuasion in Late Antiquity: Towards a Christian Empire* (Madison: University of Wisconsin Press, 1992); J. F. Drinkwater, "Patronage in Roman Gaul and the Problem of the Bagaudae," in *Patronage in Ancient Society,* ed. A. Wallace-Hadrill (London: Routledge, 1989), 189–203; and J. A. Schlumberger, "*Potentes* and *Potentia* in the Social Thought of Late Antiquity," in *Tradition and Innovation in Late Antiquity,* ed. F. Clover and R. S. Humphreys (Madison: University of Wisconsin Press, 1989), 89–104.

19. For bishops as *religione potens, potens meritis,* and *arbitrio iustitiaque potens* ("potent" in "religion," "merits," and "judgment and justice"), see Duchesne, *Fastes,* 1:188–89, 2:165–68; see also M. Heinzelmann, *Bischofsherrschaft in Gallien: Zur Kontinuität römischer Führungsschichten von 4. bis 7. Jahrhundert* (Munich: Artemis, 1976), 123–27.

20. *Carmen de providentia dei* (Poem on the providence of God), 67–80: see M. P. McHugh, *The Carmen de providentia dei Attributed to Prosper of Aquitaine: A Revised Text with an Introduction, Translation, and Notes* (Washington, D.C.: Catholic University of America Press, 1964), 262.

The ensuing chapters will help to demonstrate the extent to which such charges were justified.

Counterbalancing the aristocracy on the social scale was the great mass of the remainder of the population. Individuals who had some rank and privilege, but who lacked the prerequisites or the audacity to claim to be senators, held the rank of *honoratus* (honorable).[21] These included town councilors, well-to-do estate owners, lesser members of the clergy (such as deacons, and some priests), holders of offices that did not carry senatorial rank, and military noncommissioned officers. They and the senators had the legal status of *honestior* (more distinguished), which carried privileges such as the ability to avoid torture if arrested for a crime, or the right to a simple execution if sentenced to death.

The remainder of the population—the free, the quasi free, and the nonfree—had the legal status of *humilior* (more humble).[22] The free encompassed plebeians such as artisans, merchants, and small freeholders. The quasi free included individuals who had surrendered some of their independence in exchange for protection by a local *potens* (potentate), usually a senator or *honoratus,* who provided them with either employment or land to farm. They had designations such as *colonus* (tenant farmer), *adscripticius* (enrolled person), *originalis* (native inhabitant), *tributarius* (one upon whom taxes were due) or *inquilinus* (cottager). The unfree, of course, were the *servi,* or slaves.[23] And, as in the case of the senators, women and children generally, though not always, shared the rank and status of the male head of the family.

The Pursuit of Literary Studies

Our knowledge of social groups, and the individuals who comprised them, comes primarily from written sources, so to understand the portrayals of the people we must first comprehend the nature of the source material. Nearly all of the surviving literary material was written by

---

21. For discussion of these, see the next chapter.

22. See G. Cardascia, "L'Apparition dans le droit des classes d'honestiores et d'humiliores,'" *Revue historique de droit français et étranger* 28 (1950): 305–485.

23. *Inquilini* usually were laborers without rights to land; as with *tributarii,* taxes on them were assessed upon the landowner. *Adscripticii* and *coloni* had a rather higher status: they farmed land belonging to a lord and sometimes could be responsible for their own taxes. *Originalis* usually indicated that one was bound to one's place of origin. For the usage of these terms, see Sid.Apoll. *Epist.* 5.19, discussed in the next chapter.

men who were part of the male secular and ecclesiastical elite and who focused inordinately upon their own concerns and activities.[24] Much literary material survives from Late Antiquity—certainly more than one might expect in proportion to the prosperity of the times[25]— because the pursuit of literary studies was considered to be an essential aspect of the aristocratic ethos.[26] There were several reasons for this. It gave one an entrée into secular and ecclesiastical careers. It allowed Romans to feel a certain sense of superiority over the recently arrived barbarians. And it permitted educated Romans who might have fallen on hard economic times to continue to participate in aristocratic society. In general, an interest in classical culture served to unify Roman aristocrats who otherwise were separated by rank, occupation, wealth, and geographical distance.

Literary Circles

One manifestation of the unifying function of literary activity was that it was pursued in the public arena. Nearly every city of note had its own literary circle, which included both secular and ecclesiastical aristocrats.[27] There, compositions would be read, discussed, and evaluated. Sidonius Apollinaris said of one such soirée at Narbonne, "O the feasts, stories, and books, the laughter, solemnity, and jests, the gatherings and comradeship, one and the same . . ."[28] Although the attested participants are nearly always men, women also shared enthusiastically in literary life, as attested, for example, by the correspondence of Jerome and compositions such as the Vergilian *Cento* of Faltonia Beti-

---

24. There were exceptions: female members of the imperial family also received attention: see K. Holum, *Theodosian Empresses: Women and Imperial Dominion in Late Antiquity* (Berkeley and Los Angeles: University of California Press, 1982); and S. I. Oost, *Galla Placidia Augusta: A Biographical Essay* (Chicago: University of Chicago Press, 1968).

25. Indicators ranging from numbers of inscriptions to city size to economic productivity all indicate that, on balance, Europe was less prosperous during Late Antiquity than it had been during the Roman imperial period.

26. See Mathisen, *Roman Aristocrats,* 105–18.

27. See Nora Chadwick, *Poetry and Letters in Early Christian Gaul* (London: Bowes and Bowes, 1955), 170–86; Loyen, *Sidoine Apollinaire,* 77–98; and Ralph W. Mathisen, *Ecclesiastical Factionalism and Religious Controversy in Fifth-Century Gaul* (Washington, D.C.: Catholic University of America Press, 1989), 83–85, 93–97, 135–38, 235–53, and *Roman Aristocrats,* 105–18.

28. "O convivia, fabulae, libelli, risus, serietas, dicaecitates, occursus, comitatus unus idem" (*Carm.* 23.439–41).

tia Proba, the grandmother of Anicia Faltonia Proba, who was discussed above.[29] And this in spite of male efforts to restrict women's literary freedom, such as a canon of the early-fourth-century Council of Elvira, which decreed, "Let not women dare to write to laymen rather in their name without the names of their husbands; those who are faithful should receive even innocent letters of any person addressed to his name only."[30]

Those who took part in literary activities were expected to adhere to standard practices that not only served as social unifying factors, but also tended to produce works that were characterized by a certain sameness of approach, expression, and sentiment. One convention was to encourage each other to write. Sidonius wrote to his friend Lupus, bishop of Troyes (427–ca. 475), "For whom would you yourself not arouse to the rashness of composition? You who encourage the talents of all litterateurs, not to mention myself, even if they seek to remain concealed . . . ."[31] When such encouragement was heeded, its initiator—often, but by no means always, the social superior of the author—usually became the dedicatee of the resultant work.

"Let's Do a Play"

Several surviving dedicatory prefaces disclose something of the process.[32] One of the rare purely secular works to survive from the period after A.D. 400 is the *Querolus* (The complainer), a comedy written early in the fifth century in an ostensibly Plautine style[33] by an anonymous author. It was dedicated to a *vir inlustris* (illustrious gentleman) Rutilius, probably to be identified with Rutilius Claudius Namatianus, a Gaul who in A.D. 417 wrote the famous poem *De reditu suo* (On his return) on the occasion of a trip from Rome to Gaul.[34] The

---

29. *PLRE* 1:732. Other works by women will be discussed below.

30. "Ne feminae suo potius absque maritorum nominibus laicis scribere audeant; quae fideles sunt vel litteras alicuius pacificas ad suum solum nomen scriptas accipiant" (*PL* 84:310).

31. *Epist.* 9.11.9.

32. See Tore Janson, *Latin Prose Prefaces: Studies in Literary Conventions* (Stockholm: Ivar Haegström, 1964).

33. The twenty-one comedies of the Roman writer Plautus (ca. 254–184 B.C.) were standard reading in Roman times and were full of slapstick and earthy humor.

34. See E. Döblhofer, ed., *Rutilius Claudius Namatianus. De reditu suo sive Iter Gallicum* (Heidelberg: Winter, 1972).

Querolus's prologue illustrates not only some literary conventions, but also the kind of relationship that existed between a patron and an author:

1.5[35] O Rutilius, always to be extolled with great praises, you, who grant an honorable leisure that we devote to amusements, think that I am worthy of honor among friends and relatives and endow me with a great and a double, I acknowledge, blessing: this esteem and this fellowship. This is true dignity.

What fitting recompense, then, can I return in exchange for these kindnesses? Money, that cause and chief source of wealth and anxieties, is neither abundant for me nor valued by you. Not a little labor has yielded these wordlets to me: from this source honor and profit, from this source my recompense, will flow. And so that some element of charm might be added to our[36] endeavor, I have appropriated material from that philosophical parlance of yours:[37] do you not recall that you customarily ridicule those who deplore their fates, and that you are accustomed, in an Academic manner,[38] both to attack and to defend as it strikes your fancy? But to what extent is this permitted? In truth, therefore, what there is from this source, only he who knows will know.

I have written this little book for storytelling and table talk. This is the plot: . . . .

This little book, illustrious one, is dedicated to your name. May you live healthy and happy in accordance with my prayers and your own.[39]

The author's disclaimers of wealth and employment of his literary talent demonstrate how, as some aristocrats fell upon hard economic

---

35. *Querolus* (The complainer), preface: R. Peiper, ed., *Aulularia sive Querolus. Theodosiani aevi comoedia Rutilio dedicata* (Leipzig: Teubner, 1875), 3–5; L. Herrmann, ed., "Querolus (Le Grognon)," *Latomus* 96 (1968): 67–167; and C. Jacquemard–Le Saos, ed., *Querolus (Aulularia) Le Grincheux (Comédie de la petite marmite)* (Paris: Budé, 1994), 3.

36. At this point the author, still referring to himself, self-consciously shifts from first-person singular to first-person plural.

37. An aristocratic retreat into philosophy was fashionable. Sidonius Apollinaris wrote to Eutropius (*Epist.* 3.6.2), "While you were involved in the dogmas of your Plotinus, the exercise ground of the Platonists sucked you into the profound leisure of an unseasonable tranquility," and the Italian Asterius withdrew into a life of philosophic contemplation (Ennodius, *Epist.* 1.24).

38. The "Academics" were the representatives of Plato's academy in Athens.

39. Letters generally terminated with some form of farewell salutation, as here.

times, literary interests became a lowest common denominator that united them all. Even if the anonymous author ranked below Rutilius in wealth and status, the two still could interact as equals in the literary arena. In this case the apparently impoverished author had an additional reason to be grateful: not only had Rutilius sponsored the composition, he also had underwritten the production. The *Querolus* presumably is representative of the kinds of works that were composed in the aristocratic literary milieu of the fifth century. One might imagine that many other works like it also were written, but, perhaps as a consequence of subsequent Christian literary preferences, have not survived.

The Dedication of a Grammatical Treatise

Another classically based work, *On Orthography,* was written circa the 440s by Agroecius, who seems then to have been a layman; he may be the Agroecius who in the early 470s was the learned and elderly bishop of Sens.[40] The dedicatory preface of this volume was addressed not to a secular aristocrat, but to Eucherius (ca. 430–51), the influential and cultured bishop of Lyon:[41]

.6[42]   Agroecius, to the lord bishop Eucherius.

You have sent to me the book of Caper, *On Orthography.*[43] The subject matter is consistent with your purpose and your inclinations, because you who wish to correct us in the activities of this life likewise emend us when we are engaged in composition. You believe, therefore, that there is nothing in us that is sheltered from your castigation; all of our deeds, even those that are insignificant to mention, you pry into with a diligent investigation; you range from the act of living to the act of writing, from the spirit to the hand, from the heart to the finger. This is what it means, as you yourself say, to be the greatest priest[44] of God: both to satiate in spirit and to instruct in literature those entrusted to you.

---

40. See *PLRE* 2:39.

41. For Eucherius, see Mathisen, *Ecclesiastical Factionalism,* 79–87 and passim.

42. Agroecius, *De orthographia* (On orthography), preface: Heinrich Keil, ed., *Grammatici latini,* 8 vols. (Leipzig, 1855–80), 7:113–14.

43. Flavius Caper was a Latin grammarian who wrote works called *De latinitate* (On Latinity) and *De dubiis generibus* (On doubtful types) in the second century A.D.

44. "Summum . . . sacerdotem": that is, bishop.

Therefore, to this book of Caper, which is about orthography and about the correctness and diversity of speaking, I have appended certain items that should be added, not because a man of such great wisdom, famous especially for so many literary works and renowned even for interpreting Cicero, omitted anything, but because I think that matters that he neglected as being unambiguous are in reality difficult. I trust, moreover, that the points I cover, because they were often obscure to me, will seem unclear to some people. To you, therefore, is sent this little work, over which you will toil mightily; to you falls the necessity of emending the one who presumes to emend anything. The divine piety will grant that I, who desire to examine what has been written by you, might indeed be able to follow your model.
Farewell, be mindful of me, my glory and my bulwark.

This dedication illustrates the continuing attraction that classical, pagan literature had for ecclesiastics, in spite of the conventional aversion they sometimes purported to have.[45] It also shows that the role of the bishop had expanded beyond spiritual concerns, in this case, even to assisting in the survival of the classical tradition.[46]

Although the writers of the *Querolus* and *On Orthography* would not have known it, their undertakings represented a literary and cultural dead end. Fewer and fewer compositions in the tradition of the secular classical past were being written. Those that were, and that survived the test of time, tended to be practical in nature, dealing with topics ranging from grammar to medicine to animal husbandry.[47] This is

---

45. See P. Courcelle, "Nouveaux aspects de la culture lérinienne," *Revue des études latines* 46 (1968): 379–409; and Fr. Glorie, "La culture lérinienne (Notes de lecture)," *Sacris erudiri* 19 (1969–70): 71–76. Aversion: see the letters of Rusticus to Eucherius and Jerome to Eustochium below.

46. See, e.g., Bernhard Bischoff, "Benedictine Monasteries and the Survival of Classical Literature," in *Manuscripts and Libraries in the Age of Charlemagne,* ed. and trans. M. Gorman (Cambridge: Cambridge University Press, 1994), 140.

47. Surviving secular works include, from the late fourth century, the *De medicamentis* (On medications) of Marcellus of Bordeaux (Leipzig, 1916); from the early fifth the *De duabus partibus orationis nomine et verbo* (On two parts of speech, the noun and verb) and *De barbarismis et metaplasmis* (On barbarisms and word transformations) of Consentius of Narbonne (Leipzig, 1880), and the *Opus agriculturae* (Treatise on agriculture), *De veterinaria medicina* (On veterinary medicine), and *De insitione* (On grafting) of Palladius Rutilius Taurus Aemilianus (Leipzig, 1898); from the middle fifth, perhaps, the *Praecepta artis rhetoricae* (Precepts of rhetorical art) of Julius Severianus (Leipzig, 1863), and the *Epitoma* (Abridgment), a summary of Sallust's *Life of Marius* by Julius Exsuperantius (Leipzig, 1902) (see also

not to say, however, that literary creativity ended. Far from it. But most of the literary efforts of this period and later were expended by ecclesiastics on ecclesiastical topics for an ecclesiastically oriented audience.

As demonstrated by the dedication of Agroecius, anything that was written became the responsibility of the dedicatee as well. The priest Mamertus Claudianus of Vienne, in the dedication of his *De natura animae* (On the nature of the soul) to Sidonius Apollinaris, said in 469, "Now see to it that you remember that you share the responsibility, for if I run any risk by being the author of this work, you do so by being the editor."[48] And to the editor of his own letters Sidonius wrote, "But of course I have obeyed you, and I have entrusted these letters to your examination . . . knowing that you are an unbounded supporter not only of literature but also of litterateurs."[49]

Aristocratic authors also were concerned about how their works were received by other aristocrats. Sidonius, for example, asked a friend to whom he had sent one of his publications to let him know "what all the best people think about it."[50] There was, however, really no need to worry. It also was understood that all compositions would receive an enthusiastic response. The rhetorician Paulinus of Périgueux wrote circa 480 to Perpetuus, bishop of Tours, "You believe to be good what you choose to be good, and you admit to Your Devotion's circle even the poorer writers whom you read."[51] And Sidonius reassured a young protégé who was about to deliver a declamation, saying simply, "All who hear will approve."[52]

In general, one might suspect that it was not so much one's literary efforts themselves that were important, whatever objective merit they

---

Sid.Apoll. *Epist.* 9.15.1), and from the early sixth, the *De observatione ciborum* (On the analysis of foods) of Anthimus (Leipzig, 1877), dedicated to the Frankish king Theoderic I. Several short poems also survive in the *Latin Anthology.*

48. "En . . . tu modo faxis uti memineris non absque cura tui prodi oportere . . . quoniam, si in his secus aliquid, ego conscriptionis periclitabor, sed tu editionis" (A. Engelbrecht, ed., *CSEL* 11:20).

49. "Sed scilicet tibi parui tuaeque examinationi has <litterulas> non recensendas . . . . sed defaecandas . . . sciens te inmodicum esse fautorem non studiorum modo verum etiam studiosorum" (*Epist.* 1.1.3).

50. *Epist.* 9.1.3.

51. M. Petschenig, ed., *CSEL* 16:17. See also Sid.Apoll. *Epist.* 3.14.1: "But I realize very well that . . . it is not the . . . work itself that creates this pleasure for you but affection for the author; therefore . . . what you deny to my composition you grant to friendship."

52. *Epist.* 9.14.9.

might have had, but the purpose that these endeavors served: to give aristocrats an arena in which all could relate on common ground. Therefore, if an individual with literary inclinations was personally acceptable to other aristocrats, his creative ventures perforce would be acceptable as well and would receive fulsome and extravagant praise. Consequently, one friend of Bishop Hilary of Arles rhapsodized, "He has acquired not learning, not eloquence, but something indefinable beyond the reach of men," and another confided, "If Augustine had come after you, he would have been judged inferior."[53]

Book Collecting

Of course, to be appreciated fully compositions had to be reproduced and circulated. But in an age without photocopiers or printing presses, this was never easy. An example of how the process functioned, as well as of the pleasure taken by ordinary aristocrats in their literary pursuits, is seen in a letter written, perhaps in the 440s, to the aforementioned Eucherius by Rusticus, a classically educated priest who would have belonged to one of the premier families of late Roman Lyon.[54] The letter was preserved only because, along with letters of Hilary of Arles and Salvian of Marseille,[55] it was incorporated into a manuscript of Eucherius's *De spiritalis intellegentiae* (On spiritual understanding). It may be that Rusticus himself was the original copyist of this version of the manuscript, and that this is why this cover letter was included:

1.7[56] The priest Rusticus to Eucherius, a truly sanctified lord, a friend of God, and a father to be received by me in Christ with all reverence.[57]

---

53. Honoratus of Marseille, *Vita Hilarii Arelatensis* (Life of Hilary of Arles), 14: S. Cavallin, ed., *Vitae sanctorum Honorati et Hilarii episcoporum Arelatensium* (Lund: Gleerup, 1952), 93.

54. For the family of the Rustici, see *PLRE* 2:961–65. This Rusticus is too young to have been the famous Bishop Rusticus of Narbonne, as suggested by J. Pitra, "Sanctus Eucherius Lugdunensis," *Analecta sacra* 2 (1884): 492ff.; nor is he likely to have been the son of Taurentius mentioned below. But he just might be the Rusticus who was bishop of Lyon and died on 25 April 501: see *CIL* 13:2395; and Duchesne, *Fastes,* 2:165–66.

55. See chapter 3 below.

56. Rusticus, *Epist.* "Transcriptis exultanter": *CSEL* 31:198–99; see M. Vessey, "The *Epistula Rustici ad Eucherium,*" in *Society and Culture in Late Antique Gaul,* ed. R. Mathisen and D. Shanzer (Aldershot: Ashgate, 2001), 278–97.

57. The salutations of aristocratic letters could be extremely flowery. Some writers, such as Sidonius, affected a briefer form, usually just the name of the addressee. Of course, Sidonius was of such exalted rank that he did not have to behave ingratiatingly unless he wanted to.

Having transcribed joyfully and speedily the texts that, at my request, you sent to be copied, I have promptly sent both volumes to Your Beatitude. As to your teaching, truly unique and beyond compare, by means of which light pours forth with the intelligence of a truly spiritual[58] heart, answering most completely, with the veil removed from the eyes, questions concerning the great enigmas from each testament, I cannot express how admirable it was to me more clearly than by confessing that I cannot possibly praise it fittingly. Indeed, what can I say in praise of your writings except that I am unequal to the task? And let me say this with all due respect to those who are best educated in what are called the liberal studies,[59] and I do not think that even they can fittingly extol the marvelous qualities of your books. Because, although they claim that judgment is easier than composition, I, nevertheless, am so convinced that it is not easy that I justifiably assert that no glorifier of an outstanding work can exist more rightly than its author and initiator, because that which no one else can compose in such a manner, in a like manner no one else can praise.

But, while I meditate upon this quietly, there occurs to me something that, as a boy, I once read in passing, as the curiosity of that age often does, in the library of a scholar of secular literature. For, in the midst of statues either of orators or even of poets formed and shaped from stones or many-colored waxes, after the designer and owner of the above-mentioned room had composed suitable epigrams for the portraits of several of the authors, when he came to a poet of already established eloquence, he began thus:[60]

His own poems praise the poet Vergil better:
As long as the rivers run in their banks,
As long as shadows encircle the mountain hollows,
As long as the north pole sustains the heavens,
Your honor, your name, and your praises shall always remain.

---

58. "Spiritalis intellegentia": an allusion to the title of the work being copied.

59. "Liberalia studia," that is, a classical literary education.

60. Such poetic tags seem to have been common: see Alexander Riese, ed., *Anthologia latina* 1.2 (Leipzig: Teubner, 1906), 300–303, nos. 813–39. The images could have included statues, busts, or mosaics: see L. Stirling, "Gods, Heroes, and Ancestors: Sculptural Decoration in Late Antique Aquitania," *Aquitania* 14 (1996): 209–30.

And truly, provided that I incur no blame in your prayers for mentioning passages from secular writings among the sacred words and remembrances of saintly men,[61] the aforementioned composition deservedly returns to mind as I recall the lord Eucherius. For in times to come, when your words have been comprehended, you will be honored by the voice and love of all Christians, to be praised by future generations as long as you instruct future generations.

Pray for me, truly sanctified lord, friend of God, and father to be received by me in Christ with all reverence.

By volunteering to undertake the onerous task of copying Eucherius's work, Rusticus accomplished two things: he participated in Eucherius's literary circle, and he effected the preservation of his own little literary contribution. Like the author of the *Querolus,* Rusticus attached himself to an influential aristocratic patron. And, like Agroecius, he was sensitive to Eucherius's appreciation of the classical literary past.

Copies like the one made by Rusticus served a valued purpose. As just seen, aristocrats prided themselves on their libraries,[62] which could be expanded only by means of handwritten facsimiles. Another example of manuscript copying is found in a letter written to Ruricius of Limoges (ca. 485–510) by his friend Taurentius. The latter is otherwise unknown, and his letter survives, it seems, only because it happened to be in Ruricius's bookcase when Ruricius's collected letters were compiled.[63] Ruricius had written to Taurentius, saying, "Therefore, rendering my salutation, I ask that you send to me without delay, through the bearer of this letter, the book of the blessed Augustine *On the City of God,* as you thought it proper to promise."[64]

---

61. A typical pseudoapology, from one ecclesiastic to another, for citing secular literature.

62. Note also Tonantius Ferreolus, a retired Gallic aristocrat with an extensive library that contained Augustine, Varro, Horace, Prudentius, and a translation of Origen (Sid.Apoll. *Epist.* 2.9.4).

63. See Mathisen, *Ruricius,* 165–68.

64. "Salutem itaque dicens rogo, sicut promittere dignati estis, librum nobis sancti Augustini de civitate dei per portitorem harum sine dilatione mittatis" (Ruric. *Epist.* 2.17). Augustine's *De civitate dei* (On the city of God), written ca. 420, distinguished the heavenly city from the earthly one while appreciating the merits of each, and was one of the most famous and influential books of Late Antiquity. For another letter to Taurentius, see Ruric. *Epist.* 2.47.

Taurentius's reply indicates that Ruricius and others were in the habit of borrowing from his library to such an extent that he was scarcely able to keep track of, much less to read, his own books:

.8[65] Taurentius to Bishop Ruricius, a sanctified and blessed lord, a father to be venerated by me with all worship and honor, and a lord patron in Christ.[66]

The letter of Your Sanctity has aroused me, nourished by its spiritual food, to hope for the future, and your words, shining with prophetic clarity, have blazed forth with the purest light and have dispersed the clouds of errors. I recognize an affection full of charity, and I embrace the sincerity of your pious reproof. You demonstrate eloquence in your words, perfection in your deeds, grace in your counsel, diligence in your granting of kindness, constancy in truth, truth in admonition, and knowledge in your teaching.

You have returned the ancient interpreters of Scriptures and exegetes of the divine volumes, names that I revere, Cyprian, Augustine, Hilary, Ambrose,[67] some blooming with the flower of eloquence, some, indeed, spiritual in the revealing of what is hidden, some charming in their delighting of the senses of the uneducated, some striving in their assertion of faith. We enviously fault time past because our own times did not produce these men most worthy of admiration. But at least men of more recent times seek out the teaching of those who taught before.

I, moreover, acknowledge that my age is the result neither of clippings of graying hair nor, as Your Beatitude derived from a secular author,[68] from the color of a whitening beard,[69] because, even if there was a mistake in their reckoning, I would sense the years of old age from the lethargy of my limbs resulting from the progress of disease. But I beg with the humility of all my entreaties that you will make an appeal in your holy prayers for the correction of my character, for the inspiring in me of the desire for repentance, for the favor of our Lord,

---

65. Taurentius, *Epist.* "Litterae sanctitatis": *CCL* 64:398–400; *CSEL* 21:444–46; *MGH AA* 8:274–75; for translation, see Mathisen, *Ruricius,* 168–69.

66. Note the similarity of this salutation to that of Rusticus's letter to Eucherius above.

67. The books that Ruricius had borrowed previously. All were by ecclesiastical authors, a reflection of contemporary literary tastes.

68. None of the editors of this letter has been able to identify the source of this citation.

69. Taurentius, therefore, was up in years.

so that you, who point out, in order that one might avoid descending to the road that leads to ruin, a path straight and to be traveled with labor, might achieve both the beginning of a good work and the effect of pious emendation brought about not through the lash of discipline but through the medicine of indulgence and the gentleness of pity. Confer also this reward upon yourself: you indeed owe to the Lord interest from the treasure that was entrusted to your faith and was received by you at His recommendation. Win over the despairing, reprove the negligent, arouse those surrendered to the slumber of an idle security, excite those who have become complacent. It is fitting for a good shepherd to carry back the lost lamb upon his shoulders and enclose within better-protected folds those for whom the wolf lies in wait.

As you directed, I have found the saint Augustine, which I had thought was in the possession of our mutual son, the priest Rusticus.[70] The cost to you is that you admire my zeal, for, because I did not in fact know until now what treatises it contains, I examined the chapter headings as I was about to pass it along. It is a papyrus book and insufficiently strong to bear mistreatment, because, as you know, papyrus is quickly consumed by age. Read it, if you wish, and copy it. And I hope that, after it has become familiar to you, it will be returned to me, to whom it is unknown, because I propose to correct my negligence by repeated reading of this very document.
Pray for me.

If some aristocrats such as Rutilius, the dedicatee of the *Querolus,* sought solace in philosophy, many others, such as Taurentius, adopted an earnestly Christian lifestyle, especially in their old age.[71] For Taurentius, Ruricius, and many others, the rhetoric of religion became second nature. So, like many aristocratic epistolographers, Taurentius felt comfortable prefacing his letter with a profusion of conventional Christian platitudes before getting down to the real business at hand.

Taurentius's letter also gives some insight into why many docu-

---

70. Apparently Taurentius's son by blood, Ruricius's by religion. He would have been too young to have been the Rusticus who wrote the letter to Eucherius cited above.

71. Note, for example, Sidonius Apollinaris's descriptions of the *vir spectabilis* (respectable gentleman) Germanicus of Cantiliae (Chantelle-la-Vieille) (*Epist.* 4.13) and the presbyter Maximus (*Epist.* 4.24); both were former government officials. These assiduous Christians often were the patrons of local churches.

ments from this period have perished. Even though durable writing materials like parchment *(pergamentum)* and vellum were known at this period, they were expensive, and many documents continued to be written on papyrus as late as the early seventh century.[72] This was the case not only for lengthy manuscripts, such as Taurentius's copy of the *City of God,* but in particular for shorter ones, such as letters. And Taurentius was correct in his assessment of the fragility of papyrus, which did not bear up well under heavy usage. His own book could not have been more than eighty years old and was already crumbling. And, in general, in the modern day surviving papyrus documents are in a poor state of preservation.

The Gift Horse

On some occasions, these outwardly pompous and prating notables allowed their sillier sides to show through. Indulging in their own brand of literary-related humor, they bandied about in-jokes that fostered their sense of clubbiness. A reiterated witticism in the circle of Ruricius involved the lending of a horse, which was described differently by the lender and the recipient. In a letter to his friend Celsus, Ruricius extolled the sterling qualities of the horse that he had dispatched:

[73] Ruricius, to the lord of his heart, Celsus.

I have sent the sort of horse you requested, placid in gentleness, strong in limbs, hardy in strength, excelling in appearance, well-proportioned in form, temperate in spirit, neither, of course, excessively quick in speed nor lazy in slowness: the use of the bit and goad is at the will of the rider, and in the carrying of burdens it is both willing and able, with the result that it neither succumbs to the one superposed

---

72. Parchment was made from sheepskin, and vellum, rather thicker, from calfskin. Papyrus was made in Egypt from the inner pith of the papyrus plant, which was cut into strips *(schedae)* that were glued together in two layers perpendicular to each other. A papyrus page was known variously as a *charta,* a *pagina,* or a *scheda;* a papyrus roll was a *volumen.* An average roll was eight to thirteen inches in breadth and about forty feet long. Text was written in columns about five to ten inches wide. Taurentius's use of the word *membrana* at the end of the letter ordinarily would refer to parchment. But, given his earlier specific reference to papyrus, the use here must be a generic reference to a "document."

73. Ruric. *Epist.* 1.14: *MGH AA* 8:307–8; *CSEL* 21:367; *CCL* 64:327; for translation, see Mathisen, *Ruricius,* 126.

atop nor drops what has been imposed. Having made this known, therefore, as is fitting, having extended my greetings, and having fulfilled my promise, we demand what you have promised, that, God willing, you will deign to come to us for the festival of the saints,[74] together with our sister,[75] in order to demonstrate regard for your patrons, affection for the brothers, and consideration for the people.

Apparently, this jest was too good to let die. In September 506, after the Council of Agde, Bishop Sedatus of Nîmes continued on to Toulouse and wrote a letter to Ruricius expressing both his desire to see his aged friend and his disappointment that Ruricius had not attended the synod.[76] Ruricius responded not only with a letter, but also with a horse. Some of the words were the same (italicized below) as those in his letter to Celsus, and perhaps the horse was too:

1.10[77]   Ruricius to the Bishop Sedatus, a blessed and apostolic lord for me in Christ, a patron to be preferred to others with special worship and affection.

I received through the physician Palladius[78] letters of your fruitful heart and fluent tongue, which invited us to a mutual rendezvous in keeping with our hearts' desire. But what can I do? Because various infirmities of the limbs resist the desires of my spirit, while you are excessively robust, I am impeded by the weakness of a worn-out body; whereas four feet belonging to another are hardly able to bear your weight, my own two are scarcely able to sustain even me without exhaustion. As a result, I cannot fulfill our shared desires. Indeed, with the Lord as my witness, if I but had the strength, I would have come to the scheduled synod with all eagerness, but the necessity of weakness

---

74. This "solemnitas sanctorum," perhaps the Festival of Peter and Paul, was celebrated near Ruricius's family estate at Gourdon, located far to the south, in the territory of Cahors rather than at Limoges.

75. Perhaps a reference to Celsus's sister, or even to his wife, if she had become his "sister" as a result of their adoption of the religious life.

76. Sedatus's letter "Satis credidi" survives in the corpus of Ruricius: *MGH AA* 8:273; *CSEL* 21:446–47; *CCL* 64:400.

77. Ruric. *Epist.* 2.35: *MGH AA* 8:338; *CSEL* 21:420–21; *CCL* 64:374–75; for translation, see Mathisen, *Ruricius,* 200.

78. He is otherwise unknown.

inhibited me from the intention of the planned journey, because I can hardly tolerate the atmosphere of that region especially at this time.[79] Which I have faith that you believe, and I do not doubt that the perverse ascribe to something else.[80]

Therefore, with these things sufficiently discussed, to the extent that I can, and having given the salutation of an eager spirit, I have sent to you, if you consider it proper, a steed of the sort that I know you need: *placid in gentleness, strong in limbs, hardy in strength, excelling in appearance, well-proportioned in form, temperate in spirit,* that is, neither lazy in lethargy nor excessively swift in speed. *The use of the bit and goad is at the will of the rider, and in the carrying of burdens it is both willing and able, with the result that it neither succumbs to the one placed atop nor drops a burden.* It remains for you to indicate in your reply how you like it, to whatever extent that I can presume, based upon your personal affection for me, that the dreadfulness I have committed—I won't say transmitted—suits you. Indeed, the intensity of absolute affection is so great that nothing is displeasing in a friend, even though wickedness from a friend in fact ought to be even more displeasing. And it is for this reason that men's judgment tends to be influenced by affection or hatred, so that they do not evaluate accurately. You, truly, whom hatred does not exasperate and jealously does not inflame, tolerate my humor agreeably and inform me abundantly about your health and activities so that, when I later read your letter, I will be instructed more fully.
Pray for me.

Even though Ruricius was a crony of Sedatus, he nonetheless had to explain the pleasantry in profuse detail just to ensure that Sedatus was not offended. Meanwhile, Sedatus's reply also found its way into Ruricius's letter collection. He clearly had enjoyed the jest, and he picked up where Ruricius had left off—with a few twists of his own:

---

79. In the summer, a result of the unseasonably early meeting time of the council.

80. Ruricius's absence clearly was an issue. Bishop Caesarius of Arles, who presided at the council, rebuked Ruricius for it (Caesarius, *Epist.* "Dum nimium": *MGH AA* 8:274–75; *CSEL* 21:448–49; *CCL* 64:402–3), and in his reply Ruricius (*Epist.* 2.33) not only attributed his illness to the "heat of that area," but also complained that he had not been informed far enough in advance and that his dignity had been injured.

1.11[81]   Bishop Sedatus to Bishop Ruricius, a sanctified and blessed lord and father to be received with apostolic reverence.

I have received the horse that you sent through our brother priest, loaded[82] with the magnificent trappings of your words, vile on the hoof, precious in the letter, moving itself when it is goaded with spurs or urged with blows, and moving forward not at all. Most discouraging in form, most vile in color, more flabby than feather-down, more slow-moving than statues, trembling at solid bodies, lacking an inbred fear only, I believe, of shadows, a runaway when it is let loose, immobile when it is calmed, standing still on level ground, falling down in the rough: it does not know how to be held, it is unable to walk. Before I saw it, while I was perusing your letter, I believed it to be of the race of those,

> Whom ingenious Circe bred as bastards
> From the stolen mare she had mated.[83]

I thought then that it would be shrewd in spirit, energetic in running, blowing fire, when it is displayed, from its flaring nostrils, about to strike the ground with a solid hoof, an outstripper of the winds and rivers in speed. Such, indeed, did the most splendid description of your letter promise me. I believed then that two very strong men, lest it escape, would restrain it as it gnawed at the reins and crushed the iron with its bites. And it did not disappoint me, for several pulled it, others pushed it, and more pummeled it. When I saw it displayed thus, I wished that you always would send to those who are dear to you gifts just as they were, not such as my letter contains. Nevertheless, because you did not leave to me anything that I could say in praise of the gift you sent, lest I altogether . . .[84]

This letter demonstrates once again the pervasive use of classical allusions. Even bishops were able to dredge up appropriate tags at the

---

81. Sedatus, *Epist.* "Equum quem": *MGH AA* 8:274–75; *CSEL* 21:449–50; *CCL* 64:403–4; for translation, see Mathisen, *Ruricius,* 202–3.

82. There is a little wordplay here. The word *onoratum* (loaded) also could be read as *honoratum* (honored).

83. From Vergil, *Aeneid,* 7.282–83. Circe was the daughter of the Sun: his horses were immortal, her mare was mortal.

84. The text breaks off here, and there follows in the manuscript an extract from Sid.Apoll. *Epist.* 2.1.

drop of a hat. And it gives a welcome example of the kind of repartee that could be exchanged among the staid bishops who ordinarily are known to us only through the dry renderings of church councils and theological tracts.

A Tempest in a Teapot

Occasionally, even literary relations were not absolutely amicable, as when Bishop Avitus of Vienne (ca. 490–518), to his apparent dismay, was accused by Bishop Viventiolus of Lyon[85] of having perpetrated a barbarism. Avitus wrote a lengthy letter, with extensive grammatical exposition, in his own defense:

12[86] Avitus, bishop of Vienne, to the "rhetorician"[87] Viventiolus.

A rumor whispers from your neighborhood that you—apparently openly castigating me for having blundered in a public oration—said that I perpetrated a barbarism[88] in the sermon that I recently delivered to the people of Lyon[89] when the basilica was dedicated. I confess that this could have happened, especially to me, from whom age has borne away any literary studies there may have been in my younger days. Nevertheless, I would have preferred to have heard this particular opinion from you standing face-to-face, because even if my faculty for understanding is now diminished, my desire for learning remains unaltered. But because I have ascertained that you spoke out in my absence, I have undertaken to respond, even though I too am absent.

Therefore, people report that you that you censured me because I said "potītur" with the middle syllable long, manifestly disregarding the practice of Vergil, who shortened that same syllable, saying "vi potitur."[90] But this is excusable because of poetic necessity, for we find

---

85. Avitus's correspondence also includes *Epist.* 59, 67, and 69 to Viventiolus; and *Epist.* 68 from Viventiolus to Avitus.

86. Avit. *Epist.* 57: *MGH AA* 6.2:85–87. The author's thanks to Danuta Shanzer for providing an advance look at this letter from her forthcoming translation of Avitus's letters.

87. An ironic appellation referring to the bishop Viventiolus's presumption in criticizing Avitus.

88. A formal study of barbarisms (the misuse of Latin) had been made in the fifth century by Consentius of Narbonne (note 47 above).

89. Avitus's doing so would suggest that he was on good terms with Viventiolus; they apparently occasionally exchanged pulpits.

90. *Aeneid,* 3.55–56: "auro / vi potitur. quid non mortalia pectora cogis": the *i* in *potitur* is short.

that in his work Vergil often transgressed in the same manner, so that, disregarding barbarism, he abandoned the metric rules as the need arose, and following convention not at all, he reversed the quantity of the syllables in some certain instances.[91] As, for example, this, "non erimus regno indecores,"[92] or "fervere Leucatem,"[93] or this, "namque ut supremam falsa inter gaudia noctem egerimus."[94] Certainly, no littérateur will maintain that at least these three words, that is, *fervēre, egerīmus,* and *indecōres,* are to be shortened, but will rather recommend that they be pronounced naturally, with lengthened penultimate syllables. Vergil, therefore, used poetic license, as I have shown above: shortening the middle syllable, he presumed to say, "potitur."

Putting aside poetic license for a bit now, let us instead deal with this word by grammatical principle, according to which the middle syllable is long, as "potītris" testifies, just as the third person, that is "potītur," similarly is long. In the same manner we say, "sortior, sortītris, sortītur." Additionally, in the perfect tense, the first, second, and third person are "potītus sum, es, est"; thus, in the imperative mood, present tense in the second person, "potīre," likewise "sortīre." Similarly, in the optative mood, in the present and imperfect tenses, in all three persons, the syllable is likewise lengthened, "utinam potīrer, potīreris, potīretur." But if you make the third person short, as "potitur," you would be compelled to do the same for the second person, so that you would say "potiris," which the integrity of Latin usage excludes everywhere from each practice and application. Behold, then, the word that you criticized, upon which I dare to base my argument!

Now, however, extending an honorific greeting fortified with my prayers, I ask that, because I, according to the law of friendship,[95] expressed how things seemed to me in the manner of an outspoken page, you—having lost, as demonstrated above, the authority of your Vergilian example, which even in this case we ought not to imitate when it comes to usurping barbarisms because we are unable to match

---

91. That is, it was Vergil who violated the rules, not Avitus.

92. *Aeneid,* 7.231: "Non erimus regno indecores, nec vestra feretur."

93. *Aeneid,* 8.677: "Fervere Leucaten auroque effulgere fluctus."

94. *Aeneid,* 6.513–14: "Namque ut supremam falsa inter gaudia noctem / Egerimus, nosti; et nimium meminisse necesse est": the *i* in *egerimus* is short.

95. The "ius amicitiae" bound aristocrats together, and Avitus suggests that Viventiolus had failed to observe it.

him in the dignity of verse, even if the same Vergil had "potītus" or "potīti" long, as in the case of "ausoque potīti"[96]—in turn likewise should hand over to me, in an explanatory reply, a principle that I ought to follow. Or if indeed you choose to instruct this questioner with a compilation of some kind of testimony, I hope that you will submit something carefully sought out and unearthed in the ancient orators whom you rightly pass on to your students.[97] But if no justification is discovered by means of either grammatical art or oratory, then suffer our shared sons—whose intellects I would prefer at the present time that you primarily, albeit not solely, nurture[98]—to be content with this one error only.[99] In the midst of their formative years no less than of their studies, finally, let them drink from that rich fountain of flowing learning, for it is better to attract than to disparage a friend by means of your studies, and it is fitting for an orator to declaim rather than to defame.

Avitus's annoyance may be further conveyed by his omission of the customary farewell salutation. One can understand the vehemence of Avitus's denial of such a trivial misstep in part by realizing that Viventiolus's charge, that Avitus, in effect, not only sounded like a barbarian but was one, attacked the core of his aristocratic standing. Avitus responded to Viventiolus in kind: in the guise of asking for advice he gave him a grammar lesson, thus deftly putting him in his place.[100] Even an educated bishop as learned as Avitus was sensitive about his intellectual status. He was perfectly willing not only to quote Vergil but to gloss him as well in order to prove that he was indeed as learned as he claimed to be. Indeed, Avitus's final words, that it was better "to declaim rather than to defame," could serve as a guiding principle of

---

96. The manuscript reads "auroque potiti"; but Vergil, *Aeneid,* 6.624, has "ausoque potiti," clearly the passage Avitus had in mind; note also *Aeneid,* 3.55–56, "et auro / vi potiti." Either Avitus quoted incorrectly or a copyist copied wrongly, probably on the basis of these similarities.

97. Like many bishops of the day, Viventiolus also served as a teacher.

98. Avitus here seems to be referring to other teachers, among whom he probably includes himself.

99. That is, with the error Viventiolus made by wrongly accusing Avitus, who here suggests that a response would only result in yet another error.

100. For the continued interest in grammar, note also Agroecius's edition of Fl. Caper above, and the works of Consentius and Severianus (note 47 above).

the Roman literary elite. In his opinion, Viventiolus had crossed the line. For Avitus, the purpose of literary endeavors was to give aristocrats the opportunity to feel good about themselves and each other.

A Cultured Barbarian

The late Roman literary world was primarily an aristocratic, Roman, and male preserve. In general, it would seem that barbarians and women need not apply. Every so often, however, one encounters exceptions to this rule, exceptions that are all the more significant for their rarity. Barbarians in particular are rarely found engaging in literary activities in the fifth and even early sixth century. Yet, in the 470s one discovers Arbogastes, the count of Trier and likely the grandson of the fourth-century Frankish general Arbogastes,[101] absorbed in literary endeavors with some of the most eminent Gallo-Roman literati. For example, Auspicius, the bishop of Toul, dispatched to him an elaborate biographical poem:

1.13[102]　Letter of Auspicius, bishop of the church of Toul, to Arbogastes, count of Trier.

I, Auspicius, who esteem you, with these lines offer a fulsome
　　greeting
　　to the outstanding, respectable[103] Count Arbogastes.
I render great thanks in my heart to the celestial Lord
　　because, nearby in the city of Toul, I observe your greatness.
In the past, I was often cheered by your many accomplishments,
　　but now you have made me exult with the greatest joy.
In fact, you have customarily seemed to me to be greater than
　　everyone,
　　with the result that your illustrious intellect surpasses the degree
　　　of your authority:
This title thus is owed to you by us with a greater joy;

---

101. Master of soldiers in the West ca. 388–94. He supported the pagan revival under the usurper Eugenius (392–94) and committed suicide after his defeat by Theodosius I at the battle of the Frigidus River in 394; see *PLRE* 1: 95–97.

102. Auspicius of Toul, *Epist.* "Praecelso expectabili" = *Epistulae austrasicae* 23: *MGH Epist.* 3:135–36 = J. Strecker, ed., *MGH Poetae latini* 4.2 (Berlin, 1914), 614–18.

103. *Expectabili* (emended by some to *et spectabili*): the office of *comes* (count) carried with it the rank of *vir spectabilis.*

not yet granted in name, it has been conferred already through
    your merits.[104]
It is more praiseworthy, indeed, for a man to shine through his
    deeds
    than to display a lamp without a glimmer of a spark.
But as for you, who are greater in all regards than you claim to be,
    it will happen very soon, I think, that your merits will bestow
    fame.
Distinguished[105] indeed by birth, distinguished also by the
    character of your life,
    you are rendered just, chaste, sober, totally illustrious.[106]
Your father in all things was the noble Arigius,[107]
    whose noble fame you either restore or surpass.
But your honor is his and his persists in you,
    and thus with a doubled light you outshine everyone.
And no one doubts that you have surpassed his happiness,
    inasmuch as your mother still survives, praised by all.
She equally replenishes and equips you with all things in such a
    manner
    that you are overflowing with abilities and adorned
        with accomplishments.
You must be congratulated, O city of Trier,
    you who are ruled by such a man, the equal of the ancients.
He has descended, I do believe, from a great family of your people:
    undoubtedly, his is that virtue which one reads was that of
        Arbogastes.[108]
His triumphs likewise are inscribed in the annals,
    just as also are written those of him whom I mentioned above.
But let me add this distinction to the one who is truly greater,
      because he, dedicated to religion, invokes the name of Christ.

---

104. The title of *inlustris*, which Arbogastes had not yet officially earned, ranked above that of *spectabilis*; Auspicius accords him the title anyway and shows that the barbarian Arbogastes was as desirous of high rank as any Roman senator.

105. *Clarus*: the rank (*vir clarissimus*) of individuals born into the senatorial aristocracy.

106. Auspicius endows Arbogastes with the most traditional Roman virtues. His lack of the title of *inlustris* clearly seems to have been a cause of concern for Arbogastes, and Auspicius rather belabors his attempts to downplay it.

107. Arigius is otherwise unknown. The Roman name could suggest that Arbogastes was descended from the fourth-century general on his mother's side.

108. That is, the elder Arbogastes.

That ancestor of his, it is true, was energetic in warfare,
but he died an unbeliever, and in death he lost everything.
This man of ours, however, is vigorous, bellicose, acclaimed,
and, what is greater than all of these, a devotee of the divine
name.
Now, moreover, I beseech you, my wise son, accept graciously
this page of your admirer, which I affectionately proffer.
Firstly, I pray that you preserve within yourself my wishes
extended
with such great esteem, and that you overflow with many goods.
Avoid one sin, lest your pure heart become sullied,
for it is written in the Scriptures that the root of all evils is
Of course, cupidity, which rages in its devotees and does not
prevent
the madness of those through whose savage love it is nourished.
Suffering from a gnawing hunger, I say, it always devours them,
and like a fire it grows, rekindled when fuel is added.
But I have not spoken such words because I condemn you for this
crime;[109]
Nevertheless I affectionately pray that not even one spark will
scorch you,
For if by chance at any time, unprepared, you should trap such a
spark,
it might quickly flare up, being fanned into flames.
Cast your eyes over the world, note that the leading men of the day
either die in cupidity or live amid dangers.
Like greedy dogs, they hoard, hunt, hunger,
And they neither possess anything themselves, nor do they
bequeath it to their heirs.[110]
Nevertheless, I have not spoken these words about all men in
general,

---

109. In fact, the elder Arbogastes had been praised specifically for his lack of greed: Eunapius fr. 3; Zosimus 4.33.1–2, 53.1.

110. For a translation of these few lines, see Jack Lindsay, *Song of a Falling World: A Study of the Literature of the Roman Empire during Its Decline* (London, 1948), 201:

Turn serious eyes abroad / look on each famous lord
who dies with lusts yet ranging / or lives in midst of dangers.
The snout and yap and quarrel / like greedy dogs. The moral:
they lose what's sought with cares / nor leave it to their heirs.

but so that the disgrace of the few may serve as an example for
　　the many.
You remarkable man, moreover, a provident judge of many
　　persons,
　　as a judge examine quickly the secrets of your heart.
If you should sense in it any little drop of poison,
　　drench it with sweet oil, lest it creep into your innards.
Nor, in the best interest of your wisdom, should you ignore this oil,
　　which is the business of charity toward all of the poor.
Exercise yourself in these practices, espouse all these virtues,
　　so that my joy in you may remain and persevere.
For you know that it is too little if someone appropriates none of
　　them,
　　and with a hardened heart holds back his property from the
　　unfortunate.
He has no great consideration for himself, one who avoids the
　　madness
　　Of cupidity in such a way that at the same time he incurs that of
　　avarice.
For these two sins, as if they were related in nature
　　and duplicated in their aspect, are particularly persistent when
　　they are combined.
As for those unfortunates who pursue them, this one fault is the
　　difference:
　　because one of them is bad and the other is the worst.
Therefore, my dear administrator, you, your mother's only son, I
　　beg you:
　　refrain from outlandish acts so that your own acts might be
　　counted among the holy.
And above all, remain mindful in your heart of this,
　　that I already see in you the presaging of the priesthood.
Preserve this grace, I beg you, and grow in those merits,
　　so that the sacred preordained voice of the people may ascend
　　to the skies.[111]
Honor and esteem in your heart our bishop Iamlychus,[112] blessed
　　and

---

111. Compare the epitaph of Nymfius in the next chapter. An Arbogastes, perhaps the same person, did indeed become bishop of Chartres not long afterward; see Duchesne, *Fastes,* 2:424–25.

112. Bishop of Trier; see Sid.Apoll. *Epist.* 4.17.3.

the first among us all, so that you may be esteemed in the future.
Anything you grant to him, you prepare for yourself in Christ;
   you shall reap in the future that which you yourself sow now.
It is finished.

Even the erudite and conceited Sidonius Apollinaris addressed a letter to Arbogastes, who had written him requesting some biblical exegesis. Sidonius fulsomely replied, "Thus, the glory of Roman speech, if
it exists now anywhere at all . . . resides in you. . . . I greatly rejoice that
at least in your illustrious breast vestiges of our vanishing culture
remain," and noted, perhaps tongue in cheek, "Thus, you are familiar
with barbarians, but you nonetheless are unfamiliar with barbarisms."[113] Sidonius then referred Arbogastes to Auspicius for the
biblical instruction. Educated barbarians like Arbogastes could be
admitted on sufferance into Roman literary circles, but even they were
not allowed to forget their barbarian background.

Eucheria and the Persistence of the Classical Tradition

Aristocratic women also contributed to the literary life of late antique
Gaul.[114] A collection of poems known as the *Latin Anthology* preserves
a poem by a certain Eucheria that makes particular use of antithesis
(opposites), a popular rhetorical characteristic of late Latin literature.

1.14[115]   I wish to fuse golden threads, shining with harmonious metal,
                  with masses of bristles.
               Silken coverings, gem-studded Laconian[116] fabrics,
                  I say, must be matched with goatskins.

---

113. "Quocirca sermonis pompa Romani si qua adhuc uspiam est in te resedit . . .
granditer laetor saltim in inlustri pectore tuo vanescentium litterarum remansisse vesti-
gia . . . sic barbarorum familiaris, quod tamen nescius barbarismorum" (*Epist.*
4.17.1–2).
114. Note also the examples of Faltonia Betitia Proba (n. 29) above and Baudonivia
(chap. 6 below).
115. Eucheria, "Aurea concordi": E. Baehrens, ed., *Poetae latini minores* 5 (Leipzig:
Teubner, 1910), 360–63 = Alexander Riese, ed., *Anthologia latina* 1.1 (Leipzig: Teubner,
1894), 303–5, no. 390.
116. From Laconia, in Greece, the homeland of Sparta.

Let noble purple be joined with a frightful red jacket;[117]
   let the gleaming gemstone be joined to ponderous lead.
Let the pearl now be held captive by its own brightness,
   and let it shine enclosed in dark steel.
Likewise, let the emerald be enclosed in Leuconian[118] bronze,
   and let now hyacinth[119] be the equal of flint.
Let jasper be said to be like rubble and rocks;
   let now the moon embrace the nether void.
Now, indeed, let us decree that lilies are to be joined with nettles,
   and let the menacing hemlock oppress the scarlet rose.
Now, similarly, let us therefore, spurning the fish, choose
   to disdain the delicacies of the great sea.
Let the rock-dwelling toad love the golden serpent,
   and likewise let the female trout seek for herself the male
     snail.[120]
And let the lofty lioness be joined with the foul fox;
   let the ape embrace the sharp-eyed lynx.
Now let the doe be joined to the donkey, and the tigress to the wild ass;
   now let the fleet deer be joined to the torpid bull.
Let now the foul silphium juice[121] taint the nectared rose-wine,
   and let now honey be mixed with vile poisons.
Let us associate sparkling water with the muddy cesspool;
   let the fountain flow saturated with a mixture of filth.
Let the swift swallow cavort with the funereal vulture;
   let now the nightingale serenade with the doleful owl.
Let the unhappy coop-dweller[122] abide with the pellucid partridge,
   and let the beautiful dove lie coupled with the crow.
Let the times manipulate these monstrosities with uncertain
   consequences,
   and in this way let the slave Rusticus seek Eucheria.

---

117. *Burrae;* apparently from *burrus,* a coarse red outer garment.

118. Ms. *lenconico;* emended to *leuconico,* perhaps as a reference to Leuci (Toul) in Gaul.

119. A gemstone, possibly a kind of sapphire or dark amethyst, the color of the hyacinth flower (perhaps a larkspur).

120. *Limacem:* from *limax,* a word also used of prostitutes who preyed upon the property of their lovers.

121. *Lasera:* a bad-smelling gum resin obtained from the silphium plant and used medicinally as an antispasmodic drug.

122. *Cavannus:* perhaps the inhabitant of a *cavea,* a cave or bird coop.

A little detective work can help us to identify Eucheria. Her name and that of Rusticus suggest the area of Lyon, where these names are attested during Late Antiquity.[123] The mention of *aes leuconicum* likewise could be an allusion to the *civitas Leucorum,* modern-day Toul. Both considerations place the poem in Gaul, and Eucheria is most likely to be identified as the Eucheria whose husband, the patrician Dynamius, served in Provence in the middle to late sixth century.[124] If so, then one might wonder just what the connection was between Eucheria and "Rusticus": perhaps the poem was a juvenile effort, or perhaps Rusticus and Dynamius are the same person, or perhaps "rusticus" is not a name at all, and the phrase should be translated as "rustic slave." As for Dynamius, he was a litterateur in his own right. Two of his letters are preserved in the Merovingian collection known as the *Epistulae Austrasicae* (Austrasian letters): in one he pays his respects to an anonymous friend, and in the other he apologizes to Bishop Vilicus of Metz for his tardy reply.[125] He also is named as the author of an extant *Life of Maximus of Riez,* dedicated to Urbicus, bishop of Riez.[126]

Eucheria survived Dynamius by eight years and died circa 605; their epitaph, in the Church of St. Hippolytus at Marseille, was provided by a grandson, also named Dynamius;[127] the younger Dynamius also has been identified as the Dynamius who wrote the *Laus insulae Lerinensis* (Praise of the island of Lérins).[128] Eucheria, therefore, belonged to a literary family,[129] and her literary activities demonstrate the continued vitality of the Roman secular literary tradition.

Conclusion

For aristocrats, literary endeavors served not only as intellectual challenges but also as a means of cementing their position in society. The

---

123. For the letter of another Rusticus to Bishop Eucherius of Lyon, see above.

124. Dynamius: Greg.Tur. *Hist.* 6.7, 11; Venantius Fortunatus, *Carm.* 6.9–10; *PLRE* 3.429–30. The penultimate line of Eucheria's poem was cited by Julianus of Toledo in the early seventh century, providing a *terminus ante quem.*

125. *Epistulae Austrasicae* 12, 17: *MGH Epist.* 3:127, 130–31.

126. *PL* 80:31–62. The question of Dynamius's authorship remains open.

127. *MGH AA* 6.2:194; it is cited fully in the companion volume.

128. *Anthologia Latina* 1.2:265–66, no. 786a.

129. She may have been a scion of the family of Bishop Eucherius of Lyon, whose own literary circle is discussed in chapter 3 below.

thoughts that they expressed, especially in their personal correspondence, offer much insight into society, individuals, and personal expression. In the subsequent chapters, additional letters will be cited. But letters are not the only documents that provide social insights. This volume will feature other kinds of sources as well. And all of them, in one way or another, indicate that during Late Antiquity the old Roman aristocracy was threatened on all sides. Some aristocrats responded effectively to the changing circumstances; others fell by the wayside.[130]

---

130. On senatorial strategies for survival, see S. J. Barnish, "Transformation and Survival in the Western Senatorial Aristocracy, c. A.D. 400–700," *Papers of the British School at Rome* 56 (1988): 120–55; and Mathisen, *Roman Aristocrats.*

CHAPTER 2

The Socially Less Privileged: Decurions and Plebeians, Dependents and Slaves

Full-fledged aristocrats, even if they monopolized traditional kinds of status and authority, made up but a small percentage of the population. The rest of society possessed lesser privilege. Some, such as women and children, encountered social restrictions resulting from their gender or age; they will be discussed in the next chapter. Those rendered nonelite by their social, economic, and legal status are described here. For them, the changing times could be either a curse or a blessing, a problem or an opportunity. On the one hand, lower-ranking *honestiores,* who had some little status, confronted the possibility of losing their rung on the ladder of privilege, and *humiliores* could face bankruptcy, enslavement, and death. But on the other, the social and political disruption opened windows of opportunity to able and ambitious persons of all ranks whose aspirations might have been stifled or restricted in the past.

The Aristocratic Fringe

Aristocratic families like the Apollinares, Rustici, Ferreoli, Syagrii, Aviti, and Magni[1] may have been the "big fish" on an imperial or Gallic level, but in each municipality, smaller fry also made their marks. There, the members of town councils—who were known as *municipales, curiales,* and *decuriones*—performed their duties, carried out

---

1. For these families, see Ralph W. Mathisen, "The Ecclesiastical Aristocracy of Fifth-Century Gaul: A Regional Analysis of Family Structure," Ph.D. diss., University of Wisconsin, 1979. For the significance of names, see the previous chapter.

other activities, and pursued their ambitions outside the glare of the full-fledged aristocratic spotlight.[2] Socially, these least privileged of the *honestiores* were squeezed between the senatorial elite and the mass of the unprivileged population. In a sense, they suffered the worst of both worlds, disdained by their aristocratic superiors and distrusted by their plebeian or servile inferiors.

Salvian of Marseille, for example, portraying the viewpoint of the unprivileged, suggested that in out-of-the-way places town councillors took advantage of their niggling prominence: "What cities are there, and even towns and villages, where there are not as many tyrants as there are decurions? Yet, perhaps they glory in this designation, because it seems to be powerful *(potens)* and honored."[3] So these persons, too, avidly pursued their share of the coveted *potentia.* But their ability to exercise it was scorned by their aristocratic distant cousins. The snobbish Sidonius, for example, sneeringly described his nemesis Paeonius as *municipaliter natus* (town bred) and noted that the deposed prefect Arvandus had been returned to a *plebeia familia* (plebeian family).[4]

A Petty Aristocrat

Such individuals faced an anxious, hand-to-mouth existence. Their lot was described by the author of the *Querolus,* who put into the mouth of a slave a vignette of two fictional local notables, Querolus and Arbiter:

2.1[5] (75) Good gods! Would that I ever be granted what I now seek: would that my harsh and cruel master have to live as an ex- town councillor

---

2. See J. Declareuil, "Les curies municipales et le clergé au Bas-Empire," *Revue historique du droit française et étranger* 14 (1935): 26–53.

3. "Quae enim sunt non modo urbes, sed etiam municipia atque vici, ubi non quot curiales fuerint, tot tyranni sunt? quamquam forte hoc nomine gratulentur, quia potens et honoratus esse videatur": *De gubernatione dei* (On the government of God), 5.4; see C. Lepelley, "Quot curiales, tot tyranni: L'image du décurion oppresseur au bas-empire," in *Crise et redressement dans les provinces européennes de l'empire,* ed. E. Frezouls (Strasbourg, AECR 1983), 143–56.

4. Sid.Apoll. *Epist.* 1.11.5, 1.7.11; see *PLRE* 2:157–58 and 495 respectively. For these two as "climbing parvenus," see Barnish, "Transformation," 137; for Sidonius's difficulties with the social climber Paeonius, see Ralph W. Mathisen, "Resistance and Reconciliation: Majorian and the Gallic Aristocracy after the Fall of Avitus," *Francia* 7 (1979): 597–627.

5. *Querolus* 2.4 (75–76), ed. Peiper, 40–41; ed. C. Jacquemard–Le Saos, 48–49. The numbers represent the section numbers in Peiper and Le Saos, respectively.

(ex municipe) or as an ex–civil servant *(ex togato)* or as an ex-chief of an office staff *(ex principe officii).*[6] Why do I say this? (76) Because after being privileged, being humbled is all the more ignominious. What would I wish for Querolus except that he himself should do what Arbiter does. Let him live as a togate petitioner, an entertainer of judges, a watcher of doors, a little slave of little slaves, a round-the-forum examiner, a crafty observer, a seeker and grasper of hours and time, in the morning, at noon, and in the evening. Let him shamelessly[7] greet the snobbish, let him go to meet those who don't show up, and let him wear in the heat stockings that are new and too tight.

Such persons were at the mercy of the great men, and received scant respect from everyone else. The positions of *togatus* and *princeps officii* were the kind of middle-level imperial administrative posts that provided employment to legions of educated Gauls during the Later Roman Empire. Their disappearance in the fifth century made the social and economic position of many who had depended on them even more tenuous, including perhaps the author of the *Querolus,* who may have had personal experience with the humiliation that he described.

Big Fish in Small Ponds

Few local gentry left any record of their activities or even of their existence. One who did is Nymfius, who lived in the area of Valentine on the upper Garonne River in Novempopulana, perhaps circa 350/450.[8] He was a minor character, but one with grand pretensions, as illustrated by the fulsome epitaph provided by his wife Serena:

---

6. Even though the position of *princeps officii* was a good one, it was hardly the highest goal of a bona fide aristocrat.

7. *Impudens,* a word usually used to describe slaves (see the second passage from the *Querolus* below), indicating how far the author wishes to show that this petty notable will have fallen.

8. See H. Sivan, "Town, Country, and Province in Late Roman Gaul: The Example of *CIL* XIII 128," *Zeitschrift für Papyrologie und Epigraphik* 79 (1989): 103–14. Date: any earlier, and the inscription is unlikely to have been Christian (as indicated by the crosses); any later, and it would be unlikely that the Roman administration would have survived. For the locale, see G. Fouet, "Le sanctuaire gallo-romaine de Valentine (Haute-Garonne)," *Gallia* 42 (1984): 153–73.

.2[9] + Nymfius, having surrendered your limbs to eternal sleep,
  you are placed here. Your pious soul delights in heaven;
Your soul observes the stars; the peace of the tomb encompasses
    your limbs;
  your blessed faith tramples upon the gloomy shadows.
Your deserved fame conveyed you to the stars on account of the
    merits
  of your virtue, and it ascended to the distant pole.
You will be immortal, for your living glory will flourish
  with great praise among coming generations.[10]
The entire province[11] esteemed you as its own parent;
  public prayers sustained your life.
In days gone by, the largess bestowed at your expense received
  the joy of a people applauding throughout the auditorium.[12]
Through you, our dear homeland called forth the council of its
    leaders,[13]
  and believed that it spoke more virtuously through your mouth.
A communal grief afflicts cities that now are orphaned, and the
  leading citizens, bewildered, assemble in an anxious throng:
As a result, the torpid limbs stiffen with the head torn away;
  as a result, the listless flock grieves the loss of its bellwether.[14]
Your wife, grieving Serena, dedicates this epitaph for your tomb,
  a small solace for her great sorrow.
She, present always as a comrade of unswerving support,
  gave her undivided self to you for forty years.
Life with you was sweet; your anxious comrade, craving the
  eternal light, hopes that what remains of hers will be brief. +

---

9. *CIL* 13:128.

10. Compare this sentiment to Rusticus's statement to Eucherius (chap. 1 above), "in times to come . . . you will be . . . praised by future generations."

11. The province of Novempopulana.

12. *Per cuneos* (wedge-shaped sections of seats): apparently a reference to Nymphius's sponsorship of local entertainments.

13. *Concilium procerum;* it is unclear whether this is the town council or the provincial assembly; the reference to orphaned cities could suggest the latter. For these poorly attested councils, see E. Carette, *Les assemblées provinciales de la Gaule romaine* (Paris: Picard et fils, 1895); and J. A. O. Larsen, "The Position of Provincial Assemblies in the Government and Society of the Late Roman Empire," *Classical Philology* 29 (1934): 209–20.

14. *Princeps,* perhaps an official title, although probably not the *princeps officii* of the *Querolus.*

The poem is skillfully composed. The repetition of many of the words may be intended to convey the sense of togetherness between Nymfius and Serena. Indeed, perhaps Serena herself wrote the poem.

Nymfius might not have been a player in the "big time," but he certainly was a big fish in a little pond, even presiding, perhaps, at meetings of the provincial assembly. There must have been a multitude of such persons, whose ambitions had been thwarted during the Roman period but who now had an opportunity to blossom during the changed circumstances of Late Antiquity. The family of Gregory of Tours, for example, which enjoyed great success in the sixth century, had been of but middling local importance in the fifth.[15]

From the depths of sub-Roman Gaul, in the early seventh century, comes an epitaph from Lyon. It describes a man who, if not of the stature of Nymfius, still was far from destitute, and it continues traditions established two centuries and more before:

2.3[16] Buried under this tombstone lie the limbs of Mercurinus, nicknamed Cictato,[17] benign in goodness, perfected in charity, generous in piety, great with greatness, most delightful in faith, especially great in simplicity, born, beloved, of a family, always dutiful toward the poor. Four times ten in the tenth age,[18] he lived in peace for seventy-five years, and he died seven days before the Kalends of April in the sixth indiction, the seventy-ninth year after the consulate of the consul Justin, a most distinguished gentleman.

Mercurinus's charity toward the poor and his self-consciously modest claim to be the scion of "a family," not to mention his ability to afford a rather lavish epitaph, all attest to a social position of some note. Presumably, he exemplifies many who existed in the social gap between the eminent and the servile. In some regards, moreover, he

---

15. See Ralph W. Mathisen, "The Family of Georgius Florentius Gregorius and the Bishops of Tours," *Mediaevalia et Humanistica* 12 (1984): 83–96.

16. F. Descombes and J.-F. Reynaud, "Epitaphes chrétiennes recemment découvertes à Lyon," *Rivista di archeologia cristiana* 54 (1978): 291–96.

17. *Cictato:* the meaning is unclear; perhaps it is a reference to a scar *(cicatrix)*.

18. "Quater denus decima etate annus lxxv portavit": this apparently nonsensical phrase perhaps was uncritically copied from an earlier epitaph, such as that of Felemoda *sive* Moda (A.D. 548/549), "quater denus decimam aetatem XXXX portauit" (fully cited in the companion volume): P. Wuilleumier, A. Audin, and A. Leroi-Fourhan, *Bulletin de la Société Archéologique de la France* (1948–49), 186.

also represents a lost world. For, at a time when dating was customarily done using regnal years of kings, his epitaph employed, rather inconsistently, the antiquated and increasingly cumbersome consular dating system, giving a date no less than "seventy-nine years after the consulship of Justin" (A.D. 619).[19] The inscription also uses the Byzantine fifteen-year indiction cycle (giving a date of A.D. 618); and "seven days before the Kalends of April" translates to March 26.

"A Merchant of Clermont"

Late Antiquity saw the social and economic degradation of a number of petty aristocrats and moderately wealthy decurions-cum-landowners, as barbarians, bishops, and senators strengthened their own hands at the expense of those unable to protect themselves. Those who had the patronage of more powerful magnates could hope to survive, even if sometimes in reduced circumstances. Others faced total ruin.

The case of Amantius is instructive. He was a businessman from Clermont who regularly traveled to Provence. This made him ideal as a letter carrier for Sidonius Apollinaris, who mentioned him several times circa 470–80 in letters to Graecus, bishop of Marseille.[20] Sidonius portrayed Amantius as a likable rogue, like a stock character from a romance.[21] Amantius's pretensions and ambitions, although depicted with some conventional disapprobation, also were viewed indulgently by Sidonius—who was, after all, his countryman, bishop, and patron. In his introductory letter to Graecus, Sidonius gave a sketch of Amantius's background:

.4[22] Sidonius to the lord pope[23] Graecus, greetings.

(1) The bearer of these words maintains a poverty-stricken living by acting as a buyer; for him there is no profit in craftwork, no comfort in

---

19. Justin, sole consul in A.D. 540, was the nephew of the emperor Justinian (527–65). His full name was Fl. Mar. Petrus Theodorus Valentinus Rusticius Boraides Germanus Iustinus; see Bagnall et al., *Consuls,* 614–15. The last non-imperial consul, Basilius, served in the following year, but in Gaul it remained customary to date "from the consulate of Justin."

20. *Epist.* 7.7.1, 7.10[11].1, 9.4.1.

21. See Sid.Apoll. *Epist.* 7.2.9, "So here you have . . . a tale fit to match any that Miletus or Athens has produced."

22. Sid.Apoll. *Epist.* 6.8; for additional translations see Anderson, *Sidonius,* 2:269–71; and Dalton, *Sidonius,* 2:88.

23. At this time, any distinguished bishop could be given the title *pope (papa),* which did not begin to be limited to the bishop of Rome until the sixth century.

official service, no gain from farming. On account of this very fact, that he is known for his hired-out activities and his contracted labor, there is indeed an increase in his own reputation but in the affluence of others. But even if he has little wealth there is nonetheless great confidence in him, seeing that however often he approaches the sale of a recently arrived ship with the money of whomever you please he deposits as security with deservedly trusting creditors only their experience of his character. (2) These matters were presented to me in the midst of my dictation, but I do not hesitate on these grounds to report confidently what I heard, given that those with whom he himself is sufficiently familiar are no less familiar with me.[24] I therefore commend his youthful countenance and unpolished background, and, because the roster of readers[25] recently has received his name, understand that as he was about to set out on his journey I owed him a letter of introduction as a fellow-citizen and a canonical letter[26] as a cleric. I believe that shortly he will be a splendid merchant if, hurrying thence to pay his respects to you, he prefers the spring of a more undiluted wisdom to the chills of his municipal springs.

Deign to be mindful of me, Lord Pope.

This letter is pretty standard stuff, and Sidonius presumably wrote many like it on behalf of other parishioners. He probably would not even have included it in his collection were it not for Amantius's other appearances in his correspondence, and in particular for Amantius's past escapades, as described in a subsequent letter to Graecus:

---

24. An indication of how important it was to know the right people and be part of the right social networks.

25. There were several offices in the official church hierarchy, including, in order of increasing rank, *fossor* (gravedigger), *psalmista* or *cantor* (psalmist, singer), *ostiarius* (doorman or usher), *lector* (reader), *exorcista* (exorcist), *acolitus* (acolyte), *subdiaconus* (subdeacon), *diaconus* or *levita* (deacon), *presbyter* (priest), and *episcopus* (bishop). Only deacons, priests, and bishops were ordained by the imposition of hands. The position of *lector* was often held be persons who remained in secular life.

26. Referred to here as an *epistola formata* (form letter), also known as *litterae commendaticiae* ("a letter of recommendation," on which see below). These were letters that bishops were duty-bound to give to parishioners, and especially those who were clerics, who were traveling to different dioceses so as to allow them to participate in Christian services elsewhere.

5[27]   Sidonius to the lord pope Graecus, greetings.

(1) You overwhelm me, most consummate of all bishops, by the praises showered on any unpolished lines that I happen to write.[28] Short though my first letter was, I wish I could acquit myself of blame for having told you a whole string of things irreconcilable with fact. The truth is that a crafty traveller imposed upon my innocence. Ostensibly a trader, he persuaded me to give him a canonical letter as a reader, and this ought certainly to have contained some display of thanks.[29] For it appeared, on subsequent inquiry, that by the generosity of the people of Marseille he set out better equipped than one so moderately favored in birth and fortune had reason to expect.

(2) It makes quite a good story, if I only wielded a pen able to do justice to its humors. But as you have asked me for a long and diverting letter, permit me to relate the manner in which this messenger of ours exploited the hospitality of your city. It shall be told in a light vein, but I shall be careful to say nothing to offend the severity of your ears. You will see that on this occasion I really do know the man whom I introduce to your notice for the second time. Usage permits a writer to find his subject-matter wherever he can; why, then, should I go far afield, when the man who is to bear my letter can himself provide the theme of it?

(3) The bearer, then, is a native of Clermont, born of humble but free parents, people who made no pretense of social standing, but were above all fear of degradation to the servile state, and were satisfied with means, moderate indeed, but unencumbered and amply sufficient for their needs.[30] It was a family that had chiefly held offices under the church, and had not entered public service. The father was a most estimable man, but not free-handed with his children; he preferred to serve his son's advantage, instead of ensuring him pleasant times in his youth. The result was that the prisoner escaped to you a little too

---

27. Sid.Apoll. *Epist.* 7.2; translation from Dalton, *Sidonius,* 2:98–101; see also Anderson, *Sidonius* 2:292–303.

28. Sidonius begins with a customary disparaging of his own literary ability, which, rather than being meant to be taken seriously, was intended to put the recipient at his ease.

29. *Actio gratiarum:* a formal speech of thanks, often delivered to an emperor or other high official.

30. This was important, as it meant that the family was not directly dependent upon some potentate.

lightly equipped, and this was no small impediment to the outset of his adventure, for a light purse is the heaviest encumbrance on a journey. (4) Nevertheless, he made his first entry into your city under the most favorable auspices. Your predecessor St. Eustachius[31] received him with a two-fold blessing, in word and deed. He wanted a lodging; one was forthcoming without difficulty on the prelate's commendation. He rented the rooms in due form, entering on his tenancy without delay, and at once set about making the acquaintance of his neighbors by saluting them as often as possible and being civilly greeted in return. He treated all as befitted their several ages; respectful to the old, he always was obliging to those of his own years. (5) He was consistently temperate and moral, showing qualities as admirable as they are rare at this time of life. He was assiduous in paying court to your chief personages, and even to the count of the city himself. Alive to every chance, he began by receiving nods, went on to acquaintance, and ended in intimacy. By this systematic cultivation of important friendships, he rapidly got on in the world. The best people competed for his company. Everyone wished him well; there were plenty to offer him good advice. Private individuals made him presents, officials helped him by their influence. In short, his prospects and his resources rose by leaps and bounds.

(6) It chanced that near the house where he lodged there resided a lady whose disposition and income were all that he could have desired. She had a daughter, not quite marriageable, but no longer a child. He began to attract the girl by pleasant greetings, and by giving her (as, at her age, he quite properly could) the various trifles and trinkets that delight a maiden's fancy. By such light links he succeeded in closely attaching her heart to his own. (7) Time passed; she reached the age of marriage. You already guess what happened. This young man, without visible relations or substance, a foreigner, a minor who had left home without his father's leave or knowledge, demands the hand of a girl equal to himself in birth, and superior in fortune. He demands, and, what is more, obtains: he is recognized as a suitor. For the bishop actively supported his reader, and the count encouraged his client; the

---

31. The predecessor of Graecus, bishop of Marseille ca. 461–70 (Duchesne, *Fastes,* 1:274). He was an author of hymns; see Gennad. *Vir.ill.* 80.

future mother-in-law did not trouble to investigate his means; the bride approved his person. The marriage contract was executed, and some little suburban plot or other at Clermont[32] was put into settlement and read out with much theatrical parade. (8) This legal trick and solemn swindle once over, the pauper lover carried off the wealthy bride. He promptly went into all his wife's father's affairs, and got together some nice little pickings for himself, aided all through the imposture by the credulity of his easy-going and free-handed mother-in-law. Then, and not until then, this incomparable charlatan sounds the retreat and vanishes into the Auvergne. After he had gone, the mother thought of bringing a compensatory action[33] against him for the absurd exaggerations in the contract. But it was rather late for her to begin lamenting the exiguity of the settlement when she was already rejoicing at the prospect of a wealth of little grandchildren. It was with the object of appeasing her that our Hippolytus[34] went to Marseille when he brought you my first letter of introduction.

(9) That is the story of this accomplished young man, as good in its way as any out of Attic comedy or Milesian fable.[35] Excuse the excessive length of my letter; I have dwelt upon every detail that you might be fully informed in regard to the person whom your generosity has made a citizen of your town; and besides, one naturally has a kindly feeling for those in whom one has taken active interest. You will prove yourself in everything the worthy successor of Eustachius if you expend upon his clients the personal interest he would like to have been able to bequeath them,[36] as you already have paid his relations the legacies mentioned in his will.

---

32. This presumably was property that Amantius did not yet own.

33. *Actio repetundarum:* a formal Roman legal procedure. She seems, however, not to have pursued the matter.

34. In Greek mythology, the son of Theseus and Antiope; his stepmother Phaedra failed in an attempt to seduce him. The tale was presented at Athens in the drama *Hippolytus* by Euripides in the late fifth century B.C.

35. The erotic *Fabulae Milesiae* (Milesian tales) were written by Aristeides of Miletus ca. 100 B.C. and were later translated into Latin by Cornelius Sisenna. Curiously, Sidonius makes no attempt to play upon Amantius's name (i.e., "Lover"). Perhaps he thought the point was obvious.

36. Sidonius indicates not only that he continues to support Amantius, but also that he expects Graecus to do likewise.

(10) And now I have obeyed your commands to the full, and talked
to the limit of my obligation; remember that one who imposes on a
man of small descriptive powers a subject calling for great detail must
not complain if the response betrays the gossiper rather than the skilled
narrator.

Deign to hold me in remembrance, Lord Bishop.

At first glance, Sidonius's introductory words might seem rather
disingenuous. Could he really have known so little about one of his
own parishioners whose family, it seems, was of some moment in Clermont? If so, one might conclude that after he—a native, after all, of
Lyon—became bishop of Clermont circa 469, he not only knew little
about the local population, but also made scant effort to find out. On
the other hand, however, his discussion suggests that Amantius had
been back in Clermont long enough for him and his bride to have had
"numerous children" in the interim. So, as far as Sidonius was concerned, Amantius's escapades in Marseille might have been "ancient
history."

As for Amantius himself, for obvious reasons he would have been
close-mouthed about his shenanigans. And Sidonius's lack of mention
of any consequences upon Amantius's return to Clermont could suggest that any differences with his family were subsequently patched up.
Indeed, the niggardly parsimony that Sidonius attributes to Amantius's father could have been a necessary result of the hard times on
which the family had fallen, hard times that had forced at least one of
his sons to create a new career for himself. So, Amantius, perhaps
using his family connections, had built up a thriving business as a pur-
chasing agent. He no doubt also saw his office of lector—which he performed at both Marseille and Clermont—as a means of making new
business contacts, perhaps akin to joining the Chamber of Commerce
or Rotary Club in the modern day. Yet regardless of how Amantius
eventually was able to make the best of things, his new position as an
itinerant merchant-cum-messenger very probably was a step or two
below what he might have had reason to expect a generation before.

The Dispossessed Priest

A person who suffered greater economic ruin, and who made a more
serious commitment to the church, was the priest Possessor, whose

high ecclesiastical rank may reflect a respectable social status as well. Possessor came from Angers, where just before A.D. 500 he obtained from Bishop Eumerius[37] a letter of introduction to Ruricius, from whom he then sought a letter to Aeonius of Arles (ca. 490–502). Ruricius was happy to oblige, as seen in his cover letter to Aeonius:

.6[38] Bishop Ruricius to a sanctified and apostolic lord, and a patron for me before others to be esteemed personally by worship and affection in Christ the Lord, Bishop Aeonius.

However often any individuals, depressed by the mass of their troubles, are compelled to seek out sanctified and apostolic men, whose good deeds of compassion, services of good deeds, and life of services commend them, and who are made known by the fame of all their virtues, these individuals, when they seek solace for their distress in correspondence, confer a favor upon us, and although their distress troubles us, nevertheless, through our conferring of service, their need becomes in some way our expression of kindness, by which, when we acquiesce to their petition we satisfy our own desire, and it thus turns out that the poverty of the petitioner benefits the bestower.

Therefore, when he requested letters of attestation[39] to Your Apostlehood I readily indulged our brother and fellow priest, Possessor by name, unfortunately, rather than by property,[40] because that which he had, he lavished upon the redemption of his brother; he became a possessor of Paradise when he ceased to be a possessor of secular property. If Your Sanctity should deign to comprehend his need more fully, you may consider it sufficiently important to review the letter that our brother, Bishop Eumerius, sent through him to My Humility, and you may recognize there how fitting it is to counsel him in the customary manner and to sympathize with him for the sake of our mutual esteem. In order that he render his brother free of the enemy, he prefers himself

---

37. In office between Thalassius (last attested in 461) and Eustochius (first seen in 511) (Duchesne, *Fastes,* 2:366).

38. Ruric. *Epist.* 2.8: *MGH AA* 8:317; *CSEL* 21:382–83; *CCL* 64:341; for translation, see Mathisen, *Ruricius,* 145–46. The end of the letter is lost.

39. *Commendaticias.* The Council of Agde (A.D. 506), canon 38 (*CCL* 148:208–9), required clerics and monks to receive "epistolae commendaticiae" before going on a journey, as Amantius had done in the previous example. Technically, the recipient should be one of the writer's own parishioners, apparently not the case here.

40. Ruricius could not resist some wordplay: Possessor's name means "owner," and in particular, a property owner, which Possessor clearly no longer was.

to be a captive of creditors, and in order that he not lose his life through a most cruel death, he himself has been made an exile from his home. . . .

The letter begins with another example of an elaborate epistulary salutation. By referring to Possessor as his "fellow priest," and thus ascribing to him a status equal to his own, Ruricius not only affects humility, but also by implication augments Possessor's status in the eyes of Aeonius. And this in spite of the likelihood that Ruricius apparently knew Possessor even less well than Sidonius had known Amantius. Yet he took the trouble to use his influence with Aeonius, providing another example of the operation of the aristocratic-episcopal network that knit together the late antique world.

Ruricius claimed that Possessor had expended what wealth he had in ransoming his brother, presumably impoverishing himself in the process. As for the identity of the enemy that had captured his brother, there are several possible candidates: Angers was in an exposed frontier area, threatened by Franks, Visigoths, Bretons/Armoricans, and freebooting bandits.[41] For example, Gregory of Tours reported that in the mid-460s, Adovacrius, a leader of Saxon raiders, "took hostages from Angers and elsewhere."[42] And even though Ruricius does not specify what kind of assistance Possessor thought that Aeonius could offer,[43] Aeonius's successor Caesarius certainly had a reputation for expending resources on the freeing of captives.[44] Aeonius may have done the same.

Buried Alive

Those who, unlike Nymfius, could not stand on their own, or find powerful patrons, like Amantius and Possessor, faced coercion. Gregory of Tours told a macabre tale, worthy of Edgar Allen Poe, about what could happen to unprotected landowners who fell victim to the avarice

---

41. For slaving by Bretons, see Sid.Apoll. *Epist.* 3.9; by bandits: Sid.Apoll. *Epist.* 6.4.1.

42. *Hist.* 2.18.

43. Perhaps introductions to moneylenders, although even here it is unclear what kind of collateral Possessor could have provided.

44. See William Klingshirn, "Charity and Power: Caesarius of Arles and the Ransoming of Captives in Sub-Roman Gaul," *Journal of Roman Studies* 75 (1985): 183–203. Note also St. Patrick's letter to Coroticus in chapter 4 below.

of their more powerful brethren. It seems that the priest Anastasius had refused to turn over to Bishop Cautinus of Clermont (ca. 560–71) the *charta* (a papyrus document) he had received from Queen Clotilde granting him a choice parcel of land that Cautinus wished to use for an expansion project.[45] In an attempt to force him to do so, Cautinus applied some terror tactics:

2.7[46] Then, at the order of the bishop, he was turned over to guards so that he would die of starvation unless he turned over the documents. There was a most ancient, out-of-the-way crypt at the basilica of the sainted martyr Cassius,[47] where there was a large sepulchre of Parian marble[48] in which, it seems, was placed the body of a certain man of ancient times. The priest was buried alive in the sepulchre on top of the corpse and covered with the stone that had originally covered the sarcophagus, and guards[49] were stationed at the doors. But the guards, trusting that Anastasius was restrained by the stone, lit a fire because it was winter, and, made drowsy by heated wine, fell asleep. And from the enclosure of the tomb the priest, like a modern-day Jonah, as if from the belly of hell, likewise begged for the pity of the Lord. And because the sarcophagus was spacious, as I said, even if he was unable to turn around his whole body, he nevertheless could reach his hand freely into whatever part he wished.

Moreover, there oozed from the bones of the dead man a terrible stench, as Anastasius himself was accustomed to relate,[50] which assaulted him not only externally, but also internally in his very viscera. And after blocking his nostrils with his cloak, as long as he was able to hold his breath he smelled nothing ill. But when he removed the cloak a little from his face, he drank in the pestiferous odor not only through his mouth and nose, but even, so to speak, through his very

---

45. For Cautinus, see Duchesne, *Fastes,* 2:36: he died of the plague on 27 March 571. For Clotilde, see chapter 6 below.

46. Greg.Tur. *Hist.* 4.12: *MGH SRM* 1.1:143; for other translations, see Dalton, *Gregory,* 124–25; Thorpe, *Gregory,* 205–6.

47. A martyr, along with Victorinus, at Clermont, perhaps in the early fourth century; his church, like most early churches, was located outside the city (Greg.Tur. *Hist.* 1.33).

48. Supposedly from the island of Paros in the Aegean, and hence very expensive.

49. Given their use of the sarcophagus to imprison Arcadius, it would seem that the guards were *fossores* (gravediggers). These individuals also could serve as the "muscle" of the bishop (see Brown, *Power and Persuasion,* 103).

50. As a native of Clermont, Gregory would have heard the tale firsthand.

ears, and he thought that he would suffocate. What next? After he had communed, so I believe, with the divinity, he extended his right hand to the rim of the sarcophagus and felt the crowbar that, after the lid had been lowered, remained between him and the rim of the sepulchre. Moving this little by little with the cooperative help of the Lord, he felt the stone shift. When it had been moved enough so the priest could put his head out, he was able to make a greater opening through which his entire body could fit.

The priest then fled to King Chlothar with his patents and was reconfirmed in his ownership of the property. So in this instance, the nefarious designs of a powerful aristocrat were foiled—although one would dearly love to know whether Anastasius in fact intended to retain his controversial piece of property, or was simply looking for a better price.

Humiliores

If individuals such as Amantius had to worry about losing their grip on the bottom rung of the ladder of privilege, or if those like Possessor and Anastasius faced the loss of their property, others, the *humiliores,* who had no status or property to speak of, had little to lose and everything to gain. Of course, for most such persons, little changed, and we have scant insights into their lives. The nonelite free, or plebs, if anything, became even more dependent on either aristocrats or the church (and hence bishops) for support and continued employment. Such persons were marginalized in the literary works, where their primary function, it seems, was to be the nameless, faceless "cast of thousands" who were the clients of the great men. When persons of plebeian status behaved themselves and fulfilled societal expectations of them, they made only cameo appearances in the literature. They were seen and not heard—and only rarely seen. But sometimes, and especially when they misbehaved, they provided better grist for the literary mill.

The Tongue-Tied Reader

Sidonius Apollinaris, for example, in a letter of circa 470 to his uncles Simplicius and Apollinaris reported on a transgression committed by the family retainer, Constans. Sidonius and his son, also named Apollinaris, had been in the midst of reading Terence and Menander.[51]

.8[52] (2) . . . All of a sudden a family dependent[53] appeared, pulling a long face. "I have just seen outside," he said, "the reader Constans, back from his errand to the lords Simplicius and Apollinaris. He says that he delivered your letters, but has lost the answers given him to bring back." (3) No sooner did I hear this, than a storm-cloud of annoyance rose upon the clear sky of my enjoyment. The mischance made me so angry that for several days I was inexorable and forbade the blockhead my presence; I meant to make him sorry for himself unless he restored me the letters all and sundry, to say nothing of yours, which as long as I am a reasonable being I shall always want most because they come least often. (4) After a time, however, my anger gradually abated. I sent for him and asked whether, besides the letters, he had been entrusted with a verbal message. He was all a-tremble and ready to grovel at my feet. He stammered in conscious guilt, and could not look me in the face, but he managed to answer, "Nothing." The messages from which I was to have received so much instruction and delight all had been consigned to the pages that had been lost. So there is nothing else for it; you must resort to your tablets once more, unfold your parchment, and write it all out anew. I shall bear, with such philosophy as I am able, this unfortunate obstacle to my desires until the hour when these lines reach you, and you learn that yours have never yet reached me.
Farewell.

This little contretemps, among other things, provides a window into the lives of the dependents of the aristocratic elite. Constans, like Amantius, held the ecclesiastical rank of "reader" and possessed sufficient status that he merited having his name given. The letter also depicts an aristocrat at ease, with leisure time on his hands, during a period when the Roman world supposedly was disintegrating. It also shows, once again, how important aristocrats thought it was to maintain contact through letter writing. A single letter could relieve one's sense of isolation and provide days of pleasure. Conversely, its loss

---

51. For a fuller discussion of this occasion, see chapter 4 below.
52. Sid.Apoll. *Epist.* 4.12.2–3; translation from Dalton, *Sidonius,* 2:24–25; see also Anderson, *Sidonius* 2:113.
53. *Puer,* "lad": a word used for persons of dependent status.

would be the cause of great distress, and in this instance the unfortunate Constans suffered the consequences.

In addition, this incident provides some insight into the mechanics of letter exchange. For one thing, it was a common practice for writers also to send with the bearer a verbal message,[54] and Constans's calamity was exacerbated because he had not brought one to compensate for the lost letter. Furthermore, drafts of letters were composed on wax tablets *(pugillares)* that were preserved, and therefore created a kind of private archive for the author. The actual letter, in this case, was written on folded parchment sheets *(membrana)*.[55]

Most letters, of course, dealt with aristocratic interactions among themselves. But aristocrats, and in particular bishops, also used them in their roles as patrons and arbitrators for the less privileged. They provided letters of recommendation, patched up quarrels, interceded for those accused of crimes, and assisted in financial and legal affairs. As a result, their letters provide glimpses of some very mundane matters in the world of those who were totally dependent on the good will or good nature of the great men.

The Case of the Pilfered Pigs

The eighty-three letters of Bishop Ruricius of Limoges (ca. 485–510), for example, include several that deal with local matters and with individuals of no great status.[56] On one occasion, perhaps in the 480s, Ruricius replied to Bishop Censurius of Auxerre[57] regarding a criminal case that involved several of the latter's clients. One of them, Sindilla,[58] had accused Foedamius, a dependent of Ruricius, of stealing some pigs. Subsequently, Sindilla and several of his comrades had

---

54. Sometimes for reasons of discretion, if not simply to conserve writing material.

55. The verb *replicate* shows that a folded parchment writing tablet was used here. The example of Taurentius in chapter 1 above suggests that the word *membrana* also could refer to papyrus sheets.

56. See, e.g., Ruric. *Epist.* 2.7–8, 2.12, 2.20, 2.47–48, 2.56–57; for translations, see Mathisen, *Ruricius.*

57. Duchesne, *Fastes,* 2:445. Circa 480, Constantius of Lyon sent Censurius a copy of the *vita* of St. Germanus of Auxerre: see R. Borius, ed., *SC* 112 (Paris, 1965), 114–17. He also received *Epist.* 6.10 from Sidonius Apollinaris, concerning a deacon who had fled to the territory of Auxerre in order to escape the Visigoths.

58. His name could suggest a Germanic origin.

been taken into custody, and Censurius had written—a second time, it seems—to Ruricius on their behalf.

The first section of Ruricius's letter, expounding on the virtues of letter writing as a means by which isolated aristocrats could remain in contact, provided a means of working up to a rather ticklish topic.

.9[59] Bishop Ruricius to Bishop Censurius, greetings.

I rejoice that I have received the letter of Your Sanctity, even if on a business matter. For it makes no difference whether [our correspondence] occurs from necessity or from personal preference, as long as those who esteem one another communicate reciprocally among themselves and as long as a true conversation of their minds and senses links those whom spatial distances separate in body, because the virtue of the divine piety has granted even this greatest thing to our kind, so that we who are unable to scrutinize each other in the flesh can see with a spiritual gaze. For this reason, as the bearer of your letter returns, I have endeavored to reply to it as you enjoined, so that I respond equally both to your concern and to our mutual esteem.

I offer greetings, therefore, to Your Apostlehood, and, regarding that matter, which you wished to investigate in writing through my people's testimony, you should know that I have diligently conducted an examination of my men, as to where they were, that is, whether Sindilla lost his pigs with Foedamius's knowledge. But, just as I already ascertained before, I learned that Sindilla and the laborers were primarily responsible, and that he himself lost the pigs through his own disobedience, even though he claimed that he was in another place. But the aforementioned Foedamius was in no way culpable. For, of all these people, Sindilla ought to blame no other one for what he has suffered except for himself. How much I have labored in this matter, out of regard for you, so that your men might be freed from custody and recover your pigs, you will be able to learn more fully from their reports, because, in this matter, there was no need to discuss that in this letter. It is up to you to defend your man justly from the charge of this false accusation,[60] which you know, from my letter, that he unjustly suffered.

---

59. Ruric. *Epist.* 2.51: *MGH AA* 8:345–46; *CSEL* 21:432–33; *CCL* 64:386; for translation, see Mathisen, *Ruricius,* 222–23.

60. *Calumnia:* this was a formal legal charge: see *CTh* 9.34.

One might wonder what pigs belonging to the church of Auxerre were doing in the territory of Limoges. One possibility would be that Sindilla and his comrades were engaged in long-distance pig trading.[61] But perhaps it is more likely that they were tending property of the church of Auxerre located in the territory of Limoges.[62] And as for Foedamius, if he is to be identified as the priest Foedamius who appears elsewhere in Ruricius's correspondence, then he would have been a person of some standing, a person who, if he was accused of pig rustling, would expect his bishop to defend him from the charge.[63]

Ruricius seems to have been caught in the middle of the dispute. He did not want to implicate Foedamius, who may, in fact, have been operating on Ruricius's instructions, yet he could not deny that the pigs did in fact have to be restored to Sindilla. He also was unhappy with Censurius himself, whom he saw as being a bit presumptuous: his irritation may be reflected in his omission of the customary farewell salutation. In the end aristocratic politeness and solidarity prevailed, and Ruricius saw to it that the pigs were returned and that Sindilla was released, even if the latter did not gain any satisfaction for what he had suffered. Any more trenchant observations Ruricius might have had, which there was "no need to discuss," might have been reserved for the verbal message that accompanied the letter.

Itinerant Artisans

The letters of Ruricius also show that there was a thriving community of itinerant skilled craftsmen and artisans, apparently free plebs, who made their way among the nobility. In a letter to his friend Celsus he remarked, "Just as you requested, I have sent the glassworker *(vitrarius), whose work should be imitated for its splendor, not for its fragility."[64] He dwelt at somewhat greater length on a painter *(pictor)*

---

61. Limoges and Auxerre were not even adjacent; the territory of Bourges intervened.

62. In the eighth century, for example, the church of Sens owned twenty-five properties "in pago Lemovicino" [in the territory of Limoges]. They were worked by *coloni* (tenant farmers) or *servi* (slaves or serfs), and several paid their rents in pigs *(friscingae)*: see Michel Rouche, *L'Aquitaine des Wisigoths aux Arabes, 418–781: Naissance d'une région* (Paris: Editions Touzot, 1979), 468–70.

63. See Ruric. *Epist.* 2.14.

64. "Vitrarium, sicut iussistis, me destinasse significo, cuius opus nitore non fragilitate oportet imitetur" (*Epist.* 1.12).

who had been working for him and whom he then dispatched to the noblewoman Ceraunia, whose husband Namatius had lately died.[65]

10[66]   Bishop Ruricius to a venerable mistress and magnificent daughter in Christ, Ceraunia.

I did not send the painter to you previously for this reason, because I believed you to be occupied by the arrival of the new governor[67] and thus discouraged from thinking about such matters. But because, with God's favor, I understand both from your letters and from the verbal reports of your people that you are carrying on and doing well according to your design, I present my salutation and send the painter, although he was fully occupied here, and his apprentice, because I preferred to postpone my own need in order to satisfy your request. But because both your and our purpose[68] demands attention, I presumed to advise Your Reverence regarding these few matters, so that from the painter's efforts you might gain an example for undertaking penitence and the newly assumed vestments of a new person, so that in you aged Adam[69] might perish and He who vivifies might come forth. In the manner that he paints the walls with manifold art in varied painted colors, thus you should adorn your spirit, which is the temple of God, with different kinds of virtues.[70]

Ruricius used the painter as a metaphor for what he hoped would be Ceraunia's spiritual development. In addition, his own use of both the painter and the glassworker might have been related to his construc-

---

65. Ruricius wrote seven letters (*Epist.* 2.1–5, 15, 62) to Namatius and/or Ceraunia, who may have lived near Ruricius's family estate at Gourdon. This may be the Namatius who commanded the Visigothic naval facilities at Saintes in the late 470s (Sid.Apoll. *Epist.* 8.6); and another had been bishop of Clermont ca. 440 (Greg.Tur. *Hist.* 2.16, 21; Duchesne, *Fastes*, 2:34); a Ceraunius was bishop of Nantes in the late fifth century (Duchesne, *Fastes*, 2:366).

66. Ruric. *Epist.* 2.15: *MGH AA* 8:323–26; *CSEL* 21:394–99; *CCL* 64:351–55; for translation, see Mathisen, *Ruricius*, 159–60.

67. The identity of this new governor *(novus iudex)* is unknown; Ruricius had several friends, such as Eudomius, Freda, Praesidius, and Rusticus (qq.vv. in *PLRE*, vol. 2), who were in Visigothic service.

68. That is, both Ruricius and Ceraunia had taken up the religious life, Ruricius as a bishop and Ceraunia apparently as a *vidua* (widow). The *viduae* oversaw the preparations for the baptism of women.

69. Cf. 1 Cor. 15.22.

70. Ruricius then continued with a long description of these virtues, e.g., "We should subdue our bodies with tireless vigils and continuous fasting."

tion of a new church for St. Augustine: in another letter, he ordered ten small marble columns and an unspecified number of large ones from Bishop Clarus of Eauze, located in the neighborhood of a thriving Gallic quarrying industry.[71] One sees here continued Gallic material prosperity, even if on a smaller scale than during imperial times. And as for the artisans, none of them merited having their name divulged "in print." They merely provided the backdrop for Ruricius's spiritual exegesis.

A Slave's-Eye View

A stereotypical aristocratic view of slaves and servants is provided by the *Querolus*. There, the character filling the traditional role of the "clever slave," Pantomalus, delivered a soliloquy on servile life, supposedly from the slave's point of view. Slaves were portrayed as thieving, unreliable, unruly, licentious, shameless, and generally—as his name indicates—guilty of all kinds of wickedness.[72] Pantomalus's views are placed in the context of a discussion of the virtues and vices of two different masters, Arbiter and his own, Querolus.

2.11[73]   (67) Pantomalus: It is quite well known that all lords are wicked, and this is most clear. Truly, I know full well that none is worse than mine. He is not in fact a dangerous person, merely very ungrateful and disgusting. If a theft is discovered at home, it is denounced as some kind of crime. If something seems to be missing, he ceaselessly screams and curses as wickedly as possible. If anyone throws a seat, a table, or a bed into the fire, as we customarily do in our haste, he even inquires into this. If the roof leaks, if the doors slam, he checks into it all himself; he looks into everything. By Hercules, this is unbearable. He furthermore authorizes with his own hand all the expenses and accounts, and he demands restitution for any expense that he did not approve. (68) . . . O unjust authority! Moreover, if he himself perhaps notices some

---

71. *Epist.* 2.64; for the church see also Venantius Fortunatus, *Carm.* 6.5. For the marble industry of Visigothic Aquitania, see Edward James, *The Merovingian Archaeology of South-West Gaul* (Oxford: British Archaeological Reports, 1977), 29, 234–38; and J. B. Ward Perkins, "The Sculpture of Visigothic France," *Archaeologia* 87 (1938): 79–128.

72. In Greek, the phrase παντὸς μᾶλλον ("pantos mallon") literally means "more than everything," but a Latin reader would have seen the name as πάντα (*panta*, Greek, "all") plus *malus* (Latin, "wicked"), a linguistic pastiche that the educated Roman audience would have appreciated.

73. *Querolus* 2.4 (67–75), ed. Peiper, 36–41; ed. Jacquemard–Le Saos, 44–48.

offense, he dissembles and is silent, and then he makes an accusation when no opportunity for excuse remains, so that one cannot object in response, "I was going to do it now," or, "That's what I was going to say."

(73) . . . As to that Arbiter, to whom I now go, how irritating that man is! He reduces the slaves' food, and he orders them to do more work than is fair. By Hercules, he would snatch a shameful profit from an empty bushel[74] if he could. Indeed, if these two men ever meet, either by chance or by design, they compare notes with each other in · turn. But nevertheless, by Hercules, when all is said, if I must choose, I prefer my own master. To this point, that master of ours is such a one as I have described; but, nevertheless, he is not stingy toward his own household. It is only that he repeatedly beats us and always shouts. May god therefore be infuriated with them both.

(74) Yet, we nevertheless are not as miserable and dull-witted as certain people think. Some assume that we are somnolent because we sleep during the day. We do this, however, as a result of evening vigils, because we stay up at night.[75] The slave who drowses during the daily hours is up at all hours of the night. I think that in human affairs nature created nothing better than night. This is our day; we do everything then. We enter the baths at night, even if they are more tempting during the day. We bathe, moreover, with the lackeys and maidservants: isn't this a free life? Enough light or illumination is supplied to be sufficient, but not to give us away. I grasp naked one whom the master is hardly allowed to see clothed. I caress her flanks, I partition the spreading masses of her hair; I sit beside her, I am embraced; I caress, I am caressed: what lord is allowed to do this?

The chief element of our happiness, however, is this: that among ourselves we are not resentful. We all commit thefts, yet no one suffers loss because it is all done mutually. We monitor the masters and exclude them, for among the male and female slaves there is a collective kinship. Unfortunate are those whose masters drag out their activities deep into the night. For the slaves, you cut off as much from their lives as you detach from the night. How many free persons are there who would wish to transform themselves like this: to be masters during the day and slaves at night? What need is there for you, Querolus, to think

---

74. Perhaps the empty bushel of the food owed to the slaves.
75. *Causa vigiliarum:* perhaps an allusion to Christian vigils, as in Ruricius's letter to Ceraunia above.

about lawsuits and taxes when we carry out all these other activities? For us, furthermore, there are daily weddings and birthdays, spoofs and parties, and revelries with the maidservants. Because of this, not all slaves wish to flee; because of this, some of us do not want to be set free.[76] What free person, indeed, can flaunt such great expenditure and such great impunity? (75) . . . But what will happen now? Injury must be accepted and bemoaned. They are the masters; they say what they want. For however long they wish, it must be tolerated.[77]

A Marriage in the Family

To portray the slave as a stock character from drama, as here, was one thing; to give lengthy accounts of slaves in the real world was something else altogether. A rare insight comes from Sidonius, who in a letter of circa 470 interceded with another magnate on behalf of a female dependent of his own who wished to marry an *inquilinus* (cottager) of his friend. Sidonius purported to believe that his friend knew nothing of the affair, and his letter reveals something of the social and legal status of the unfree or quasi-free.

2.12[78] Sidonius to his friend Pudens, greetings.

(1) The son of your nurse has eloped with the daughter of mine. It is a shameful action, and one that would have destroyed our friendly relations, had I not learned at once that you knew nothing of the man's intentions. But though you are thus acquitted in advance, you yet do not scruple to ask that this crying offense should be allowed to go unpunished. I can only agree on one condition: that you promote the ravisher from his original position of bound cottager[79] by changing your relation to him from that of master to that of patron. (2) The woman already is free, but she will only be regarded as a lawful wife instead of a mere con-

---

76. This sentiment may represent the wishful thinking of the masters, if it does not also reflect some social realities.

77. In the complete text, this section is followed immediately by the section beginning "Good gods," quoted above.

78. Sid.Apoll. *Epist.* 5.19; translation from Dalton, *Sidonius,* 2:75–76; see also Anderson, *Sidonius,* 2:239–41.

79. *Inquilinus originalis: inquilini* customarily worked for a lord but did not farm; the reference to this person also as a *colonus,* or tenant farmer, suggests that he did in fact work land, even if, as indicated by the word *originalis,* he was bound to the soil, and therefore a *tributarius,* that is, a person whose taxes were paid by the landlord.

cubine if our criminal, whose cause you espouse, ceases to be your taxable dependent and becomes your client, assuming the status of a plebeian in place of that of a *colonus.* Nothing short of these terms or these amends will in the least condone the affront. I only yield to your request and your protestation of friendship on condition that, if as ravisher he is not to be bound to justice, liberty shall make him a free bridegroom. Farewell.

Sidonius, as the social superior, felt free to get right to the heart of a delicate matter without any polite preamble. And once again, as in the case of Amantius, he fully supported one of his own clients, even if a very humble one. He not so subtly threatened Pudens with personal enmity if the latter refused to raise the status of his own cottager to that of a free plebeian.[80] This incident illustrates not only the complications that could arise through associations of individuals of different status, but also what could result if nonelite individuals had powerful patrons. Another incident, also related by Sidonius, shows what could happen if one did not.

Kidnapped

In a letter of circa 470 to Lupus, bishop of Troyes, Sidonius reported on the case of a hapless woman who had been captured and sold as a slave, apparently a common practice. Her relatives had set out to find her.[81] The humble social status of them all is indicated by Sidonius's failure to cite the names of any of them.

13[82]   Sidonius to the Lord Pope Lupus, greetings.

(1) I render you the observance ceaselessly due, even if it is endlessly paid, to the incomparable eminence of your apostolic life. I commend

---

80. Sidonius, however, might not have been doing the *inquilinus* any favors unless the agreement with Pudens included the right to farm land; given that Sidonius assumes that the man will remain as Pudens's client and that the fellow already had access to land, it probably did, and in point of fact very little would have changed as a result.

81. Faustus of Riez discusses a similar case (*Epist.* "Gratias ad vos": *MGH AA* 8:274–75; *CSEL* 21:414–15; *CCL* 64:414–15), that of the priest Florentius, who was "traveling for the sake of the freeing of his sister." For refugees in general, see Ralph W. Mathisen, "Emigrants, Exiles, and Survivors: Aristocratic Options in Visigothic Aquitania," *Phoenix* 38 (1984): 159–70.

82. Sid.Apoll. *Epist.* 6.4; translation from Dalton, *Sidonius,* 2:84–85; see also Anderson, *Sidonius,* 2:259–63.

to your notice, based upon our new relationship,[83] an old trouble of the bearers in whose case I have recently become interested. They have journeyed a great distance into the Auvergne at this unfavorable season, and the journey has been undertaken in vain. A female relative of theirs was carried off during a raid of the Vargi,[84] as the local bandits are styled. They received trustworthy information, and following an old but reliable clue, discovered that some years ago[85] she had been brought here before being removed elsewhere.

(2) In the meantime, this same troubled woman died in the house and under the authority of my agent,[86] having been sold in open market before their arrival. A certain Prudens (this is the man's name), rumored now to be resident in Troyes, endorsed the contract of men unknown to me; his signature appears in the market records[87] in the capacity of a suitable attestor. By the fortunate fact of your presence you will be able, if you think fit, to see the parties confronted and use your personal influence to investigate the whole course of the outrage. I gather from what the bearers say that the offense is aggravated by the death of a man upon the road as a sequel to the abduction.

(3) But as the aggrieved parties who wish to bring this scandalous affair to light are anxious for the remedy of your judgment and for your neighborly aid, it seems to me that it would no less become your character than your position to bring about an equitable arrangement, thus affording the one side some comfort in affliction, and saving the other from an impending danger. Such a qualified decision would be most beneficial to all concerned; it would diminish the misery of one party and the guilt of the other, while it would give both of them a greater feeling of security. Otherwise, in regions and times like these of

---

83. Sidonius apparently had just become a bishop, which would date this letter to circa 470.

84. According to Anderson (*Sidonius,* 2:260 n. 1), "A Teutonic word meaning outlaw or exile." The Vargi are otherwise unattested.

85. Apparently, therefore, before Sidonius had become bishop.

86. *Negotiator:* one is reminded of the Arvernian agent Amantius, discussed above.

87. "Cuius subscriptio intra formulam nundinarum tamquam idonei adstipulatoris ostenditur": an ostentatious use of legal terminology. See chapter 3 for several legal formulas in use in Merovingian Clermont. Such examples demonstrate that normal business activities continued even after the disappearance of Roman authority.

ours, the last state of the dispute may well prove no better than the beginning.

Deign to keep me in remembrance, Lord Bishop.

Cases such as this demonstrate the disruptive effect that these unsettled times could have upon ordinary persons, who would have lived in some security during the imperial period, but who now were threatened by lawlessness and the rule of the strongest on every side. At the same time that Sidonius showed the continued existence of both secular criminal courts and ecclesiastical civil ones, he also recognized the possibility of more rough-and-ready self-help methods of settling disputes.[88]

In this instance, with their relative already having died, one might doubt whether the bereaved family members ever were able to obtain much redress. Left to their own devices, the unprivileged easily fell victim to those who were only too willing to take advantage of them, be they senators, bishops, or bandits. Even Sidonius, who discussed the affair in a most matter-of-fact manner, seems to have been involved (prior to his becoming bishop) in the sale of the unfortunate woman, who died in the custody of Sidonius's own agent. Better, perhaps, for individuals of her status to place themselves safely under the protection of a powerful lord, as the female dependent of Sidonius discussed above had done.

The Rise and Fall of Andarchius

An even more detailed depiction of a most remarkable slave is found in Gregory of Tours's lengthy account of the escapades, in the early 570s, of the ambitious and resourceful slave Andarchius of Marseille. This tale, which has similarities to descriptions of the clever slave (such as Pantomalus above) in comedy, would have been of interest to Gregory and his readers, as often was the case, because of the way in which societal standards were violated.

---

88. Such methods, of course, also were customary in Germanic society.

2.14[89]   I now will tell you about the death of Andarchius. First I will describe his birth and where he came from.[90] He was, so they say, a slave of Felix, who himself came of a senatorial family. Andarchius acted as personal servant to his master. He joined in the literary studies of Felix and he distinguished himself by his learning. He became extremely well informed about the works of Vergil, the books of the Theodosian Code of laws and the study of arithmetic.[91] He was proud of his knowledge and began to despise his masters. When Duke Lupus visited Marseille on the order of King Sigibert [561–75], Andarchius placed himself under his patronage. When Lupus left Marseille, he asked Andarchius to go with him: Lupus recommended him strongly to King Sigibert and found employment for him at court. The king sent him on missions to various places and used him in the public service. He already seemed a person to whom some honor was due.

He came to Clermont and wormed his way into the friendship of a man called Ursus, who lived in that city. Andarchius had a keen eye to his own advantage and he decided to marry the daughter of this Ursus. He placed a mail shirt in a case in which legal documents were usually kept, and said to the wife of Ursus, "I have put in this case a quantity of gold coins which belong to me, more than sixteen thousand of them, as a matter of fact. I leave them in your charge. They might perhaps become yours, if you were to let me marry your daughter."

  . . . Accursed lust for money,
  to what do you not drive the hearts of men?[92]

The woman was simple enough to be taken in by this and in the absence of her husband she promised Andarchius that he should marry the girl.[93] He went back to see the king and then returned once more with a royal license, which he showed to the local magistrate, saying that he was to marry her. "I already have made a deposit for her," he

---

89. Greg.Tur. *Hist.* 4.46: translation from Thorpe, *Gregory,* 241–43; see also Dalton, *Gregory,* 154–56.

90. Gregory begins this brief excursus as if it were a standard biography, a genre with which, as a hagiographer, he was quite familiar.

91. The standard course of studies for young aristocrats in the mid–sixth century.

92. Gregory's editorial comment comes from Vergil, *Aeneid,* 3.56–57, perhaps a back-handed allusion to Andarchius's supposed Vergilian expertise.

93. Simple or not, Ursus's wife must have had sufficient legal competence to have been able to make such a promise in the first place.

maintained. Ursus denied this, saying, "I do not know who you are, or where you came from, nor have I received any of your property." A quarrel arose between them and became worse and worse, until Andarchius demanded that Ursus should appear before the king. Andarchius went to the royal villa at Berny, where he produced another man also called Ursus. He brought him secretly before an altar and made him swear the following oath: "By this holy place and on the relics of the saints I swear that if I do not give you my daughter in marriage I will immediately repay you sixteen thousand pieces of gold." There were witnesses standing in the sacristy, listening unobserved to what he said, but they could not see the man who was making this oath. Andarchius spoke reassuringly to the true Ursus and persuaded him to return home without having had an audience with the King.[94] After the oath had been sworn, Andarchius showed a copy of it to the King. "Ursus has written this out and given it to me," he said. "I therefore ask your Majesty to give me a license that shall make him let me marry his daughter. If not, I am to take possession of his property, and when I have my sixteen thousand gold coins back I will withdraw from the affair."

Andarchius took the document and went off with it to Clermont, where he made public the king's decree. Ursus fled to Velay, but, as his property was sequestered to Andarchius, the latter followed Ursus there. He went into a house belonging to Ursus and ordered a meal to be prepared for him and water to be heated so that he could wash. The house-servants refused to obey the orders of so rude a person, but he beat some with sticks and others with rods, hitting them over the head until the blood flowed. The household was coerced by this: supper was prepared and Andarchius washed himself in the water that they heated. He then drank himself silly with some wine and retired to bed. He had only seven servants with him. They, too, went to bed where they slept soundly because of the wine that they had swallowed.[95] The household then assembled and closed the doors, which were made of wooden planks. First they removed the keys, then they broke open the grain-ricks, which stood near by, and piled all round the house and even on top of it the stooks of grain, which was still in sheaves. When they had finished, the house was completely covered and you could not

---

94. Ursus, apparently, was as simple-minded as Gregory claims that his wife was.
95. Cf. the guards of Anastasius above, who also fell into a drunken stupor.

have told that it was there. They then set fire to it in a number of places. The charred fragments of the building fell in on the unhappy wretches within. They shouted for help, but there was no one to hear them. The whole house was burnt down and they were roasted alive. Ursus was terrified by what had happened and fled for sanctuary to the church of St. Julian. In the end he received all his goods back, but only after giving the king a bribe.

The Andarchius story provides several lessons. For one thing, it shows how a knowledge of Roman law and literature provided a boost for an ambitious slave wishing to appropriate a place in aristocratic society. Furthermore, for Gregory, it demonstrated how the climbing parvenu ultimately received a just retribution: Andarchius might have been able to gain status and authority, but he did not know how to exercise them in the proper measure. And for us, Andarchius's example demonstrates that phenomenal changes in status were possible for some, even if most of those who lived in the world of the unprivileged were not as fortunate as he—at least before his untimely end.

Persons ranging from Nymfius to Amantius to Andarchius were rendered, in their own ways, respectively less elite by their social status. Another category of nonelite persons consisted of the less privileged members of families, women and children, for even in wealthy and aristocratic families not everyone was able to benefit equally from the family status. The next chapter will discuss them.

CHAPTER 3

Family Life: Women and Children, Husbands and Wives

The family provided the glue that held society together. For individuals, it always remained the most important social unit. It provided a focus for one's loyalties, and one's position in society was determined by the status of one's family. Participation in family activities often provided opportunities that were available nowhere else. This was especially true for those who were disadvantaged by their age or gender. The activities of women and children nearly always occurred in private; in matters of a public nature, a father, husband, or other male usually was the participant, spokesperson, and decision maker.

Children

In antiquity, children (like the slaves and servants discussed in chapter 2) were to be seen and not heard, and accounts of them, their activities, and their concerns are infrequent.[1] The literary remains contain only scattered references to children. Circa the 460s, in a letter to his wife Papianilla, Sidonius Apollinaris mentioned one of their daughters: "Roscia, our shared care, greets you. She is being nurtured in the most indulgent lap of her grandmother and aunts, which rarely happens when grandchildren are raised, with a strictness that does not harm her tender years but which strengthens her intellect."[2]

---

1. The most famous autobiographical account of a childhood is that of Augustine in his *Confessions.*

2. Sid.Apoll. *Epist.* 5.16.5. This is the only letter in Sidonius's corpus addressed to a woman, and the topic was family matters, in this case not only Roscia, but also the elevation of Papianilla's brother Ecdicius to the rank of patrician.

An Illness in the Family

Elsewhere, in a letter to Papianilla's brother Agricola, Sidonius expressed their concern over the illness of another daughter.

3.1[3]   Sidonius to his Agricola, greetings . . .

(2) Severiana, our common cause of concern,[4] at first was agitated by the annoyance of an intermittent cough, and now is exhausted by fevers that worsen during the night. As a result, she longs to get away into the country, and when we received your letter, we were already preparing to depart for our little country place. With that being the case, regardless of whether you come now or later, with your supplications please bolster our prayers that this activity in and of itself will have a beneficial effect upon the one who desires the country air. Indeed, your sister and I have been suspended between hope and fear; we thought we would run the risk of causing further distress for our invalid if we opposed her wishes. (3) Accordingly, with Christ's guidance we are freeing ourselves and our entire household to boot from the heat and languor of the city, and at the same time we also avoid the advice of the persistent and disagreeing doctors, who through their ignorance and endless visits conscientiously kill many of their patients. Only Justus shall be of our party, but in the quality of friend.[5]

These are the only mentions Sidonius makes of his daughters in his entire corpus; a third, Alcima, is not mentioned at all.[6]

A Family Tragedy

Where parents often did have something to say about their children, and where their depth of feeling remains achingly clear, was on the youngsters' epitaphs.[7] One still sympathizes with an unfortunate cou-

---

3. Sid.Apoll. *Epist.* 2.12; for additional translations, see Anderson, *Sidonius,* 1:470–73; Dalton, *Sidonius,* 1:57–58.

4. Cf. Sidonius's reference to "Roscia . . . our shared care," cited above.

5. That is, rather than as a physician. The Latin is "iure amicitiae" (by right of friendship), a powerful element of the aristocratic ethos.

6. For Alcima, see the next chapter, and *PLRE* 2:116.

7. For other translated epitaphs, see J. N. Hillgarth, ed., *The Conversion of Western Europe, 350–750* (Englewood Cliffs, N.J.: Prentice-Hall, 1969), 13–15.

ple of Vienne who, perhaps in the fourth century,[8] lost three sons within less than a month, and commemorated them as follows:

.2[9]   I, their father Vitalinus, and their mother
         Martina write not of great glory[10]
         but of our grief for our children.
         Three children within twenty-seven days
         we laid here: our son Sapaudus, who
         lived seven years and twenty-six days;
         our daughter Rustica, who lived four years
         and twenty days; and our daughter Rusticula, who
         lived three years and thirty-three days.[11]

The death of three children within so short a time suggests that they may have been lost to an illness of some kind, even to an epidemic.[12] Sidonius's daughter Severiana apparently survived her illness, but she had access to both health care and a salubrious country estate. Vitalinus's and Martina's children might not have had the opportunity for either, even though it would seem that the family was rather well-to-do, as suggested not only by the expensive epitaph, but also by the implication, at least, that the children had lost their chance to obtain "glory."

Proba the "Approved"

Other epitaphs, especially those from the fifth century and later, were more clearly Christian in character. A rather more detailed marker commemorating a girl named Proba, dated to A.D. 498 and in elegiac couplets, was found outside Lyon:

8. The script is dated to the fourth or fifth century; the lack of clear Christian sentiment or symbolism would seem to argue for the earlier date.

9. *CIL* 12:2003.

10. This may be an allusion to the common self-congratulatory epitaphs that one often encountered, such as those of Proba and Celsa below.

11. Note the enumeration by days only, not months: perhaps doing so cut down a bit on the cost of the epitaph.

12. Gregory of Tours mentions several sixth-century plagues: near Trier and Reims ca. 543 (*Vit.pat.* 17.4, *Glor.conf.* 78); in the Auvergne in 571 (*Hist.* 4.30–32, *Vit.pat.* 9.2); in Albi in 581 (*Hist.* 7.1); at Nantes in 582 (*Hist.* 6.15); at Narbonne in 582 and 584 (*Hist.* 6.14, 33); and at Marseille and thence to Lyon in 588 (*Hist.* 9.21–22). For a plague and famine ca. 400, see chapter 5 below.

3.3[13]   +   [vine leaves]   ☧ [14]   [vine leaves]   +

    Of noble birth, "Approved" by name and approved in spirit,[15]
        Proba, who was suddenly snatched away, lies entombed here.
    God, who grants all things beautiful, bestowed upon her
        whatever the wishes of all her relatives desired.
    Here remain her grieving father and the endless grief of her aunt
        and mother. [leaf]
        Oh, the shame! Their purpose and responsibility are lost.
    Take heart, you who gush with tears, pray ceaselessly, [leaf]
        look toward life everlasting: death is nothing.
    She, who lived five years and nine months, died on the third day
        before the Ides of October, while the distinguished gentleman
        Paulinus <was consul>.

   [dove]   [leaf]   [dove]
+   [vine leaves]   ☧   [vine leaves]   +

Proba's well-to-do, and perhaps aristocratic,[16] family spared no expense in commemorating their lost child.

    The epitaph of the girl Artemia, probably dating to the fifth century, was found at Cologne:

3.4[17]   Here lies[18] Artemia,
    a sweet and most delightful
    child, both pleasing to the eye and
    most dulcet to hear.
    She gave us four whole years;
    in the fifth she went to Christ.
    An innocent, she abruptly departed
    for the celestial kingdom.

---

13. *CIL* 13:1655; Franciscus Buecheler, ed., *Anthologia latina* 2.2 (Leipzig: Teubner, 1926), no. 1361.

14. An abbreviation for ΧΡΙΣΤΟΣ, the Greek spelling of the name of Christ.

15. "Proba mente, mente probata," a play on Proba's name, which means "approved."

16. Her name was a distinguished one, as seen in the cases of Anicia Faltonia Proba and the Christian poetess Faltonia Betitia Proba (chap. 1 above), both of the late fourth century. Note also the dedicated virgin Proba of Rome (*PLRE* 2:907), daughter of Q. Aurelius Symmachus, consul in 485, and Aurelia Proba of Seville, a *clarissima femina* buried in the fifth century (*PLRE* 2:908).

17. *CIL* 13:8478.

18. *Hic iacet* was a common introductory formula for epitaphs in Gaul, and elsewhere, during the fifth century in particular.

Another epitaph, of a similar date and also from Cologne, commemorated the boy Leontius:

5[19]   Here lies Leontius, a faithful
boy, most sweet to his father, most
dutiful to his mother. He lived seven
years and three months and six days, an
innocent, snatched by death, blessed and happy in spirit,
and he departed in peace.[20]
[dove]   α   ☧   ω[21]   [dove]

All of these touching farewells demonstrate the tenderness that parents felt toward their children. One notes the repeated themes of the children's innocence contrasted with the unexpected suddenness with which they were snatched away. And in the examples dating to the fifth century and later, the solace provided by Christian beliefs also is manifest.

An Army Brat

One literary genre that often did include a discussion of childhood was hagiography, although the accounts often tended to be fairly standardized and to include little information that was specific to a particular individual.[22] Sulpicius Severus, however, was an exception. In his life of St. Martin of Tours, written circa 400, he dwelt in some detail on Martin's youth:

6[23]   Martin, therefore, was born in the town of Sabaria in Pannonia,[24] but was raised in Italy at Pavia. His parents were of not ignoble birth, in a

---

19. *CIL* 13:8482.

20. *In pace recessit:* A typical Christian funerary formula.

21. That is, a Christogram between the letters alpha and omega.

22. Some hagiographers were more forthright, and if they knew nothing of a saint's childhood, they simply omitted it, as in Eugippius's *Vita Severini* (Life of St. Severinus [of Noricum]) and the *Vita Aniani* (Life of St. Anianus [of Orléans]).

23. *Vita Martini* (Life of St. Martin), 2: *Sulpice Sévère Vie de Saint Martin,* ed. J. Fontaine, vol. 1, *SC* 133 (Paris, 1967); *CSEL* 1; for English translation, see *Sulpicius Severus et al. The Western Fathers: Being the Lives of Martin of Tours, Ambrose, Augustine of Hippo, Honoratus of Arles, and Germanus of Auxerre,* trans. F. R. Hoare (New York: Sheed and Ward, 1954), 12–16.

24. Modern Stein-an-Anger, in Hungary.

secular sense, but in addition were pagans. His father first was a soldier, then a military tribune.[25] In his youth, Martin himself pursued an armed military career in the units of the *scholae*[26] under the emperor Constantius [337–61]. Then he served under the Caesar Julian [355–60], but not of his own will, because almost from his earliest years the sacred infancy of the illustrious[27] boy aspired rather for divine servitude.

For when he was ten years old, against the will of his parents, he fled to a church and asked that he be made a catechumen.[28] Soon he was totally converted to the work of God in a wonderful way. When he was twelve years old, he yearned for solitude, and he would have fulfilled his vows if his youthful condition had not impeded him. Nevertheless, his spirit, always intent either on the monastery or on the church, meditated then in his boyhood age upon that which he later devotedly accomplished. But when he was fifteen years old, when there was an edict of the emperors that sons of veterans were to be entered on the military rolls,[29] his father, who opposed his joyful activity, turned him in, and after being taken captive and shackled he was bound by the military oaths.[30] He contented himself with only one slave as a comrade, whom, as the master, he nevertheless served in his turn, to the extent that he himself often both removed his slave's shoes and cleaned them; they also ate together, and Martin in fact catered more often. He was in the army for nearly three years before his baptism; he nevertheless remained free from those vices in which that kind of men are accustomed to indulge.

---

25. That is to say, he had risen to quite a respectable rank, being in command of what passed at that time for a legion or similar unit, perhaps about two thousand men.

26. Note that *militia,* "military service," could be either in the civil service or in the army; Sulpicius correctly indicates that Martin served in the latter. In the west, there were five "schools" (regiments) of imperial guards, very elite units.

27. The word *inlustris* shows how terms used to describe secular nobility came to be applied to ecclesiastics. In this case, Martin was ennobled by his divine calling.

28. *Catechumeni* were those who were receiving instruction before becoming full communicants in the church.

29. Edicts such as this one, intended to ensure that necessary services were provided, were repeated many times, indicating how difficult they were to enforce; see, e.g., *CTh* 7.1.5 (29 April 364).

30. The enlistment of a fifteen-year-old in these times of military need is not as strange as it might seem; the American Civil War, e.g., saw service by boys as young as twelve or thirteen.

Along with the assertions, typical in this genre, of the youthful holiness of the saint-to-be comes some quite realistic information. The statement that Martin contented himself with but a single slave, for example, in the modern day seems a bit incongruous.

A Consular Installation

Aristocratic teens, of course, enjoyed a more privileged existence than Martin's, and could participate in some very exalted activities, as when Sidonius Apollinaris, at about the age of seventeen, attended the installation of the consul Astyrius[31] at Arles on 1 January 449. He heard the orator Nicetius deliver the panegyric:

[32] (5) I heard him speak when I was a young man just recently emerged from boyhood. My father was at that time president of the tribunals of the Gallic provinces as praetorian prefect,[33] and of course it was during his tenure of office that the consul Astyrius had entered upon his year as wearer of the coveted consular robe. I was standing close to the curule chair (for though my age forbade me to be seated, my rank entitled me to some prominence); and so mingling with the crowd of cloaked census-officials[34] I was next to those who were next to the consul.

Sidonius, of course, was always happy to let his readers know about his lofty status, even as a child.

Education

In antiquity, it was the responsibility of the parents to arrange for the education of their children. This was certainly the case during Late Antiquity, when the educational system in some places was not as elaborate as it once had been. The parents—in most attested instances the

---

31. The same Astyrius whose diptych was discussed in chapter 1 above.

32. Sid.Apoll. *Epist.* 8.6.5; translation from Anderson, *Sidonius,* 2:423; see also Dalton, *Sidonius,* 2:146.

33. See *PLRE* 2:1220. Sidonius never gives the name of his father; it may have been Alcimus: see Mathisen, "Epistolography."

34. *Censuales:* officials who kept property and tax assessment records, and also were responsible for the collection of some taxes.

father—either retained the services of a teacher, or served as teachers themselves. And in this regard, parents could be either natural or spiritual.

Home Schooling

Sidonius Apollinaris, for example, participated directly in the education of his son Apollinaris, as he related in a rare domestic vignette in a letter to his uncles Simplicius and Apollinaris:

3.8[35]   (1) . . . The other day I and the son of all of us[36] were ruminating on the wit of Terence's *Mother-in-Law*.[37] I was seated beside him as he studied, following my natural inclination and forgetful of my sacred calling, and in order to spur his receptive mind and enable him to follow the comic measures more perfectly, I had in my own hands a play of similar content, the *Arbitrants* of Menander.[38] (2) We were reading, praising, and jesting together, and, such are the desires we all share, he was charmed with the reading, and I with him.

Sidonius's pride in his son's proficiency is clear. At this time, moreover, Sidonius was a bishop and, technically, should have been devoting himself to sacred literature. But, in reality, many aristocratic bishops preserved their interest in classical literature and were largely responsible for its preservation. Sidonius's description of his and Apollinaris's literary diversion sounds very much like the way that the literary circles described in chapter 1 functioned, and provides insight into how young aristocrats were trained to function in aristocratic life as adults.

---

35. Sid.Apoll. *Epist.* 4.12.1–2; translation from Anderson, *Sidonius,* 2:111; see also Dalton, *Sidonius,* 2:24.

36. *Filius communis;* cf. Sidonius's references to his daughters above as "our shared care" and "our common cause of concern."

37. Six plays of the Roman republican dramatist Publius Terentius Afer (ca. 190–159 B.C.) survive; this one was titled *Hecyra.*

38. Most of the works of the Greek comic playwright Menander (342–291 B.C.) are lost, but much of this play (the *Epitrepontes*) has been recovered, on papyrus, from the sands of Egypt.

Engaging a Rhetor

Ruricius, bishop of Limoges circa 485–510, on the other hand, educated his sons by retaining the services of the rhetor Hesperius,[39] to whom he also gave some advice on what the position entailed:

9[40]   Ruricius, to a most steadfast and always magnificent[41] son, Hesperius.

Affection has opened to me the opportunity, which my ignorance had obstructed, of writing to Your Single-Mindedness. And piety, the governess of all, through whom rigid things are bent, stony are softened, swollen are collapsed, harsh are refined, gentle are excited, savage are mellowed, mellow are made savage, dull are sharpened, barbarous are tamed, and monstrous are placated, fulfilling her work even in me, has unbarred my inarticulate mouth, drawing me forth from the safest retreat of silence to public and frightening judgment, and compels me, in a life already old, to undergo something new.[42] I, of course, as one who hitherto followed the ancient sentiment by which it is said that it is generally preferable to be silent rather than to speak,[43] would prefer to conceal my ignorance in the taciturnity of modesty rather than to display it impudently in awkward speech. But now, as much negligent of my own habit as forgetful of my rusticity, as if changed suddenly from Arion into Orpheus,[44] with a garrulous tongue I would appear to your most learned ears not so much dutiful as injurious, as I both attempt the unknown and undertake the unaccustomed.

----

39. Hesperius received the next two letters in Ruricius's collection as well. The young Hesperius was a protégé of Sidonius Apollinaris (Sid.Apoll. *Epist.* 2.10, 4.22.1), and probably came from Clermont. See *PLRE* 2:552.

40. Ruric. *Epist.* 1.3: *MGH AA* 8:301–2; *CCL* 64:316–17; *CSEL* 21:355–56; for translation, see Mathisen, *Ruricius,* 107–9.

41. The title *magnificus* probably is a gratuitous honorific applied by Ruricius and not a formal designation of aristocratic rank (pace *PLRE* 2:552).

42. That is, invitations to write or publish something, a common element of aristocratic interchange.

43. An ancient commonplace.

44. Arion, a mythical minstrel from Lesbos, invented the dithyramb, a hymn to Dionysus. He jumped from a ship to escape pirates and was carried to shore by dolphins. Orpheus was an equally mythical poet who invented music after being given a lyre by Apollo. In general, Dionysus represented the senses and Apollo the intellect, and this contrast may lie behind Ruricius's comparison. Note also Vergil, *Eclogues,* 8.55–56, "let Tityrus be Orpheus / Orpheus in the forests, Arion among the dolphins."

But you, I presume, will grant pardon to one approaching from the necessity of a necessary need,[45] because a breast aware of a shared passion recognizes that which affection in the minds of mortals appropriates for itself through the power of nature. Therefore, lest by delaying any longer in excuses I extend my page to such an extent that my rather inelegant language not only does not produce < . . . >[46] in you, but even produces disgust through its inordinate length, I now burst forth in the voice of devotion and blurt out words of desire, commending to you my security,[47] your deposit, through the receipt of whom you have grasped hold of me. To you, indeed, to you alone, I have entrusted all my prayers, my hope in the present life and my consolation, if the divinity assents, for the future. I have chosen you as the stimulator and shaper of my noble jewels,[48] you as the assayer of gold, you as the discoverer of hidden springs, you, who know how to restore the gems concealed in stones[49] to their unique excellence: amid such worldly confusion they would indeed lose their nobility if they did not have you as an example.[50] Similarly, gold, mixed in with the vilest sands, unless it is washed in water and smelted in fire with the skill of the craftsman, can retain neither its splendor nor its worth. Likewise, unless the industry of the seeker most diligently excavates the enclosed channels of running water and the cavity for the flow covered by the land, the ripples of the liquid will not flow.[51] Thus also, the perspicuity of the youthful senses, until now hemmed in by the murk of ignorance as if by the density of rough blight, unless it is brightened by the ceaseless polishing of the teacher, cannot shine of its own will. Therefore, it now is up to you yourself to answer equally to your own expectation and to my judgment, lest either you appear to have presumed falsely or I to have chosen thoughtlessly.[52]

---

45. "Ex necessitudine necessariae necessitis," a rather heavy-handed use of a rhetorical trope, in this case *traductio*. The word "necessitas" could suggest that there also was a blood relationship between Ruricius and Hesperius.

46. At least one word apparently has dropped out here.

47. That is, his sons. Ruricius had five: Constantius, Ommatius, Eparchius, Leontius, and Aurelianus.

48. Once again, Ruricius's sons.

49. It was commonly believed in antiquity that cut jewels were hidden in the raw gemstones.

50. A striking affirmation of the perceived value of a classical education.

51. An allusion, it seems, to the building of aqueducts, which traveled largely underground.

52. Perhaps a veiled threat to Hesperius's continued employment.

Ruricius, like Sidonius, saw the value of a traditional classical education. His own literary technique exemplifies some of the characteristics of late Latin carried to extremes, including the repetitious use of antithesis, alliteration, and long lists of metaphors. One could suggest that his enthusiastic style might have been more akin to that of the run-of-the-mill Roman litterateur than that of, say, Sidonius Apollinaris or Avitus of Vienne.

A Dutiful Mother

Aristocratic women, too, oversaw the education of their children. In the early fifth century, for example, Jerome wrote to Rusticus, a young man of Marseille,

[53] (6) I hear that you have a religious mother, a widow of many years, who raised you and who instructed you in infancy, and who, after your Gallic studies, which were most successful indeed, sent you to Rome so that Roman solemnity would restrain the extravagance and elegance of Gallic speech,[54] sparing no expense and bearing the absence of her son through her hope in the future.

In this instance, the untimely death of her husband left Rusticus's mother responsible for overseeing the education of her son.

Parental Responsibility

Two parents who shared the role of educator, in a broad sense, are encountered in a rather convoluted letter written by Avitus of Vienne (ca. 490–518) to his friend Heraclius. It also accented the importance of literary pursuits in general.

[55] Avitus, bishop of Vienne, to the illustrious gentleman Heraclius.
If, stricken in spirit, I were not lamenting the doleful death of a

---

53. Jerome, *Epist.* 125.6: *CSEL* 56:126.

54. Gaul and Rome had reputations as centers for the study of rhetoric, and this kind of contrast was a commonplace (note the citation from the *Vita Germani* (Life of Germanus) in chapter 5 below); see Theodore J. Haarhoff, *Schools of Gaul: A Study of Pagan and Christian Education in the Last Century of the Western Empire* (London, 1920).

55. Avit. *Epist.* 95: *MGH AA* 6.2:102. This translation benefited from the helpful suggestions of Danuta Shanzer.

friend, I surely would wax eloquent, inasmuch as a concern for scaling mountains rather than scanning verses motivates you as you lie abed through fear of a groundless gout[56] while you are being invigorated by the customary art of the physician more than you are struggling with the feet of poetry. I dictated these words truly saddened and in haste, seeing that I have been summoned to the burial of our former shared son Protadius;[57] perhaps my presence, at least, in and of itself will provide some consolation for his father.

Moreover, if it is agreeable to you to be protected from fearful invasions[58] by the protective Rhône, given that I have suffered a complete loss, until I return keep safe also our Ceratius,[59] who has some things from me and several from you, whereby he asserts that he is studious on my account and martial on yours, appropriating from the wisdom of his mother that he freely shuns barbarians, and from the virtue of his father that he does not turn his back on literature.

In this instance, the father, mother, and bishop all are portrayed as sharing in the son's education—the father and bishop both overseeing his literary schooling, and the mother, it seems, being in charge of inculcating good sense in the choice of associates.[60]

Monastic Education

Another aristocrat who undertook the responsibility for educating his sons was Eucherius, a monk of Lérins who later became bishop of Lyon (ca. 430–50). Eucherius, who certainly was more committed to the religious lifestyle than aristocrats like Sidonius and Ruricius, composed a religious educational tract for each of his two sons: the *Instructiones* (Instructions) for Salonius and the *Formulae spiritalis intellegen-*

---

56. "Montium scandendorum magis moveat cura quam versuum": Avitus's rather strained antithesis suggest that Heraclius was more worried about his physical feet, impaired by gout, than his poetic feet, with which he should be more concerned.

57. *PLRE* 2:927 suggests that Protadius was the son of Heraclius, but, given Avitus's levity and Heraclius's absence from the funeral, not to mention the rest of this sentence, this seems unlikely. He more probably was a spiritual son of them both.

58. Perhaps a reference to campaigns by either the Franks or Ostrogoths, if not to a Burgundian civil war, in the course of which Avitus has experienced some losses.

59. The son of Heraclius; omitted in *PLRE,* vol. 2.

60. For other examples of an ecclesiastical role in education, note Eucherius's sons in the following passages, and Avitus's letter to Viventiolus in chapter 1 above.

tiae (Formulas of spiritual understanding) for Veranus.[61] In his dedicatory preface to the former, he wrote:

2[62]   Eucherius to his son Salonius, greetings in Christ.

You often ask me for an elucidation of the many matters in the
divine volumes that call for an explanation; I will assemble, to the
extent that they come to mind, those questions that in your eagerness
for learning you diligently and abundantly have brought forth, and I
will respond to them based not upon my own opinion but upon the
judgment of illustrious teachers, not upon my personal temerity but
upon the authority of others, striving not so much for the circuitous-
ness of a boastful eloquence as for the straightforwardness of a necessary brevity. Thus, indeed, not only will I be able to satisfy your innumerable questions, but I also will have the opportunity to insert
additional material that I deem useful for your education, such as, for
example, what *alleluia, diapsalma,* and *amen* signify; what are *cidaris,
ephod, siclus,* and so on, matters that, either repeated in the sacred
books or firmly established in ecclesiastical usage, have need of an
explanation. Because these topics continually present themselves to
readers throughout the whole body of the Scriptures, I did not think
that it was improper to point them out to you in this work, crammed
together, as it were, with their meanings.

For it is fitting that through my care, such as it is, your intellect
should be enriched, seeing that having entered the monastery, in the
hands of the saints, when you were scarcely ten years old, you were not
only taught but also raised by father Honoratus, that first master, I
say, of the islands, later a master of churches as well; when the learning
of the most blessed Hilary, then an insular novice but already now the
highest priest, molded you there in all the disciplines of spiritual matters; with the saintly men Salvian and Vincentius,[63] preeminent equally

---

61. The boys had accompanied Eucherius and their mother Galla to the monastery their
parents had founded on the island of Lero (Ste-Marguerite) ca. 410; before 420, when Salonius was ten, they all had entered the monastery of Honoratus on the neighboring island of
Lerinum (Lérins).

62. Eucherius of Lyon, *Instructiones ad Salonium* (Instructions to Salonius), preface:
CSEL 31:65–66.

63. Honoratus was bishop of Arles from 426 to 429, and Hilary succeeded him until 449.
Salvian moved to Marseille ca. 425, and Vincentius, the brother of Bishop Lupus of Troyes,
wrote works such as the famous *Commonitorium* (Reminder). For these persons, see also
Eucherius's *De laude eremi* (In praise of the wilderness), discussed in chapter 5 below.

in eloquence and wisdom, later perfecting you to this end. Having availed yourself of so many and such great teachers, you shall hear also from me, the least of all of them, the answers to your questions. In this work now recognize yourself asking and me responding.

Farewell, my Salonius, my dearest son in Christ.

A Review Copy

Honoratus, Hilary, Vincentius, and Salvian all were monks of Lérins, and in the quasi-familial environment of the monastery they partici- pated in the education of Eucherius's children. Circa the early 430s, after both had become bishops, Eucherius sent Hilary a review copy of the *Instructiones*.[64] Hilary subsequently was obliged to return it before he was quite ready, as indicated in his cover letter:

3.13[65] Bishop Hilary to Pope Eucherius, a lord blessed and deservedly accept- able and most steadfast in Christ.

Because I indicated in my preceding letter that I was going to restore the books of yours in my possession, I could not at all forestall the insistence and demand of the lad whom you sent. I returned, therefore, the blooming works of Your Beatitude not a little anxious lest they be ruined, not yet transcribed, by the tears pouring as continuously as they do abundantly. In a state of admiration, I skimmed over the entire work only once. May the Lord grant that at some time, with your guid- ance in your own pages, I might examine the splendid work of Your Glory, *Our Instructions in Christ.* I pray for this one thing, that you not for long undertake to defraud me of these *Instructions,* and, to the extent that the senility of age afflicts me with the nescience of youth, that you consider me to be one of your offspring, for whose instruction you have composed them, and wish me to have them at once.

May the Lord keep you always mindful of me to the profit of the Church, most blessed bishop.

In this instance, an aristocrat had the opportunity to make his own copy of a new composition, but failed to do so, and the piece continued

---

64. By 430, Salonius (apparently the elder son) would have been at least twenty years old, suggesting that, unless Eucherius had actually written the works some time before, his tracts were intended not for children but for young adults.

65. Hilary of Arles, *Epist.* "Cum me libellos": *CSEL* 31:197–98.

to circulate. A copy—perhaps the same one, once it had been retrieved from Hilary—was sent to Salvian, now at Marseille, who dutifully responded with a laudatory missive of his own:

14[66]   Salvian the priest to his lord and gentle bishop, Eucherius.

I have read the books that you sent to me. They are succinct in style but abounding in erudition, easy to read but perfect for instruction. They are worthy both of your intellect and of your piety, nor do I wonder that you have produced such a useful and beautiful work especially for the instruction of your holy and blessed children, because you have in fact constructed in them a choice temple to God, you have bedecked the inculcation of new erudition as if it is the culmination of your greatest edifice, and in order that the education and life of your blessed offspring might be ennobled, you have adorned with spiritual education those whom you have molded by moral guidance. It remains that our Lord God, to whose gift these most admirable young people are to be likened, may make them equal to your books, that is, that whatever the books contain, wrapped in mystery, both of the students may have in their understanding. And because, by divine dispensation and judgment they have already even begun to be masters of churches,[67] may the goodness of a most kindly God grant this, that their learning be to the profit of the churches and of you, and that with this most excellent beginning they may ornament him by whom they were begotten as well as those whom they have begotten by their own teaching. May the merciful God grant me this, if not in this life then certainly in the next, that those who once were my pupils[68] will pray daily for me.
Farewell, my lord and dear friend.

Educational tracts like these filled an important niche and found a ready audience in the Christianized pedagogical world of Late Antiquity. Ultimately, not only Eucherius's compositions but also Hilary's and Salvian's letters circulated as a package. Even if neither Hilary nor Salvian took the opportunity to copy Eucherius's works, at least one

---

66. Salv. *Epist.* "Legi libros tuos": *CSEL* 31:97. For partial translation, see Jeremiah F. O'Sullivan, trans. *The Writings of Salvian, the Presbyter* (New York: Cima, 1947), 255–56.

67. *Magistri ecclesiarum:* and, in fact, both went on to become bishops, Salonius at Geneva (ca. 440) and Veranus at Vence (in the early 450s).

68. Salvian was particularly attached to Salonius, with whom he corresponded (*Epist.* 9) and to whom he dedicated his own *De gubernatione dei* (On the governance of God).

copy was later made by the priest Rusticus, whose cover letter was cited in chapter 1, and this copy also included Hilary's, Salvian's, and Rusticus's letters.

Of course, the preceding examples of education all relate to the literary education that was received only by a privileged minority. The kinds of education received by other children were surely different, and more practical in nature, but as to their exact nature, we can only speculate.

Running with a Bad Crowd

Sometimes parents expressed concern about the way that their children were maturing. Sidonius, for example, was worried about his son's choice of companions, and, in a letter illustrating the fine art of character assassination, counseled him on the need to avoid disreputable associates. Sidonius also stressed the kinds of attributes that were considered acceptable in genteel aristocratic society.

3.15[69] Sidonius, greetings to his own Apollinaris.

(1) The love of purity that leads you to shun the company of the immodest has my whole approval; I rejoice at it and respect it, especially when the men you shun are those whose aptitude for scenting and retailing scandals leaves nothing privileged or sacred, wretches who think themselves enormously facetious when they violate the public sense of shame by shameless language. Hear now from my lips that the standard-bearer of the vile troop is the very Gnatho[70] of our country. (2) Imagine an arch-stringer of tales, arch-fabricator of false charges, arch-retailer of insinuations. A fellow whose talk is at once without end and without point; a buffoon without charm in gaiety; a bully who does not stand his ground. Inquisitive without insight, and three-times more the boor for his brazen affectation of fine manners. A creature of the present hour, with ever a carping word ready for the past and a sneer for the future. When he is after some advantage, no beggar so importunate as he; when refused, none so bitter in depreciation. Grant his request and he grumbles, using every artifice to get better terms; he moans and

---

69. Sid.Apoll. *Epist.* 3.13.1–2, 10; translation based on Dalton, *Sidonius,* 1:81–85; see also Anderson, *Sidonius,* 2:48–57.

70. Gnatho was the parasite in Terence's play *Eunuchus* (The eunuch), a good choice given Apollinaris's interest in Terence shown above.

groans when called on to repay a debt, and if he pays, you never hear the end of it. But when any one wants a loan of him he lies about his means and pretends he has not the wherewithal; if he does lend, he makes capital out of the loan, and broadcasts the secret abroad; if debtors delay repayment, he resorts to calumny; when they have absolved the debt he tries to deny receipt. (3) Abstinence is his abomination, he loves the table; but a man who lives well wins no praise from him unless he entertains well too. Personally, he is avarice itself; the best of bread is not for his digestion unless it is also the bread of others. He only eats at home if he can pilfer his viands, and seize them amid a storm of buffets . . . (10) He suffers from an itching for prurient talk, but he is particularly to be feared by patrons with secrets. He praises those with good fortune and betrays those in difficulties; let a tempting moment but urge the disclosure of a friend's secret, and instantly this Spartacus will break all bars and open every seal. He will mine with the unseen tunnels of his treachery the houses which the rams of open war have failed to breach. This is the fashion in which our Daedalus crowns the edifice of his friendships, sticking as close as Theseus in prosperity, but when adversity comes, more elusive than any Proteus. (11) Therefore, you will heed my wishes if you avoid even a first introduction to such company; especially those for whose prostituted and theatrical talk there is neither bar nor bridle. For when a man exults in leaving all seemliness and decency behind, and fouls a loose tongue with the dirt of all lawless license, be sure his heart is no less filthy than his language. Finally, it will happen more easily that someone who speaks seriously will live indecently than that one can be found who at the same time appears squalid in speech and upright in character.
Farewell.

It would appear that Sidonius's concerns were justified. Apollinaris did indeed fall in with a Visigothic collaborator, the count and duke Victorius, who, fearing for his life at Clermont because he was "excessively carnal in his love of women," fled to Rome, accompanied by Apollinaris.[71] There, Victorius still could not keep out of mischief, "and, attempting to practice similar luxury, he was stoned to death" in 481.[72]

---

71. Greg.Tur. *Glor.mart.* 44, *Hist.* 2.20.

72. "Dum nimium esset in amore mulierum luxoriosus . . . ibique similem temptans exercere luxoriam, lapidibus est obrutus" (Greg.Tur. *Hist.* 2.20).

Apollinaris was imprisoned and then exiled to Milan, whence he escaped and returned home.[73]

A Close Call

Nor, it seems, did Apollinaris learn his lesson. Subsequently, he was unable to steer clear of either trouble or friendly advice. His distinguished cousin Alcimus Ecdicius Avitus, bishop of Vienne (ca. 490–518), gave him some additional admonitions after he had become involved in some kind of altercation in the Visigothic kingdom, apparently in the early sixth century:

3.16[74] Bishop Avitus to the illustrious gentleman Apollinaris.

It is certainly repeated in a common yet true saying that the passions of concordant spirits discern themselves by the recognition of their mutual esteem. For do we not have such a solicitude for each other that I could have answered your letter, which my son the bearer brought, if I had put my mind to it, even before it arrived? For in the page of servitude that I sent with good cause through my bearers, I exhaled, more through affection than in words, a joy conceived from your prosperity, and I touched upon our relationship[75] and that of our common fathers, with exultation mixed with tears.

Furthermore, may the divine pity, which has established in the dignity of your person the hope of generating offspring and conceded also that we will become fathers with you alone as the begetter of our future posterity[76] while you repeatedly trample upon the conspiracy of your enemies and the spitefulness of the perfidious with a successful resolution, grant that the first stage of your victory will be to restore completeness to your sense of well-being, that the second will be that when your case is considered you will be approved at the hearing,[77] that the

---

73. Greg.Tur. *Glor.mart.* 44.

74. Avit. *Epist.* 52: *MGH AA* 6.2:81.

75. *Necessitatem:* see Ruricius's letter to Hesperius above. Avitus and Apollinaris were first cousins (see Mathisen, "Epistolography"), meaning that they had the same ancestors.

76. The fate of Apollinaris's son Arcadius is discussed in chapter 6 below. Apollinaris had only sisters (see above), and Avitus's brother, also named Apollinaris, was also a bishop and thus unlikely to have any offspring.

77. *Audientia:* a technical legal term.

third will be that mercy will be shown to your accusers after the sentencing. Indeed, a defeated enemy is tormented in spirit on account of the pardon that is extended to him, with a double benefit for us and a double punishment for him, inasmuch as he laments that you could not be deceived and he grieves because he is an object of pity.[78] Thus, having been placed under your authority at least to the extent that he has not lost his life, as long as he continues to be angry, embittered because of the pardon that was spontaneously offered, he will be compelled in some way to begrudge his own life.

For the rest, my most dutiful lord brother, care of my heart, glory of your family, accept for a little while the quaking ineptness of a brotherly admonition. Attentively beware evil men and beware blandishments with the hissing tricks of biting tongues and poisons with their machinations; after your experiences do not think that you know better. Nor should your shrewdness make you less cautious than your innocence can demonstrate that you are secure.[79] If in fact the opportunity for inquiry and injury has been cut off, for this very reason you ought to endeavor less frequently to assail their undertakings, because, leaving vengeance to the divine judgment, you have decided always to forgive those who are harass you. Although, as I already confessed above, he is not considered to be totally unpunished whom your triumph infuriates.

One cannot say for certain what kind of trouble that Apollinaris had gotten into here, except that it seems to be related to a reconciliation with the Visigothic king Alaric II (484–507) mentioned in the previous letter in the corpus.[80] By 507, Apollinaris was in sufficient good graces to be the leader of the Arvernian contingent at the battle of Vouillé.

Regardless of the specific circumstances, it is apparent that Avitus, like Sidonius before him, had fears about Apollinaris's common sense and good judgment. But Apollinaris seems to have continued to have a nose for controversy, as seen by his subsequent involvement, discussed in chapter 6, in a squabble over an episcopal election in Clermont.

---

78. Avitus may have had in mind here Sidonius's description (*Epist.* 1.11) of his own defeat of his rival Paeonius in 461.

79. Avitus apparently thought that Apollinaris was too clever by half.

80. Avit. *Epist.* 51: "You wrote that all is well and that the esteem of King Alaric toward you remains secure and pristine."

Living the Good Life

Constantius, one of the sons of Ruricius of Limoges, also seems to have been a somewhat wayward youth. As a result he received two pithy letters from his father.

3.17[81]   Bishop Ruricius to his son Constantius.

Even though I know that you are given to Bacchus, serenades, and diverse musical activities, and in fact even to girls' choruses, nevertheless, because while adolescence mightily seethes[82] it is good occasionally to retreat from such things and to spend time more with the Lord than with Liber, and to pay attention to parents rather than to melodies, I direct that tomorrow, which will be the fourth celebration,[83] you hasten to fast with me at Brive,[84] and in a timely manner, which I do not at all think that you are planning to do.

Ruricius's concern may have arisen, in part, because such activities were expressly forbidden to clerics: the Council of Agde of 506, for example, decreed, "Nor are they to mingle in those gatherings where romantic and shameful songs are sung, or where obscene movements of bodies with singers and dancers are presented, lest their vision and hearing, dedicated to the sacred mysteries, be polluted by the contagion of shameful utterances and exhibitions."[85] All of which would suggest that such entertainments were all the rage.

---

81. Ruric. *Epist.* 2.24: *MGH AA* 8:332; *CCL* 64:364–65; *CSEL* 21:409–10; for translation, see Mathisen, *Ruricius,* 180.

82. "Pervalde fervet adulescentia"; cf. *Epist.* 2.17, where "adulescentiae regnet cupido" [the libido of adolescence reigns] even in mature people.

83. *Quarta feria:* in the Gallic church calendar, each day of the week had its own *feria* (service), with Monday being the second, Tuesday the third, Wednesday the fourth (as here), and so on to Friday, the sixth. In particular, the days after Easter were identified as the *feria secunda, tertia,* etc., and each had its own liturgy. If it is to these *feriae* that Ruricius refers, then the time of year would have made Constantius's revelry all the more reprehensible in Ruricius's eyes.

84. Briva Curretia (Brive-la-Gaillarde), south of Limoges; there was a church there of St. Martin of Brive, a disciple of Martin of Tours. See J.-M. Desbordes, J.-M. Desbordes, C. Gautrand-Moser, G. Lintz, and F. Moser, *Les origines de Brive* (Brive, 1982); and M. Gady, "Saint Martin martyr de Brive," *Bulletin de la société scientifique historique et archéologique du Corrèze* 68 (1946): 46–70.

85. "Nec his coetibus admisceantur, ubi amatoria cantantur et turpia, aut obsceni motus corporum choris et saltibus efferuntur, ne auditus et obtutus sacris mysteriis deputatus turpium spectaculorum atque verborum contagio polluatur" (Council of Agde, canon 39: *CCL* 148:209–10).

Ruricius's exhortations, however, seems not to have had their desired results, as seen in the subsequent letter in his collection:

18[86] Another of the same person.

With God as your witness, you promised me something different, that you would worship Him, not Iacchus;[87] you even want me to be a participant in this crime, so that I would provide delicacies for the cultivation of this error and pour oil on the fire, which you know would benefit neither of us. But perhaps you say, "You promised." With what effrontery do you seek that promised by me, when you have violated your own oaths? Whence you will release me from my promise as long as I know that you serve your own appetite, lest I seem to encourage the activity, whose manner I rebuked, and lest I serve as a stumbling block for one to whom I should be an example.

One doubts whether Ruricius's threat to cut off Constantius's stipend was actually carried out. For on another occasion, Constantius and Ruricius exchanged *deliciae* (treats): Constantius sent Ruricius some fowl for his table, and the latter repaid him with a side of bacon and a brief homily advising him not to "pursue worldly concerns."[88] This exchange of goodies would suggest that Ruricius was reconciled to Constantius's worldly and self-indulgent lifestyle, which in fact was probably more characteristic of Gallic gentry than the exaggerated pseudoasceticism that aristocrats sometimes affected in their correspondence and other writings.

Children, then, regardless of their social status, were integral parts of the family unit and had little opportunity for independent action—the case of Martin of Tours, at least according to his hagiographer, being an exception. But children eventually grew up and then could enjoy what perquisites of adulthood were available to them. Apollinaris, as will be seen, went on to become a bishop in spite of his spotty past. Women, on the other hand, were endowed with their gender for life, and one now can consider what traditional roles were available to them.

---

86. Ruric. *Epist.* 2.25: *MGH AA* 8:332; *CCL* 64:365; *CSEL* 21:410; for translation, see Mathisen, *Ruricius,* 180–83.

87. Properly, a minor deity connected to the Eleusinian mysteries at Athens, but more commonly identified by the Romans with Bacchus and Dionysus.

88. Ruric. *Epist.* 2.43.

The Status of Women: Traditional Roles

Unlike children, women did have the opportunity to act independently. Depending on the individual and the circumstances, their role could be a quite substantial. Several women are attested as having established reputations for themselves in conventional family contexts and will be discussed here. Women who expressed themselves outside of the family context will be considered in subsequent chapters.

A Virtuous Matron of Vienne

When women did appear in their own right, it often was only in death. The epitaph of Celsa, found in the church of St. Peter in Vienne, presents an image of the ideal Late Roman matron.

3.19[89]   Here lies the body of Celsa,
       thus likewise by merits and by name,[90]
       for she has restored her
       celibate spirit to the heavens.
       Having subdued the flesh through the nurturing
       cross, she spurned worldly things,
       and apprehensive of prosperity
       and laughing at adversity,
       thus having both as devoted comrades,
       she offered herself to all
       as a foster parent, not unequal
       to the ten wise maidens,[91]
       with her oil [lamp] alight,
       awaiting her bridegroom, Christ.
       Her burial took place four days before the Nones of March
            [in the year] after the consulate of Agapitus.[92]

---

89. A. Riese and F. Buecheler, eds., *Anthologia latina* 2.1 (Leipzig: Teubner, 1906), 330–31, no. 700.

90. This epitaph, like that of Proba above, begins with a play on words: the word *celsa* means "exalted."

91. Matt. 25.1–13; in fact, of the ten maidens, only five wisely remembered to bring oil for their lamps; the others did not and were excluded from the wedding celebration.

92. I.e. "p(ost) c(onsulato) Agapiti": given that it was still relatively early in the year, it is likely that the consuls for the year were not yet known, hence the dating by the consul of the previous year.

Celsa died, therefore, on 4 March 518.[93] It is unclear whether, having dedicated her life to Christ, she actually became a nun, or merely lived an exemplary life. Regardless, she fulfilled all of society's expectations for a respectable Roman gentlewoman.[94]

Senatorial Matchmaking

The most prevalent family activity in which women engaged was marriage, where issues of property ownership and personal autonomy often were a concern. To what extent were women able to choose their own mates and manage their own property? Some Late Roman legislation, such as this ruling issued on 16 July 371, detailed women's rights in such regards.[95]

20[96] The emperors Valentinian, Valens, and Gratian, Augustuses, to the Senate.

Widows being less than twenty-five years of age, even though they enjoy the freedom derived from emancipation,[97] shall not enter into a subsequent marriage without the consent of their fathers or by giving a pledge. Therefore, the go-betweens and intermediaries, the silent messengers and corrupt informers, shall cease. No one shall purchase, no one shall solicit, noble marriages; but a marriage relation shall be discussed publicly, and a number of nobles shall be put forward. (1) But if in the choice of a marriage the woman's desire should conflict with the decision of her near kinsmen, it is our pleasure that, as has been sanctioned in the case of marriages of girls who are orphans, the authority of a judicial hearing shall be added to the investigation that must be held, with the result that if the suitors are equal in birth and character, the person whom the woman herself approves, consulting her own

---

93. The nones, usually on the fifth of the month, are on the seventh in March.

94. The name Celsa was a distinguished one: a Marcia Romania Celsa was the wife of Fl. Januarinus, consul in A.D. 328 (*PLRE* 1:453, which omits her).

95. See E. Clark, "Ideology, History, and the Construction of 'Women' in Late Ancient Christianity," *Journal of Early Christian Studies* 2 (1994): 171 n. 86, for an extensive bibliography on the extent to which women could control their property in the Later Roman Empire.

96. *CTh* 3.7.1 (16 July 371), the first entry in the section entitled *De nuptiis* (On marriages); for partial translation, see Pharr, *Theodosian Code,* 70.

97. That is, after the death of her husband, she was no longer under his legal control and had become *sui iuris* (under her own authority).

interests, shall be adjudged preferable. (2) But lest perchance even honorable marriages should be impeded by those persons who, as kinsmen in the nearest degree, would succeed to the widows' inheritances, if a suspicion of this kind should arise, it is our will that the authority and judgment of those persons shall prevail who, even though death should intervene, could not receive the benefit of the inheritance.

Given on the seventeenth day before the Kalends[98] of August in the year of the consulship of Gratian Augustus, for the second time, and of the most distinguished Probus.[99]

This law was addressed to the Senate of Rome because it was senators who were most concerned with its primary thrust, which really involved not marriage but property. Even if the woman was *sui iuris,* it didn't count for much, at least when property was concerned. And the bit of independence seemingly given to women in the choice of a spouse in this law was circumscribed by constraints in other laws. For example, a ruling of the emperor Honorius in 422 stated that marital arrangements made by a father were to remain in force even after his death, "Because often even the resolution of a woman herself is found to work against her own best interests."[100]

Both rulings do indicate, however, that women did seek to choose their own mates. And this inference is supported by another piece of legislation, issued by Honorius in 409, that began, "Certain men, having disregarded the rule of previous legislation, imagine that marriages, which they are aware that they do not deserve, can be sought from us by devious pleas, pretending that they have the girl's consent."[101] So, it would appear not only that, in spite of legal or social restrictions, women and men were arranging their own marriages, but also that they were willing to take their cases to the emperor himself.

---

98. The Kalends was the first day of the month.

99. A typical subscription added to imperial laws.

100. *CTh* 3.5.12: "cum plerumque etiam ipsius feminae adversus commoda propria inveniatur laborare consilium."

101. *CTh* 3.10.1: "Quidam, vetusti iuris ordine praetermisso, obreptione precum nuptias, quas se intellegunt non mereri, de nobis aestimant postulandas, se habere puellae consensum confingentes."

A Flattering Marauder

The upheaval of the fifth century and later appears to have created additional opportunities for women to assert themselves in matters of the heart. Circa 470, during the last throes of the barbarian occupation of Gaul, Bishop Faustus of Riez posed a hypothetical case, in which women chose to leave their old lives and take up with the pillagers:

¶[102]   If some legate or bishop, acting as an intercessor for his captured city, pays a great ransom and frees from the grip of captivity his entire people, who were being held by right of conquest, and if all condition and necessity of servitude is altogether removed, and, in the midst of this, if perhaps either the delight of intimacy or a flattering marauder wickedly solicits some of the captives, the slave of their desires, to refuse the gratuitous favor [of release], does the contempt of the ungrateful one not lessen the favor of the ransom?

In this conjectured instance, the disruption of the old social system caused by the arrival of the barbarians allowed for a greater latitude in one's choice of companions—in spite of official prohibitions of such practices.[103]

Defining Incest

This is not to say, of course, that one could choose one's mate with total impunity. Far from it. Sometimes when couples violated official secular or ecclesiastical standards, a public spectacle was created. This happened circa 518 when Stephanus, an official of the Burgundian king Sigismund, married Palladia, the sister of his deceased former wife. This union blatantly contravened a canon that had just been promulgated at a church council held at Epaon in 517:

---

102. Faust. *De gratia* (On grace), 1.16: *CSEL* 21:50–51.

103. A law of the early 370s prohibited inhabitants of the provinces "of any rank or place" from marrying barbarians, "Because in these [marriages] something suspect or noxious is detected" (*CTh* 3.14.1: 28 May 370/373).

3.22[104] (30) We offer no pardon whatsoever to incestuous unions except when they have cleansed the adultery by a separation. Indeed, besides those that are shameful even to name,[105] we consider these to be the incestuous unions, not to be disguised by any designation of marriage: if anyone should violate by carnal union the widow of his brother, who was previously almost his sister; if anyone, as a brother, should marry the sister of his wife; if anyone should wed his stepmother; if anyone should unite himself with a first cousin or cousin. We prohibit this from the present time. Thus, should anyone be bonded with the widow of a maternal uncle or be polluted by sexual relations with a paternal uncle or stepdaughter, we do not dissolve these marriages that were instituted previously. As for those to whom an illicit union is forbidden, they of course will have liberty to enter a more acceptable marriage.

A Case of Incest

The *vita* (life) of Bishop Apollinaris of Valence, the brother of Avitus of Vienne and apparently one of the chief hard-liners, provides an enthusiastically fulsome account of the ecclesiastical response to this couple's brazen violation of their brand-new prohibition. Here, the Nicene bishops attempt to take full advantage of the influence they have with King Sigismund, who recently had converted from Arian to Nicene Christianity:

3.23[106] (2) Therefore, it happened that a certain man from the staff of King Sigismund, Stephanus by name, who was in charge of the control of the entire administration of the fisc, after the death of his wife united to himself in an illicit marriage his wife's sister. For this reason, the saintly and blessed apostolic men Avitus[107] and Apollinaris—who were brothers according to the flesh, and most famous brothers indeed in the work of Christ, always engaged in divine works, with the prudence of their nobility known far and wide, and learned, with a fiery spirit, in the sacred teachings—preserving the conciliar institution,

---

104. Council of Epaon, can. 30: *CCL* 148A:31.
105. That is, the bishops declined to mention incestuous unions of an even closer degree.
106. *Vita Apollinaris Valentiniensis* (Life of Apollinaris of Valence), 2: *MGH SRM* 3:258.
107. That is, Avitus, bishop of Vienne. His involvement would date the incident to between the Council of Epaon, on 15 September 517, and Avitus's death, on 5 February 518.

having gathered together with the other bishops, decreed that this same Stephanus was deprived of Holy Communion, so that, with the indecency of human frailty having been trampled underfoot, disrespectful presumption would not dare to support one guilty of incest, a thing that the supernal justice condemns.

(3) Then the king, aroused by the fury of a fearful insanity, did not cease to afflict the blessed pontiffs by most skillfully setting traps. But the apostolic and venerable men, fortified by celestial powers, feared the threats of this earthly king not at all; they entwined themselves in the bond of righteousness, so that, whatever punishments were inflicted on them, they endured the savage torments of their sufferings. In fact, having been sentenced equally to exile, it seemed best to them that they should share each other's company, with the help of God, in a town in the territory of Lyon called Sardinia.[108] Seeing that their constancy was incorruptible, the king, not letting up from his anger, ordered that the pontiffs, who were residing there together, should return home and wait upon him separately on a monthly basis. And because the most blessed Apollinaris seemed to be persevering in his condemnation of Stephanus, the king determined to observe him first. Then, together tearfully beseeching the divine power that it not abandon them, they said farewell with repeated prayers and set out. . . .

(5) And when the king chose not to see that blessed apostolic man, but attempted to set more traps, He who is the judge of the most righteous deeds and of immensely laudable virtue, demonstrating his speedy vengeance, at once caused the king to incur such a potency of fever that he seemed to be more dead than alive. Then the queen, aroused by the bishop's faith, went with fleet swiftness to the place where the blessed pontiff was staying, and entreated with eager devotion that through his intercession her husband might receive the gift of good health. But the man of God, having renounced the excessive pride of worldly elation, refused any kind of servitude. So in addition, wetting his feet with her tears, the queen beseeched him to show her his cloak, which he ought to spread over the king. Overcome by her weeping, he yielded. After it had been draped over her husband with trusting steadfastness, by the benefaction of the Lord, with the infestation of fever, or any other

---

108. The town of "Sardinia" is otherwise unknown; it may be allusion to the island of Sardinia, where North African bishops were exiled by the Vandals in the late fifth century.

attack there seemed to be, immediately put to flight, he merited the gift of restored health.

(6) After this, the king, remembering the crime that he had perpetrated, even though he was filled with a great confusion exulted nonetheless because, with the aid of the pontiff by means of the covering of his clothing, he had managed to regain his earlier health. Hastening forward he first desired, as if by the bounty of such a great miracle and of such great virtue, that he would be able to see with corporeal eyes the sweet springs that the Lord granted to his servant through the gift of his kindness. Having acknowledged the grace of Apollinaris's virtue, he went to the man of God and, embracing his ankles, publicly begged pardon with tears of exultation, saying, "I have sinned, I have acted unjustly, insofar as I have often inflicted undeserved tribulations upon just men, for celestial justice knows not how to be defeated; it is stronger than that by which it is attacked." O indulgence of the celestial King, who does not want the souls of sinners to perish but just their sins! O glory of virtues, which through their servant Apollinaris, who subdues worldly cares, showed forth in the double grace of virtue! Ultimately, Apollinaris, in the defense of justice, dispelled the insanity and the inflated pride of the king and, through the efficacy of his prayer, freed him from the deadly weakness by which he was gripped.

The Bishops Back Down

This account leaves one believing that the sentence against Palladia and Stephanus was upheld. By a stroke of good fortune, there survive the acts of a church council that met at Lyon circa 518/523 for the purpose of reconsidering the case. They allow us to compare the account of the *vita* with the actual dénouement:

3.24[109] (1) In the name of the Trinity, having gathered together a second time in the case of Stephanus, who was polluted by the crime of incest, and abiding in the city of Lyon, we decreed that we would inviolably preserve our ruling, to which we had unanimously subscribed regarding the condemnation of him and her to whom he had illicitly joined him-

---

109. *Council of Lyon,* can. 1: *CCL* 148A:38–41.

self. This ruling should be enforced not only with respect to the aforementioned individuals but also with respect to any individuals who are
apprehended engaged in this perversity at any place or time. (2) We
also add this, that if any one of us, perhaps, is forced to suffer any
tribulation or grief or interference from the authorities, all of us shall
suffer together in the same spirit, and that no matter what hardship or
penalty one of us suffers as a result of his support of this case, fraternal
consolation shall lighten his suffering anxieties. (3) But if, in addition,
the most excellent king suspends himself from the communion of the
church or the bishops,[110] let the blessed bishops, giving him the opportunity of returning to the lap of the blessed mother [church], betake
themselves to monasteries without any delay, to the extent that each
has the opportunity to do so, until the king, influenced by the prayers
of the saints, and in consequence of his power and piety, thinks it
fitting to restore unblemished communion for the sake of preserving
the fullness of charity, so that not a single one will depart from the
monastery in which he chose to reside until communion has been
promised or returned to all the brothers in common.

The bishops therefore were well aware that persevering in their sentence could result in royal punishment, and at this point in the proceedings they bravely proposed to bear up under whatever travails
threatened them.

But their brave words then were followed by some Realpolitik, for
after two additional canons dealing with other matters, there then
appears an addendum:

In addition, having agreed with the recommendation of our most glorious lord king, we bestow this alleviation, that we provide to the
aforementioned Stephanus and Palladia the opportunity to pray in the
sacred places up to the address to the people, which is after the reading
of the Gospels.

So in spite of their posturing, the bishops eventually caved in to the
king, and not only permitted Stephanus and Palladia to continue their
illicit relation, but even issued them a personal invitation to attend

---

110. That is, in case the king decided to return to Arianism.

church services up to the point when noncommunicants had to depart. Once again, therefore, an influential patron was able to smooth the rough spots keeping two lovers apart.

Aunegilda Changes Her Mind

The Burgundian kingdom provides another example, from the very same time and place as the case of Palladia and Stephanus, of an institutional interest in regulating marriages. In this instance, Aunegilda, a Burgundian woman, not only chose her own spouse, but even made her way into the Burgundian law code, where an entry dated 29 March 517 reads:

3.25[111]

Concerning betrothed women who, incited by adultery, pass over to consorting with others.

(1) However many times cases of this sort arise, regarding which the statutes of earlier laws ordain nothing, it is thus fitting to resolve any doubt about the matter, with the result that a published judgment gains the force of perpetual law, and that an individual case acquires general legality.

(2) Therefore, having heard and considered the merits of the criminal charge that was pending between Fredegisclus, our sword-bearer,[112] on the one hand, and Balthamodus along with Aunegilda on the other, we issue a judgment that curbs this recent crime and imposes a means of punishment for future times.

(3) And because, after the death of her previous husband, Aunegilda, acting on her own authority,[113] betrothed herself to the aforementioned Fredegisclus not only with the consent of her parents but even by her own decision and will, and had received the greater part of the bride-price, paid out by her fiancé, and because, aroused by the ardor of a pleasurable passion, she broke her faith and did not so much rush into commitments to Balthamodus as return to an accustomed crime, and on this account she ought to expiate so great a crime and so great a disgrace in no way other than by the shedding of her

---

111. *Liber constitutionum sive lex Gundobada* ("Book of Constitutions" or "Law of Gundobad," commonly known as the *Lex Burgundionum,* or "Burgundian Code"), 52: L. R. de Salis, ed., *MGH Leg.* 1.2.1 (Hannover, 1892), 85–87; for another translation, see Kathleen F. Drew, trans., *The Burgundian Code: Book of Constitutions or Law of Gundobad. Additional Enactments* (Philadelphia, 1949), 59–60.

112. *Spatharius:* a *spatha* was a broad unpointed two-edged sword.

113. "In sua potestate": cf. the "freedom of emancipation" of the hypothetical woman in the Theodosian Code above.

own blood, nevertheless,[114] prefering reverence for these days[115] to public punishment, we direct that Aunegilda, dishonored by divine and human judgment, be compelled to pay a penalty[116] to Fredegisclus, that is, three hundred *solidi.*[117]

(4) Nor, indeed, do we liberate from the deserts of the same condemnation Balthamodus, who presumed to take a woman owed in matrimony to another and whose death this matter demanded. But consideration for the sacred days restrains our sentencing him to death, under this condition: that, unless with eleven others he swears indisputable oaths in which he affirms that at that time, when the aforementioned Aunegilda was quite frequently joined to him as if in the status of a wife, he was unaware that she was already promised to Fredegisclus, he shall not delay paying his price, that is, one hundred and fifty *solidi,* to Fredegisclus. But if he will have sworn, he will suffer neither penalty nor peril.

(5) Truly, we command that the judgment rendered in this case is to be maintained forever in the status of permanent law. And lest the temperance of the settlement now permitted tempt someone subsequently to carrying out the risk of such a great crime, we command that whomever guiltiness of a similar deed confronts will not so much suffer a loss of property as will be smitten by capital punishment. It is indeed more fitting that the multitude be corrected by the condemnation of a few, than that, under the guise of an unsuitable gentility, an opportunity be introduced that grants license to lawbreaking.

Given at Lyon on the fourth day before the Kalends of April during the consulate of Agapitus.[118]

---

114. It was common practice to use legislation for the purpose of granting some kind of special exception or exemption on the one hand, while forbidding such practices in the future.

115. Easter in 517 was on March 26, i.e., three days before the issue of this ruling on March 29. For such pardons granted by Roman emperors at Eastertime, see, e.g., *CTh* 9.38.3 (5 May 367).

116. The "pretium," or wergelds was a person's "value," and was determined by social class. A slave was valued at 30 solidi, a *minor persona* (lesser person) at 75, a *mediocris* (middling person) at 100, and an *optimas nobilis* (noble optimate) at 150. Aunegilda's wergeld of 300 solidi may represent a punitive doubling of her nominal valuation.

117. The solidus was a gold coin initially issued by the emperor Constantine in the year A.D. 314 and weighing one-seventy-second of a Roman pound, or one-sixth of an ounce. A common laborer could expect to earn three solidi per year, and a soldier about seven. So these fines would have been quite onerous for all but the most wealthy.

118. This ruling was promulgated on the same occasion as the Burgundian Code itself: *MGH Leg.* 2.1.30, "editus sub die IIII. Kalendas Aprilis Lugduno" [issued on the fourth day before the kalends of April (March 29) at Lyon]. The subscription to this Burgundian law looks exactly like subscriptions to Roman imperial laws.

Aunegilda, therefore, was able to act on her own legal authority, at least in the choice of a husband, and was in fact able to enjoy "the ardor of her desire."

Marital Companionship

Once a marriage had occurred, life went on. But the kinds of interactions that occurred between husbands and wives, and the feelings that they had for each other, are only rarely mentioned. In the midst of the disruption of the early fifth century, an anonymous Gaul addressed the following poem to his wife.

3.26[119]   Come now, I pray, steadfast   [1]
              Comrade of my activities
              And let us dedicate
              our brief life to God the Lord . . .
              You alone, faithful comrade, embark with me upon
                   this campaign,   [115]
                In which God offers help to the infirm.
              Solicitously restrain me when I am elated, console me when I
                   grieve:
                Let us each provide an example of a pious life.
              Be a guardian of your guardian, render reciprocal support:
                Encourage me when I waver, arise with the hope of consolation,
              So that for us not only our flesh is shared, but our intellect
                As well, and so that each of us nourishes two spirits.

Such sentiments demonstrate how traditional marital relations, when the couple had not undertaken celibacy, were incorporated into the Christian ideology.

A Domestic Enemy

Technically, the male was the head of the household. But in reality, women often asserted themselves. A letter of Ruricius of Limoges of circa 495 to his friend Volusianus, the bishop of Tours, gives some

---

119. *Poema coniugis ad uxorem* (Poem of a husband to his wife), 1–2, 115–22: *PL* 51:611–16. It is preserved variously among the works of Prosper of Aquitaine and Paulinus of Nola, but was not, it seems, written by either of them.

tongue-in-cheek insight into a family where Ruricius, at least, thought that his friend's wife called the shots in the family.

120   Bishop Ruricius to his brother bishop Volusianus.

Thus, what is worse, long forgetfulness has destroyed the ancient and inherent affection in us,[121] caused partly, as it must be confessed, by our own negligence, partly by the exigencies of the times,[122] partly by infirmity of the body, so that having become completely forgetful, we demand from ourselves not only no reciprocal duties but not even letters. I marvel that Your Nobility sends a letter to me like to a son, because without any regard for religion or family ties my injuries are so pleasing to you that you do not wish to make up for them. For this reason, if I had not taken heed of my status and office, I would have sent back to you the bearer of your letter in such a state as my men were rendered not by your wife, but by an excessively froward and unrestrained governess,[123] whose manners—even if you tolerate them for so long, either voluntarily or by compulsion, to the diminution of your reputation—you should know that others neither wish nor are content to bear. For—because you write that you are rendered stupefied by fear of the enemy[124]—he who is accustomed to endure a domestic enemy ought not to fear a foreign one.

Volusianus did in fact run into trouble after being accused of collaboration with a foreign enemy circa 498, as reported by Gregory of Tours: "Having been considered suspect by the Goths because he wished to subject himself to the rule of the Franks and having been condemned to exile in the city of Toulouse, he died there."[125]

---

120. Ruric. *Epist.* 2.65: *MGH AA* 8:350; *CCL* 64:394; *CSEL* 21:441–42. Volusianus, a relative of his predecessor Perpetuus, apparently is the Volusianus who had been abbot of the monastery founded by the monk Abraham outside Clermont and who received a letter from Sidonius (*Epist.* 7.17).

121. This comment is almost an epitaph for the times and is appropriate for the final letter in Ruricius's collection.

122. "Necessitate temporis"; perhaps an allusion to Frankish raids.

123. "Domina procax nimium et effrenata."

124. "Metu hostium": the Franks, who raided the Visigothic kingdom in the 490s, would seem to be the only people who could be referred to in this manner in this context. In addition, the city of Tours was situated right on the border, and most of its suffragan cities were north of the Loire River in Frankish territory.

125. "Suspectus habitus a Gothis, quod se Francorum ditionibus subdere vellet, apud urbem Tholosam exilio condempnatus, in eo obiit" (Greg.Tur. *Hist.* 10.31, cf. 2.26).

Economic Considerations

In other regards, too, women were able to exercise mastery over their own affairs. The adoption of the religious life, for example, as seen above in the case of Celsa, provided several sorts of opportunities. In the matter of property, women found that by devoting themselves to the church, they could gain greater control over the disposition of their property than they ordinarily had. Of course, in this case they had a powerful ally: the church itself, in whose interest it was to see to it that women who wished to expend their resources on its behalf would be allowed to do so.[126] Religious women also acted independently by performing pilgrimages.[127] In other regards, however, Christianity was a mixed blessing for women, for it also cast them in the roles of "seductresses and blamed."[128]

Economic Tutelage

In Gaul, meanwhile, after the disappearance of Roman authority in the west, the legal establishment continued to use Roman law to attempt to restrict the economic autonomy of women. For example, a ruling of 8 March 414 in the Theodosian Code laconically stated,

3.28[129]   The emperors Honorius and Theodosius, Augustuses, to Julianus, proconsul of Africa for the second time.

    And with regard to women and minor children, in those matters that they either avoid or ignore, it is established that reference must be made to innumerable authorities. Given on the first day before the Nones of March, at Ravenna, when Constantius[130] and Constans, most distinguished gentlemen, were consuls.

---

126. See Averil Cameron, *The Later Roman Empire* (Cambridge: Harvard University Press, 1993), 127–28.

127. See H. Sivan, "Who Was Egeria? Piety and Pilgrimage in the Age of Gratian," *Harvard Theological Review* 81 (1988): 59–72. Jerome corresponded with a number of Gallic women who had traveled to the Holy Land: see Jerome, *Epist.* 120 (Hedybia) and 121 (Algasia).

128. See Cameron, *Later Roman Empire,* 127–30.

129. *CTh* 2.16.3 = *Codex Justinianus* (Code of Justinian), 2.21.8; for another translation see Pharr, *Theodosian Code,* 51.

130. This Constantius later married Galla Placidia, the sister of the emperor Honorius, and in 421 was made emperor; he died a few months later.

But when the Theodosian Code was summarized and reissued in Gaul in 506, as discussed in chapter 4 below, *interpretationes* (interpretations) were added to the laws that had been selected for inclusion, and the interpretation appended to this ruling gave a much more copious opinion that differentiated between minors, who could not act on their own legal authority, and emancipated women, who could.

Interpretation: Aid thus is given to minor women, just as to minor men, in all cases. But as for women of the age of majority, just as the law itself says, it commands that consideration be made on account of the frailty of their sex regarding many matters that they have overlooked through ignorance; that is, if they have become sureties for any person, they are not held obligated on account of the said suretyship. If in rather difficult cases, through ignorance of the law and statutes, they should perhaps sign a document of mandate *(mandatum)* relating to their own business affairs, in order that the person to whom they have given the mandate should transact some business of theirs, and if this person should write himself into the document not only as an agent but also as principal, relief is given to the women who have been deceived through such fraud. Moreover, all other contracts that women of legal age make publicly and in formal documents shall remain valid.

A Day in Court

Shortly thereafter, these official opinions, and an example of such a *mandatum,* were gathered up for inclusion in a local legal guidebook at Clermont. In one entry, mature women were classified with children and the mentally incompetent: the property of all three categories was felt to require special (that is to say, male) oversight. The first section gave the correct formula for the paperwork, the second the means by which the paperwork was confirmed. In both instances, the surviving Latin is extremely corrupt and often difficult to construe correctly. The proceedings were overseen by the *defensor civitatis* (defender of the city), a position that had originated in the late Roman period.

3.29[131]   Mandate.

Ancient custom[132] ordains, and the laws decreed by the emperors[133] sanction, that, should anyone be less able to govern their own affairs, his own or her own, through a torpor of the senses or their feminine sex or a weakness of body or mind, oversight by chosen individuals is permitted. I, (that woman) [or] most esteemed son of mine, (so-and-so) and (so-and-so),[134] request and enjoin and entreat Your Graces that, concerning all my affairs, either in my own business or anything regarding the property of my parents or from my own gain or from my marriage, whatever contention arises against me, whatever can be said or enumerated regarding my affairs, I institute [this] for you, lords and agents, so that concerning all my affairs or my properties—including my landed property and my purchased property and my other property, which it would take too long to enumerate—both in the presence of the lords and in any jurisdiction at all, either before counts or judiciary authority, you may make decisions and proposals in my place, and that whatever in this regard for the sake of truth you define, do, or carry out, shall be published as established, confirmed, and completed in advance. Assuredly, if anyone, either I myself or another . . .[135]

Here is the procedure.[136]

At Clermont, in the presence of the praiseworthy gentleman[137] (that defender) or of the public assembly of this same city, (that woman) said, "I beseech you, best defender or public assembly of this city, to permit me to examine the public documents: I have something that I wish to confirm by an examination of past proceedings."[138] The aforementioned defender said, "Let the public documents be accessible to you; examine whatever you wish,[139] because (that woman) enjoined me

---

131. *Formulae Arvernenses* (Arvernian formulas), 2: K. Zeumer, ed., *MGH Leg., Sectio V, Formulae* (Hannover, 1886), 29. The *mandatum* cited here would be akin to the one specified in the interpretation of the regulation in the Theodosian Code just cited.

132. "Mos . . . antiqua": the most fundamental regulations governing the operation of Roman society were the "ancient customs."

133. As seen in the regulation and interpretation just cited.

134. The form includes a number of blank spaces for the appropriate phrases and names to be inserted.

135. The text of this section breaks off here.

136. "Hic habet gesta"; the "gesta" being the words of the actual court hearing that would result in the production of the enabling document.

137. *Vir laudabilis:* an honorific occasionally used in imperial times for officials of middling rank.

138. *Gestarum:* presumably the records of past cases and transactions.

139. It seems that an interval of time now may pass, during which the documents are examined, unless the preceding clause was strictly pro forma.

through this mandate, that, according to custom, I ought to present to you a written affirmation, and she asks me to countersign and affirm in all cases this mandate, which has been issued in her stead on behalf of her children, (him) and (her), [and] I ought to add and confirm [it] in the municipal records." The aforementioned defender and membership of the assembly then said, "And this mandate, which you present, ought to be shown to us so it can be read." Then one of the notaries read the mandate in public. The aforementioned defender said, "I deliver this measure, as it is written, confirmed by my hand, this matter and none other, to determine or regulate anything from now on. Let this measure, as it is written, be handed over to me without delay after it has been confirmed by your hands." (That defender) along with his fellow council members handed over and countersigned the records themselves, subscribing with their own hands.

Such guidebooks, which also survive from the sixth and seventh centuries for cities such as Angers and Tours,[140] show that Roman-style legal and administrative practices, such as the continued existence of the *curia* (municipal council) and the *defensor civitatis,* continued uninterrupted right on into the early medieval period. The formula cited here and others like it, of course, represented a legal "ideal." It remains to be seen to what extent the legal subordination of women, for example, was manifested in the real world.

In-Law Problems

The changed circumstances of Late Antiquity also could result in family difficulties. The new lifestyle that some individuals found in the church did not always sit well with their relatives. Salvian of Marseille's adoption of the religious life, for example, led to an estrangement from the family of his wife, Palladia.[141] Rather early in his career, it seems, he penned a letter to his in-laws in which he purported to be attempting to patch things up.[142] But Salvian's attitude and manner of

---

140. These collections of *formulae,* or legal forms, were compiled ca. 700, in the early Merovingian period, by a certain Marculfus (see *MGH Leg., Sectio V, Formulae*). The term *formula,* referring to the proper form of a legal proceeding, goes back to the very earliest days of Roman law.

141. Coincidentally, the same name as the wife of Stephanus above.

142. Salvian's conversion had occurred only about seven years before, so he was perhaps twenty-five at least. This letter may have been written ca. 425.

expression, which also reflect, it seems, Salvian's rhetorical and legal education, suggest that it may not have been so much with Salvian's religious persuasion that his relatives had difficulty, but with Salvian's insufferable personality. Indeed, throughout the letter Salvian intimates that he really wasn't sorry for anything.

3.30[143]   Salvian, Palladia, and Auspiciola,[144] send greetings to their parents, Hypatia and Quieta.

[After a brief introduction about the unity among the apostles:]

(2) Now, therefore, we too, small imitators of great models, write, not, like those apostles, with the authority of teachers but with the humility of servants, to you, whom we have as parents through nature, brothers through faith, and lords through respect, so that you, who hitherto have been unmoved by our individual letters, even now might be moved by our collective pleas. And you should know—lest you have any unnecessary fear—that we your children are together and are of the same opinion and that we fear, and implore in the same manner, not because we are concerned with whether you are angry at us all, but because we cannot be divided in our cause.

(3) Our fear is quite the same, even if our offense does not seem the same. To be sure, our mutual fondness had the effect that even if you, perhaps, are not upset with both of us, nevertheless, when one is guilty, the other is unable to be without sorrow for this guilty condition. It certainly is this that makes us contend against something and contest jointly, namely that, whereas both of your children are equally guilty, each of us nevertheless fears more for the other than for himself.

(4) Dearest parents, most reverend parents, we ask permission to question you. Can children who love thus not be loved? Why have we merited so much evil, from either a most esteemed loved one or a most reverend lord, with the result that favor is not rendered to us, as done for children, and offense is not forgiven, as done for slaves?

(5) It now is nearly the seventh year since you have sent no letters to us, located so far from you.[145] Such a long time for grief is imposed

143. Salv. *Epist.* 4: *MGH AA* 1.1:110–14; for another translation, see *Writings of Salvian,* 241–50.

144. The daughter of Salvian and Palladia.

145. Salvian and Palladia had fled south in the early fifth century, leaving their families in the area of Trier and Cologne.

upon nearly none who trespass against God; absolutely no one [guilty] of the greatest crimes *** with the result that [God] loves [them] more, namely so that the actions of the father may be not detrimental but profitable for affection, because however much chastisement provides for the correction of one person, the correction renders that much to their mutual fondness.

(6) Although it is more proper for those parents to do this who have true justification for anger at their children regarding certain affairs, why are you angry, you who since the time you became Christian have ceased to have even false reasons? Granted that you, as a pagan, indeed once did not accept my conversation with equanimity; then, indeed, our difference of wills had to be borne on account of the dissimilitude of our backgrounds. Then, even if affection was not upset with us, nevertheless superstition opposed us. For even though the father did not hate the son, error, nevertheless, hated the truth.

(7) Now it is far different. Ever since the time you professed belief in God you have spoken out on my behalf. If you pursue past reasons for anger, blame yourself, you who gave your daughter to a Christian. If this is not the case, why are you angry with me because I desire the very religion to grow in me that you have begun to approve in yourself? Why, I ask, do you not esteem in me that which you are, you who yourself condemned in yourself what you were?

(8) But words must be spared for a little while, because even in a good cause the speech of a son to his parents ought to be humble to the extent that the topic of discussion permits. Forgive me, dearest loves; my love of God makes me rather more free in His affairs. If you have some other reasons for being upset, I do not deny that I had the ability to sin. Truly, in regard to what upsets you, because I appear to love Christ, pardon what I am about to say.

(9) I seek forgiveness, in fact, because you are angry, but I am unable to say that what I have done is evil. These words are therefore placed before you in my name and, so to speak, with a personal plea. Now you, o most esteemed and venerable sister, you who are as much dearer to me than before to the extent that it is befitting for love to be esteemed more greatly by one's own people, in whom Christ made Himself to be loved: discharge your duties and mine at the same time. You implore so that I may obtain my request; you entreat so that we both may prevail. Because you are absent you are unable to kiss your parents with your

lips; at least, by means of your plea, kiss their feet like a servant, their hands like a foster child, and their faces like a daughter.

(10) Do not be apprehensive, do not be afraid: we have good judges.[146] Love itself beseeches on your behalf, nature itself entreats for you, you have support for your case in the minds of your own people. They who themselves are overcome by their own affection quickly render a favorable decision. Plead, therefore, and say as a suppliant: "What have I done? Why have I deserved this? Grant pardon for whatever it is, I seek forgiveness even if I do not know the crime."

(11) As you yourself know, I never have offended you by irresponsibility or disobedience, I never have harmed you by any harsh word, never have I offended you by a rather brazen look. I was surrendered to my husband by you, transferred by you to my spouse. I heed, if I am not mistaken, your commands, the hallowed mystery of your kind advice clings tightly to my senses. You ordered me, I recall, before all else to be obliging to my husband. I obeyed your will, I complied with your command. I have obeyed in all things the one whom you wished me to obey.

(12) He encouraged me to religion, he encouraged me to chastity. Grant forgiveness, I thought it shameful to resist. Chastity seemed to me to be the moral thing, the modest thing, the sanctified thing. I confess that when he discussed such a subject with me, I was chagrined because I had not undertaken it already. At this point reverence and love of Christ also entered into the reckoning: I believed that whatever I did out of love of God I did honorably.

(13) I, your Palladia, your jackdaw, your little mistress, kneel at your feet, o dearest parents, the one with whom, with so many words like these, you once played with a most indulgent tenderness, she who, by different names, was to you at one time mother, at another little bird, at another mistress, because, of course, one was an expression of the family, one of infancy, and a third of station. Behold, I am that one through whom both the status of parenthood and the joys of grandparenthood first came to pass for you, as well as that which is superior to both, to have both of these happily, along with the joy of having children and the blessedness of enjoying them . . .

(14) . . . but so much for this. O dearest sister, we now have pled enough through ourselves; the rest must be dealt with through our daughter.

---

146. Salvian pretends that they are in court.

(15) Therefore, we employ — for indeed, it is fair to try anything for the sake of regaining the love of one's parents — we employ the practice and example of those who at the very end of trials, in order to arouse the pity of the judges, sometimes proffer certain things to the arbiters who are about to pass sentence, introducing either lamenting mothers or old men in filthy clothing or wailing children, so that, of course, those who already had embellished the preceding parts of the case with words would plead the subsequent parts with the objects themselves.

(16) Therefore, we also present to you, o dearest parents, your grandchild, with a commendation the equal of those others but more pleasing. We offer a child who is not foreign but domestic, not someone else's but one's own, nor, as in the case of those orators, is she a stranger both to them and to the judges, but she is known likewise to us and to you: she who, like the quality of your own blood, does not coax you to the esteem of unknown persons but recalls you to the esteem of your own, nor does someone else commend someone else's children to you, but your own commends your own . . .[147]

(27) Therefore, I now crave forgiveness, not because I know that I have caused offense, but so that I might not leave any possibility at all of offense, not out of knowledge of crime, but for the reason and duty of affection, so that the entreaty of one who is innocent may merit greater favor of affection and so that a supplication lacking guilt may be beneficial for love, and so that you may have more to value in the plea of your son if you do not have anything to pardon.

(28) Perhaps, however, not knowing what you feel about us, we rashly flatter ourselves regarding our innocence. Indeed, the reason for your attitude more so than for our feeling must be considered. It remains, therefore, that if there is something else, whatever it is, that we have done, you, who think this worthy of offense not consider it also to be unworthy of pardon. You yourself will admirably provide satisfaction for yourself regarding the guilt of your children. A father who pardons his son loses nothing with regard to vengeance, because it is much more blessed and praiseworthy to pardon one's own, even undeservedly, than to exact punishment, even deservedly, against one's own family. Farewell.

---

147. The emphasis on grandchildren suggests that this was the issue. There follows a lengthy legalistic discussion in which Salvian dredges up analogies of Ninevites, Sabines, and Servius Galba, where children were used to mollify the anger of judges—did Salvian notice that in the cases of the Ninevites and Galba, the defendants were in fact guilty as charged?

One might wonder whether Salvian really did not know what the supposedly undisclosed reason for the estrangement was, or whether he was simply being disingenuous. According to him, his in-laws only cause for complaint was his conversion to Christianity, and—he argues—their own subsequent conversion ought to have removed that obstacle. But is Salvian purposely misrepresenting his in-laws' position? The only specific element of his and Palladia's Christian practice that Salvian brings up is Palladia's chastity. Likewise, the whole latter half of the lengthy letter is devoted to arguments for showing pity for the sake of children. Perhaps Hypatius and Quieta were not upset with Salvian's Christianity per se—after all, their own conversion would seem to belie this suggestion—but with the extremes to which Salvian took it. Not all Christian couples felt the need to live a completely chaste life, and in Salvian's and Palladia's case, their doing so would have deprived the grandparents of a grandson, and this, in turn, could have led to concerns about the disposition of the family property.

One also might wonder what the ultimate dénouement of this crisis was. Palladia and Auspiciola are never mentioned again in Salvian's extensive writings. Did Palladia and her daughter return to her parents, in Cologne or elsewhere? If they did, it may mean that Palladia, too, eventually tired of the priggish, pompous, and self-satisfied Salvian. After the departure of his wife and child, Salvian would have been able to take his zeal for the religious life to even greater extremes.

In general, the transformations of the social, cultural, religious, and economic worlds that were occurring during Late Antiquity certainly had effects on family life. Even if children remained, by and large, under the thumbs of their parents, women do seem occasionally to have benefited from the breakdown of some established institutions by being able to enjoy rather greater self-expression than in the past, especially in their choices of mates. And, as will be seen in a later chapter, some women were able to satisfy themselves in other ways as well.

CHAPTER 4

Social Turmoil: "New Men" and Bandits, Romans and Barbarians

Those who lived in late antique society interacted in many different ways. A complex system of status, both de jure and de facto, governed the relations among individuals from dissimilar backgrounds. There were many kinds of social differentiations: rich and poor, legally privileged and unprivileged, Christian and pagan, Roman and barbarian, male and female, and young and old. Other kinds of social interactions involved equals vis-à-vis equals, superiors vis-à-vis inferiors, and inferiors vis-à-vis superiors.

Exercising Authority

Circa the 460s, Faustus, bishop of Riez, described how social status could affect the way one related to others:

.1[1] Finally, if some powerful person *(potens)* does us an injury, even if he insults us to our face, we do not dare to make any harsh response, nor, I might say, to respond in kind. Why not? Lest we suffer as a result a greater injury from that powerful person than we bore initially. . . . If, therefore, a powerful person rages against us, we are silent and dare to say nothing, but if an equal or, perchance, an inferior person abuses us, like wild beasts, without any forbearance and without any consideration of God, we arise and we either avenge our injury immediately or we certainly prepare our spirit for rendering a greater response. Why is it, that when a powerful individual inflicts injury upon us, we bear it

---

1. *Sermo in natali s. Stephani* (Sermon on the birth of St. Stephen): *CSEL* 21:232–36.

patiently, but when one inferior in rank does so, we are aroused with excessive fury?

In this world, one knew exactly where one stood with respect to everyone else.

Of course, most writers of works ranging from histories to the canons of church councils had a vested interest in maintaining the kind of social stratification that they not only described but also legislated to preserve. Yet, much evidence demonstrates that late Roman society was not as structured as such sources might suggest. The various elements of society interacted in many different ways. Often, an individual who presumably was in a disadvantaged social position prevailed in some mundane activity. One encounters instances of Romans triumphing over barbarians, lesser clerics harassing their bishop, and women gaining the upper hand over men. Society was in flux. The established orders were in transition: new men were making their way into the ranks of the nobility, barbarians were usurping much of the privilege and status of the old Roman aristocracy, and careers in the church were coming to be as important as, or more important than, secular careers.

Wishful Thinking

An intriguing perception of the social status accorded to different types of individuals is found in the aforementioned early-fifth-century comedy, *Querolus* (The complainer). The protagonist lived up to his name. At one point, he expressed dissatisfaction with his lot in life, and his interlocutor, the *Lar Familiaris* (a family guardian spirit), responded by asking him what he would rather be or do. Even though some aspects of the comedy—such as the standardized characters—are commonplace aspects of this genre that go back hundreds of years, Querolus's proposals—written, one must recall, by one of the educated aristocratic elite—describe some contemporary social perceptions and conditions.

4.2[2]   *Lar.* What more would you like to know?
        Quer. Why others are better off?

---

2. *Querolus* 2 (29–34), ed. Peiper, 15–18; ed. Jacquemard–Le Saos, 18–22.

Lar. Now, this relates to envy.

Quer. But I envy with cause, because I'm worse off than my inferiors.[3]

Lar. What if I prove to you that you're better off than those whom you're going to speak about?

Quer. Then you would henceforth cause the Complainer not to allow anyone to complain.

Lar. To make the matter quicker and clearer, I'll skip the argumentation. You just specify the fortune whose condition is attractive to you; I'll immediately give you the consequence that you yourself desire. Just remember this: don't think that you can protest and evade something that is consequent upon your choice of something.

Quer. This freedom of choice is a pleasure. Give me wealth and military honors even to a middling extent.

Lar. I can give you that. But consider this, whether you can fulfill the requirements of what you seek.[4]

Quer. What do you mean?

Lar. Can you wage war? Can you evade a sword? Can you break through the line?

Quer. I could never do that.

Lar. Then leave the reward and honors to those who can do all that.

Quer. At least grant me something in the civil sphere, even something pitiful.

Lar. Do you therefore want to collect and pay out everything?[5]

Quer. Oh! That takes care of that! Now I don't want either one. If, then, there is anything you can do, Lar Familiaris, make it so I can be a powerful civilian.[6]

---

3. *inferioribus:* in this status-conscious society, this was always a significant concern. The law was replete with distinctions between superior and inferior status; see, e.g., *CTh* 1.6.5 (A.D. 368), "ut inferior gradus meritum superioris agnoscat" [so that an inferior status might acknowledge the merit of a superior one].

4. The Lar then proceeds to introduce riders (the consequences he alluded to above) to each of Querolus's suggestions.

5. Generally, minor imperial bureaucrats did not perform both of these functions at the same time. The author probably has in mind the *curiales* (decurions), the members of town councils who were responsible for local tax-collection and overseeing local expenditures.

6. *privatus et potens:* private persons who exercized overweening authority were a regular feature of the late antique landscape and an embodiment of the aristocratic ideal; e.g., an imperial ruling of 416 stated that wills were not to be overturned "in Our name or in the name of powerful private persons" [nostro vel etiam privatorum potentium nomine] (*CTh* 4.4.5).

Lar. What kind of power do you want?

Quer. Let me be able to despoil those who owe me nothing, to slaughter those I don't know, to despoil and slaughter my neighbors.

Lar. Hoo hah! You want banditry, not power. By Pollux, I don't know any way that this can be granted to you. [*He pauses*] Ah, I've found it! You can have what you desire: go live on the Loire.[7]

Quer. What then?

Lar. Folks there live according to the law of nations; there is no deception there. There capital sentences are pronounced from an oak tree[8] and are written on bones; there even yokels present cases and private citizens pronounce judgments; everything is permitted there. If you are rich, you are called *patus,*[9] as it is said in our Greek. O forests, O solitudes.[10] Who said that you are unconstrained? There are many greater things that I'm silent about; but for the time being, this is enough.

Quer. I'm not rich, and I don't want to use an oak tree. I don't want those sylvan laws.

Lar. If you're not able to brawl, then ask for something gentler and more respectable.

Quer. Give me honor like that togate fellow[11] gets, that wicked one.

Lar. And do you reckon togate persons among the fortunate?

Quer. Yes, indeed!

Lar. Now you ask for something very simple. We can do that without even trying. Do you want it to be given to you?

Quer. There's nothing I'd like more.

----

7. This section often is assumed to refer to the Bacaudae, a term whose meaning has been much debated, but which apparently refers to brigands: see J. Drinkwater, "The Bacaudae of Fifth-Century Gaul," in *Fifth-Century Gaul: A Crisis of Identity?* ed. J. Drinkwater and H. Elton (Cambridge: Cambridge University Press, 1992), 216–25. But the Bacaudae are not mentioned here, and the reference probably is to any backwoods area not under close imperial supervision.

8. *de robore:* a curious phrase; some see it harking back to the Druids, whose name was derived from the word for oak tree.

9. There have been several suggestions regarding the word from which *patus* is derived; Greek suggestions include *pachus* (great); *patulos* (rich); *upatos* (leader); and *pepamai* (acquire). It also has been derived from a Gothic word meaning "master": see J. Whatmough, *The Dialects of Ancient Gaul* (Cambridge, Mass.: Harvard University Press, 1970), 1337.

10. An example of apostrophe; cf. Cicero's famous statement, "O tempora, o mores!" [Oh the times! Oh the conduct!].

11. A reference to some kind of public official, perhaps an advocate, given the duties cited below.

Lar. I'll omit some of the most serious aspects. Put on therefore a garment shortened in the winter and doubled over in the summer, put on woolen buckins,[12] perpetually loose fetters that the rain loosens, the dust fills, and mud and sweat glue together; put on baggy boots with a cheap covering that stick to the ground and like-colored scum conceals. Spend the summer with covered knees, the winter with naked shins; the winters in slippers,[13] the summers in long stockings. Endure disordered labors, predawn meetings, entertainment of a judge either first thing in the morning[14] or in the afternoon, or in the heat or in the cold, or on matters demented or serious. Sell your voice, sell your tongue, contract out your hatred and anger; in sum, be a pauper and bring home little money, but a lot of trouble. I now could add more, if it were not better just to bury such people rather than to speak ill of them.

Quer. I don't want this choice! Give me riches such as those who deal in documents acquire.[15]

Lar. Accept therefore the sleepless nights and the labors of those whom you envy. Seek gold in your youth but a homeland in your old age, be a newcomer to a small estate but a veteran of the forum, an erudite arguer but a novice landowner, familiar to those you don't know but new to your neighbors, spend your entire life hated, so that you might provide an elegant corpse; god, moreover, will provide you with heirs.[16] I don't want you to envy such people, Querolus. Often the hoarded wealth of wolves becomes the booty of foxes.[17]

---

12. *cothurnos:* laced-up boots reaching to midcalf. One kind was worn by hunters, and the other, no doubt what the author had in mind, by tragic actors: they had thick cork soles to give the actors additional stature.

13. *soccis:* a low-heeled Greek shoe, worn by comic actors, in contrast to the *cothurni* mentioned above.

14. *primum postmeridianum:* the Theodosian Code (1.20.1 [A.D 408]) specified that judges were not to meet with litigators during the midday hours (*meridianis horis*).

15. *qui chartas agunt:* probably a reference to imperial bureaucrats. According to the contemporary *Notitia dignitatum,* the *secundicerius* of the *Comes rerum privatarum* (count of privy purse) was a clerk "qui tractat chartas" [who handled documents] (*Not.dig.occ.*12, *Not.dig.or.*14).

16. Because he will not have any of his own.

17. This sounds gnomic. Perhaps it derives from Aesop's fable of "The Fox, Wolf, and Ape," where "A wolf accused a fox of theft, but the fox entirely denied the charge. An ape undertook to judge the matter between them. When each had fully stated his case the ape announced this sentence: 'I do not think you, wolf, ever lost what you claim; and I do believe you, fox, to have stolen what you so stoutly deny'": G. F. Townsend, *Aesop's Fables* (London, 1877).

Quer. Well! I don't want documents. Then at least grant me now the income of that foreigner and of the overseas merchant.

Lar. Go, then, and take to the seas, and entrust yourself and your property to the winds and waves.

Quer. I never wanted that. At least just give me the coffers of Titius.

Lar. Accept, then, the gout of Titius[18] too.

Quer. Not me.

Lar. Then you won't get hold of the coffers of Titius.

Quer. I don't want that. Give me dancing and little concubines, like that greedy moneylending newcomer has.

Lar. You certainly shall have what you wholeheartedly demand. Accept what you desire along with the whole chorus.[19] Take Paphis, Cytheris, Briseis,[20] but along with them the burden of Nestor.[21]

Quer. Hoo hah! Why is that?

Lar. He has the destiny that you sought. See here, Querolus, have you never heard the saying, "No one is well-off without cost"? Either some things must be endured along with others, or some things must be forsaken along with others.[22]

Quer. I've finally found what I need. At least give me impudence.[23]

Lar. Well said, by Pollux. You now crave everything that I've denied. If you want to do so openly, be impudent. But in that case you must discard your wisdom.

Lar. Why?

Quer. Because no wise man is impudent.

---

18. In Roman jurisprudence, "Lucius Titius" was the equivalent of our "John Doe"; he (or "Lucia Titia") customarily served as the principal in hypothetical legal cases. The large number of conjectural cases involving "Titius" and inheritances might have led to jokes about his wealth. For the traditional relation between wealth and gout, see Juv., *Sat.* 13.96, "pauper locupletem optare podagram."

19. Recall the son of Ruricius in chapter 3 who enjoyed choruses of girls.

20. Famous women known for sexual liaisons: Paphis was an epithet of Aphrodite; Cytheris was a Roman courtesan, mistress of Mark Antony; Briseis was a slave girl over whom Achilles and Agamemnon quarreled.

21. *cum pondere Nestoris:* the meaning is unclear; Catullus uses the word *pondus* (weight) to refer to genitalia, which seems to be the sense that is meant here. Suggestions regarding the nature of Nestor's "burden" range from impotence to excessive virility. Nestor was the aged king of Pylos known in the *Iliad* for his wisdom, not his sexual exploits. Cf. also Juv., *Sat.* 6.326, "Nestoris hirnea" (the cup of Nestor).

22. In modern parlance, "It comes with the territory."

23. Subsequently in the play, slaves are characterized as *impudens* (see chap. 2).

This interchange provides an aristocratic perception of the different options available to a privileged person. Even if presented tongue-in-cheek, an underlying message seems to be that life was unpredictable, and that one never could be sure of one's position and status.

What was true for the well-to-do also was true for the less privileged. Changing circumstances opened up new opportunities for virtually everyone. This is seen in several kinds of social venues. In the past, for example, the most prestigious offices had been monopolized by the most influential aristocratic families. Late Antiquity, however, saw old-guard aristocrats being challenged by *novi homines* (new men), who often came from the small-town landed gentry, if not from even less privileged elements of society.

Rebellious Clerics

Opposition from below threatened the Gallic blue blood par excellence Sidonius Apollinaris, prefect of Rome in 468, then bishop of Clermont, and later a saint. In palmier times, Sidonius could make fun of ambitious individuals of lesser birth.[24] But late in his life, after the final disappearance of Roman authority, he could not even control his own clergy. Gregory of Tours, who recounted several anecdotes about the most famous and accomplished litterateur of his birthplace, reported that Sidonius was bedeviled by two of his own priests, an occurrence that exemplifies a prevalent aspect of social conflict during Late Antiquity: bishops defied by their clergy.

4.3[25] (22) In fact, the saintly Sidonius was so articulate that he often expressed extemporaneously whatever he wished, without any delay and most eloquently. It happened one day, moreover, that, invited to a celebration, he arrived at the basilica of the monastery that I mentioned above,[26] and when his notes, with which he customarily conducted the blessed rituals, were disgracefully purloined from him, he was so proficient that he completed the entire task of the celebration extemporaneously, to the marvel of everyone, and the bystanders

---

24. Recall Sidonius's patronizing descriptions of Paeonius and Arvandus in chapter 2.

25. Greg.Tur. *Hist.* 2.22–23: for other translations, see Dalton, *Gregory*, 61–62; and Thorpe, *Gregory*, 134–35.

26. See *Hist.* 2.21. This was the monastery of Abraham, whose fractious inhabitants were discussed by Sidonius Apollinaris (*Epist.* 7.17.3).

thought that it was not a man that had spoken there, but an angel. I wrote more fully about this in the preface of the book that I wrote about the masses he composed.[27] Because, moreover, he was of marvelous saintliness and, as I said, from the first ranks of the senators, he often used to remove silver vessels from his house without the knowledge of his wife[28] and give them to paupers. When she learned this, she scolded him, and he then restored the valuables to the house after paying the needy for them.

(23) And after he had become devoted to his holy duty and was leading a saintly life in this world, there arose against him two priests, who, with all control of church affairs removed from him and leaving him a scant and tenuous livelihood, rendered him the greatest disrespect. But the divine clemency chose not to leave his injury unavenged for long. For one of these most disgraceful individuals, unworthy to be called a priest . . . after entering his privy, expelled his spirit as he attempted to purge his bowels. . . . Whence there is no doubt that he was guilty of no less a crime than that Arius,[29] for whom likewise the innermost parts were expelled in the privy by a discharge of the lower part.

What is left unsaid is that Sidonius, who after all was a foreigner—a citizen of Lyon who had married an inhabitant of Clermont—may have been faced with opposition from the native Arvernian clergy.[30] Some locals, clearly, were happy to have the influential and articulate Sidonius as bishop, but others equally clearly resented him. Gregory, who at Tours also was a foreigner—an Arvernian—and had experienced a similar insurrection by his own clergy, would have had a personal interest in a case that had a bishop triumphing in the end over seditious priests.[31]

---

27. Neither this discussion of Sidonius's *missae* (masses) nor the *missae* themselves survive, although some may be embedded in the voluminous collection of anonymous Gallic homilies from this period known as the "Eusebian Collection" (*CCL* 100).

28. Papianilla, the daughter of the emperor Eparchius Avitus (455–56).

29. The originator of Arianism, which taught that the Son (Christ) was subordinate to the Father (God); it was adopted by several Germanic peoples, such as the Visigoths, Vandals, and Burgundians.

30. For civic dissension in Clermont, see Sid.Apoll. *Epist.* 3.2, where not all of the townsfolk agreed with Sidonius's policy of resisting the Visigoths.

31. See Mathisen, "Family"; and note Greg.Tur. *Hist.* 5.49, where the priest Riochatus rebels against Gregory.

The Bishop and the Bandit

The decline in Roman authority also resulted in a massive breakdown of law and order, and an increasing recourse to violence as a means of achieving one's goals.[32] Nor were barbarians the sole disruptive element. There also was an increase in old-fashioned brigandage, such as that pursued by the Vargi, and perhaps by the Bacaudae. Another case of lawlessness involved two Romans, a bishop and a bandit.[33] The bishop was Patrick, who was of British curial stock and became the self-proclaimed bishop of the Irish. Patrick would have been one of the aforementioned "new men" who benefited from the disruption in social relations to attain a position that he probably could not have hoped for in the past. Coroticus the bandit, on the other hand, may have been of Celtic origin. By taking advantage of the withdrawal of Roman authority to set up his own little principality in northern Britain, he demonstrated another kind of opportunism.[34] Patrick's letter to Coroticus, laced with biblical citations, gives precious insight into life on the post-Roman frontier:

4.4[35]   (1) I, Patrick, a sinner and unlearned, declare that God made me bishop in Ireland.[36] Most surely I hold that it was from God that "I received what I am,"[37] and therefore for the love of God I remain a pilgrim and an exile among a barbarous people.[38] He is witness that I

32. For the role of violence in sixth-century society, see Mathisen, *Roman Aristocrats,* 176–86.

33. See E. A. Thompson, "St. Patrick and Coroticus," *Journal of Theological Studies* 31 (1980): 12–27.

34. For these developments, see Michael Jones, *The End of Roman Britain* (Ithaca, N.Y.: Cornell University Press, 1996); and Christopher Snyder, *An Age of Tyrants: Britain and the Britons, A.D. 400–600* (University Park: Pennsylvania State University Press, 1998).

35. Patricius, *Epistola ad Coroticum* (Letter to Coroticus): L. Bieler, ed., *Classica et Mediaevalia* 11 (1950): 5–105; *PL* 53:813ff.; for translation, see D. Brooke, *Private Letters Christian and Pagan* (London, 1929), 188–91; and note also L. de Paor, *Saint Patrick's World* (Notre Dame: University of Notre Dame Press, 1993), 109–13; and A. B. Hood, *St. Patrick: His Writings and Muirchu's Life* (London: Phillimore, 1978), 55–59. The surviving text lacks a salutation.

36. This statement could suggest that Patrick had not in fact been canonically ordained bishop by other bishops, and that the Palladius who is said to have been made bishop of the Irish in 431 in Prosper's *Chronicle* (see de Paor, *Saint Patrick,* 79) was in fact the "legitimate" bishop of the Irish.

37. 1 Cor. 15.10.

38. A common Christian theme: note the *Poema coniugis ad uxorem* (Poem of a husband to his wife), 97: *PL* 51:611–16, "I do not fear exile; the entire world is a home for everyone." For this poem, see also chapter 3.

speak the truth. It was not my wish to utter the language of harshness and severity, but zeal for God constrains me, and the truth of Christ, who has stirred me up for the love of my sons after the spirit, for whom I have left my country and my kindred, and am ready to give my life also, if so be that I am worthy. I have made a vow to God to teach the heathen; let him despise me who will. (2) With my own hand I have composed and written these words, to be communicated to the soldiers of Coroticus; not to my fellow-citizens, nor to those who are fellow-citizens with the holy Romans, but to those who are fellow-citizens with devils, by reason of their evil deeds. Enemies of truth, they die even while they live, allied with the Scots and the apostate Picts,[39] eager, as it were, to glut themselves with the blood of innocent Christians, multitudes of whom I have begotten to God and confirmed in Christ. (3) For a cruel slaughter and massacre was committed on the persons of the newly baptized, while they were yet in their white robes, on the morrow of their anointing, while the holy oil still shone upon their foreheads. Wherefore I sent a letter by a holy priest, whom from his infancy I had taught, together with other holy men, to entreat that they would restore some of the booty, or the baptized captives; but they scoffed at my envoys. (4) Therefore I am in doubt for whom I should rather mourn, whether for the slain, or for the captives, or for those whom Satan has so grievously ensnared, who shall be delivered over to him to eternal pains of Hell; for "whosoever commits sin is the bondservant of sin, and is called a son of the devil."[40] (5) Wherefore let all men that fear God know that parricides and fratricides are strangers from me and from Christ, my God, whose ambassador I am, for "they are ravening wolves, eating up the people of the Lord as they eat bread."[41] As He says, "Lord, the wicked have destroyed thy law,"[42] which in this latter day was auspiciously and excellently planted in Ireland, and established by the favor of God. (6) I do not falsely set myself up; I have a part with those who have been called and predestined to

---

39. The Picts were natives of modern Scotland (ancient Caledonia); the Scots were Irish raiders who at this time were settling there and in Wales; only later did they give their name to modern Scotland. By calling them "apostates," Patrick seems to be saying that the Picts once had been Christian, but had returned to paganism.

40. John 8:34, 8:44.

41. Eph. 6:20; Matt. 7:15.

42. Ps. 13:4, 52:5.

preach the Gospel[43] amid no small persecutions, even to the end of the earth, even though the evil eye of the enemy is upon me through the tyranny of Coroticus, who fears not God nor his chosen priests, to whom has been granted the high and divine power, that those whom they bind on earth shall not be bound in heaven . . . (12) I am envied. What shall I do, O Lord? Men despise me. Lo, around me thy sheep are pillaged and torn by these robbers aforesaid, by the order of our enemy Coroticus. Far from the love of God is he who delivers Christians into the hand of the Scots and Picts. Ravening wolves, they have devoured the Lord's flock which in Ireland was increasing, verily, with all speed, watched over with the greatest care. The sons and daughters of the Scottish chieftains, in numbers beyond my reckoning, were becoming monks and virgins of Christ. For this reason, "Injury to the just ought not please you," indeed, "it should not please you all the way to perdition."[44] . . . (14) It is the custom of the Gauls to send to the Franks and to other alien peoples holy and fit men, provided with thousands of solidi, to redeem baptized captives.[45] But you who so often slay them or sell them to foreign peoples ignorant of God, delivering them over, as it were, to a brothel, what manner of hope have you in God, or he who consents with you, or flatters you? God will judge, for it is written, "Not only that those who commit evil, but those who acquiesce with them shall be damned."[46] (15) I know not what more to say or speak about the sons of God departed, slain with the sword, for it is written, "O weep with them that weep,"[47] and again, "If one member suffer, let all the members suffer as well."[48] Wherefore the church "weeps and laments for her sons"[49] and daughters whom the sword has not yet slain, but who are exiled, carried off to far lands, where sin openly and shamelessly abounds. There Christian freemen are sold and reduced to slavery, and worst of all, to the vile, degraded, and apostate Picts. (16) Wherefore I grieve for you, I grieve, my well beloved, for myself, but at

---

43. "Quos advocavit et praedestinavit evangelium praedicare": Patrick's reference to predestination could indicate that he partook of this Augustinian view, which was considered to be heresy in Gaul.

44. Eccles. 9:17.

45. For examples of such ransoming in Gaul, see below in this chapter.

46. Rom. 1:32.

47. Rom. 12:15.

48. 1 Cor. 12:26.

49. Matt. 2:18.

the same time rejoice that I have not labored in vain, and that my pilgrimage has not been fruitless. A crime has been committed that is dreadful and unspeakable. Thanks to God, it was as baptized believers that you departed into Paradise from this world. I behold you, you have begun your journey to that region where there shall be no night nor sorrow nor death anymore, but you shall leap as calves loosened from their bonds, and you shall tread down the wicked and they shall be ashes under your feet . . . (19) Where then shall Coroticus and his accursed followers see themselves, who distribute baptized damsels among their depraved followers, and all for the sake of a wretched temporal kingdom, which passes away in a moment . . .

(21) I earnestly entreat whatever servant of God is willing to bear this letter that it may on no account be kept back, or concealed by anyone, but rather may be read before all the people, in the presence of Coroticus himself—if God may inspire them at some time to amend their lives and return to Him—so that they may repent, even late, of their evil deeds, and, even though murderers of the Lord's brethren, they may release the baptized women captives, and become worthy to live for God, and be made whole from now to all eternity.
Peace, in the Father and the Son and Holy Ghost, Amen.

Patrick began ministering to the Irish circa 432 and died circa 462. His statement that he had raised from infancy the priest mentioned in the letter would date the Coroticus incident to the very end of his life, perhaps to circa 455/460. This would mean that Patrick was too old and infirm to undertake the journey, and the risk, himself.

Life with the Barbarians

One of the most omnipresent realities of the social world of the western Mediterranean during Late Antiquity was the presence of the barbarians, not only as political rulers, but also as friends and neighbors. After their initial intrusion into Gaul in 406, there was a widespread concern over just what the barbarians' role would be. How would they interact with the Roman population? How would they "fit in"?

The Barbarian Invasions

In the opinion of some contemporary observers, the arrival of the barbarians was terrible indeed. St. Jerome, writing circa 411/412, described the situation in an often-cited passage:

4.5[50]   Innumerable and most ferocious nations occupy all Gaul. Whatever is
between the Alps and the Pyrenees, that which is bounded by the ocean
and the Rhine, the Quadian, the Vandal, the Sarmatian, the Alans, the
Gepids, the Heruls, the Saxons, the Burgundians, the Alemans, and, O
unfortunate Republic, the Pannonian hordes devastate. "And, indeed,
Assur comes with them."[51] Mayence, once a noble city, has been taken
and overturned, and in the church thousands were slain. Worms has
been destroyed by a long siege. Reims, a strong city, Amiens, Arras,
distant Thérouanne, Tournai, Spire, Strasbourg, all carried into Germany. Except for a few cities, the provinces of Aquitania, Novempopulana, Lugdunensis, and Narbonensis all have been devastated.
Indeed, the same things that the sword destroys outside, hunger
destroys inside.

Not a very pretty picture. Orientius, bishop of Auch in the 430s, went
so far as to claim that "all Gaul smoked in a single funeral pyre."[52]

A "Good Barbarian"

Others, however, were more sanguine, and their views of the barbarians were not so bleak. An anonymous Gallic traveler relayed to
Jerome a conversation that he had had with the Visigothic chieftain
Athaulf at Narbonne circa 413. Even though Jerome himself, whose
portrayal of the barbarian occupation was so melancholy, never mentioned the tale, it was repeated in the *History against the Pagans* of the
Spanish priest Orosius, who had made a pilgrimage to the Holy Land
in the early part of the fifth century and had heard the story there.[53]

4.6[54]   For in the town of Bethlehem in Palestine I myself also heard a certain

---

50. Jerome, *Epist.* 123.16: *PL* 22:1057–58.

51. Ps. 82:9.

52. "Uno fumavit Gallia tota rogo": *Commonitorium* (Reminder), 2.5.184: *CSEL* 16:234.

53. Orosius had fled from Spain to escape the barbarians and settled in North Africa,
where Augustine suggested he write his history in order to counter pagan assertions that the
decline of Rome was a result of the abandonment of the old pagan gods. The resultant *Historia contra paganos* (History against the pagans), however, did not accomplish its purpose,
and Augustine then composed his own response, the famous *De civitate dei* (On the city of
God).

54. Orosius, *Historia contra paganos* (History against the pagans), 7.43: C. Zangemeister
ed., *CSEL* 5 (Vienna, 1882); for another translation see I. W. Raymond, *Seven Books of History against the Pagans* (New York: Columbia University Press, 1936), 396.

pious, prudent, and serious man of Narbonensis,[55] who held illustrious office under Theodosius,[56] recounting to the most blessed priest Jerome that he was a particular friend of Athaulf[57] at Narbonne and that he often had learned from him in serious discussion that which he was accustomed to relate when he was in excessively good spirits, health, and temperament. Athaulf said that initially he ardently had desired to obliterate the name of Rome, and to make and name all of Roman territory a Gothic Empire, and that, to speak colloquially, what had been "Romania" would become "Gothia" and that Athaulf now would become what Augustus Caesar once had been. But when much experience had proven that the Goths in no way were capable of obeying laws on account of their unrestrained barbarism and that it was not right to annul the laws of the Republic, without which a Republic is not a Republic, he chose rather to seek glory for himself by restoring in whole and augmenting the name of Rome with the strength of the Goths, and to be viewed by posterity as the author of the revival of Rome given that he was unable to be its transformer.

The opinions presented here, of course, are not those of Athaulf himself, but of the Roman author, and they reflect the Roman concept of the "good" barbarian. In spite of this rosy vision of a Romano-Germanic rapprochement, the changes wrought by the barbarian settlement did in fact cause a great deal of disruption.

Hard Times

Many inhabitants of Gaul had their lives dreadfully disturbed by the barbarian presence. Some were uprooted and fled, while others had to make whatever kind of private peace they could. The problems people faced are reflected in a piece of imperial legislation issued on 1 March 416 that was intended to mitigate the predicaments in which some found themselves:

---

55. The southern Gallic province of Narbonensis Prima had its metropolis (capital city) at Narbonne.

56. The identity of this individual is unknown.

57. Athaulf had succeeded Alaric as king of the Visigoths in 410. He married the captive Roman imperial princess Galla Placidia in a Roman ceremony at Narbonne in 414 but was soon murdered and replaced by another short-lived chieftain, Sigeric.

.7[58] Honorius and Theodosius, Augustuses, to Constantius, count and
patrician.[59]

If, during the catastrophe of the barbarian spoliation,[60] any acts
were done improperly or spitefully, either because of flight or because
of the congregation of accursed peoples, let them not be summoned
before the spitefulness of an avenging law by the crafty charges of litigants. Let those who, perhaps, had no opportunity to flee be free from
punishment for all crimes, unless they themselves assisted in the same
crimes, nor let anything be called a crime that was done under threat of
death. On these grounds it is fitting that all litigators understand that if
they learn of anything that has been stolen, they can recover it, provided that they are able to prove that it is stored and situated amid the
property of those whom they accuse.

Issued at Ravenna on the Kalends of March in the consulship of our
lord Theodosius Augustus, for the eighth time, and Palladius, a
notable gentleman.

Many individuals and families were displaced and faced life as captives—as seen in Patrick's letter above—or as exiles. Cases like that of
the woman sold by the Vargi seem to have been all too common.
Indeed, there seems to have been a regular commerce in captives, and
aristocratic correspondence is replete with pathetic tales of those
whose lives were disrupted.

Exiles, Refugees, and Captives

Ruricius of Limoges, for example, seems to have had a particular interest in displaced persons. His attention to the case of the priest Possessor was discussed in chapter 2; in that instance, the captive brother was
successfully ransomed, even though it threw Possessor into the grip of
creditors. Ruricius's letter collection also contains eight missives written to him by various individuals, several of which are relevant here.

---

58. *CTh* 15.14.14.

59. Constantius's full title was "count and patrician and master of both services" (that is,
the infantry and the cavalry). He later married Galla Placidia, the erstwhile bride of Athaulf,
and served briefly as emperor in 421.

60. Resulting from the crossing of the Rhine on 31 January 406 by Alans, Burgundians,
Suevi, and Vandals, and the entry of the Visigoths into Gaul in 412. Tactfully unmentioned
are the Gallic usurpations of Constantine III (407–11) and Jovinus (411–13), which were supported by many Gauls.

For example, just after he became bishop circa 485 Ruricius received a letter from Bishop Faustus of Riez asking a favor:

4.8[61] Faustus to Bishop Ruricius, a most blessed lord, and a brother to be received with fitting piety and most worthy of an apostolic see.

Thanks be to you, while I write from my homeland, you who made a homeland for me amid my wandering, you who tempered my desire for home with untiring liberality, conferring through successive benefactions something like the force of divine justice, so that whatever pertained to castigation[62] it converted to honor, it adapted to consolation, it changed to peace; it neglected my deserts so that it might magnify yours, forgiving my debts and multiplying your wealth; exercising the magnitude of its goodness on both sides, it enriched me with your indulgence while it enriched you with my exile. For this reason, it turns out that already, at the present, impatient of the future, it dispenses a benediction and lifts its most faithful servant atop the candlestick of its house with the cooperation of pity, justice, sincerity, continence, and kindness, that is, with domestic supporters. Behold, at what price has my Ruricius procured the highest priesthood! What he purchased it with is itself the thing that he purchased, and with his own supporters shouting their approval, as a fugitive from office he revealed in himself reasons for office. Therefore, one who knows how to acquire such a great burden also knows how, in the name of Christ, to administer it.

I, who as an agreeable mediator brought this opportunity upon myself, commend to you the bearer of this letter, the holy priest Florentius—known to me for a long time now and adorned both with the model of his master[63] and with the blossoms of his character—because he is traveling for the sake of the freeing of his sister. I bless your entire house, the seniors along with the juniors, with a paternal affection. My fellow servants, your debtors and admirers, give their blessing most reverently along with me.

May our Lord preserve Your Beatitude, to be magnified by me, to the profit of his church, and with a long life made perfect by my joy, my most blessed lord, and a brother to be received with fitting piety and most worthy of an apostolic see.

---

61. *Epist.* "Gratias ad vos": *MGH AA* 8:270; *CCL* 64:414–15; *CSEL* 21:218–19; for translation, see Mathisen, *Ruricius,* 104–5.

62. I.e., the punishment of exile.

63. "Exemplis magistri": perhaps a reference to Florentius's unnamed bishop.

Faustus reminded Ruricius that the latter had sheltered him after he himself had been exiled by the Visigothic king Euric circa 477, hoping, no doubt, to make Ruricius sympathetic to the plight of another refugee.

A Family in Captivity

On a subsequent occasion, Faustus wrote in support of an unnamed letter-carrier, reprising some of the same themes of the previous letter:

1.9[64] Faustus to Bishop Ruricius, a most blessed lord and a brother to be esteemed singularly by me before all others with the greatest honor.

I have such great faith in the kindness of your spirit that no longer am I content to gulp alone from its most pure waters, but I also invite others, who might be revived along with me through its use; especially because its extended largess redounds to the profit of the bestower, and the recipient is so enriched by its goodness that the one imparting is not lessened but is augmented, as if with profit, through his expenditures, my lord most blessed and to be cultivated singularly by me before all others with the greatest honor.

Therefore, with this letter I exhibit the irrepayable payment of charity, by which the property of the bestower is further enriched, and I presume to offer the opportunity for a good deed through my commendation of those in trouble, because I have faith that my intercession pertains to your profit, and therefore I was unable to deny pity, which ecclesiastical humanity is accustomed to offer to the miserable, to the bearer of this letter, who has suffered captivity in Lugdunensis. Would that the largess of the faithful could be as prompt as the need of this individual is all too obvious. And because, having gained freedom to an extent with regard to his own person, he is yet held captive through the servitude of his wife and children, having extended my good offices I beg you to adhere to your customary kindness even in the consolation of this one and to pursue through letters what he has requested with regard to those concerned.[65]

---

64. *Epist.* "Tanta mihi": *MGH AA* 8:270; *CCL* 64:413–14; *CSEL* 21:217–18; for translation, see Mathisen, *Ruricius,* 103–4.

65. "Apud antepositos": the only "aforementioned persons" are the wife and children, but Faustus seems to be asking Ruricius to pursue the case with some other individuals, i.e. "the authorities."

My fellow servants, especially your admirer, my brother, the priest Memorius,[66] give their blessing most reverently with me.

May our Lord God keep your pious beatitude mindful of me through happy longevity to the profit of His church, my brother, a lord most blessed and to be cultivated singularly by me with the highest honor before all others.

It is unclear just what kind of aid Ruricius—who lived nowhere near Lugdunensis—was expected to provide; perhaps nothing more than another similar letter to present to the next bishop on the traveler's route. Given that the latter was passing through Limoges, he probably was headed in the direction of Tours and Angers, where, as seen in chapter 2, Ruricius had contacts.

The Searcher

Yet another letter to Ruricius, from Victorinus, bishop of Fréjus, included an additional request for assistance for an unfortunate letter carrier:

4.10[67]   Victorinus to a Lord most blessed and reverend, and a patron in Christ to be respected singularly by me with fitting worship, Bishop Ruricius.

Although I have deserved to see Your Beatitude both for a very short time and only in a single instance, nevertheless you so watered my senses with the purest fountain of a kind heart at my first opportunity of recognizing and contemplating you, that however much I was unable to capture the precious gifts of your words, I possessed nevertheless your presence within the depths of my mind, so that even if I did not receive opportunities externally of refreshing my desire, I nevertheless could find them within myself as long as I remembered Your Grace. Nor, indeed, is it right that this blessing have need of reinforcement only from chance circumstances, because it is constant, infused within my marrow. For this reason, it happens that the charity that sweetens in my innards at the renewed memory of our bond promises a reciprocation of your charity toward me. And thus my affection

---

66. Memorius seems to have accompanied Faustus in exile and thus also to have enjoyed Ruricius's hospitality.

67. Victorinus of Fréjus, *Epist.* "Cum beatitudinem vestram": *CSEL* 21:443–44 = *CCL* 64:397–98 = *MGH AA* 8:271–72; for translation, see Mathisen, *Ruricius,* 210–11.

toward you stands forth for me as a guarantor of your spirit and in some way my interior conscience assists, as a witness for me of your affection; and I question my mind, which burns with the full ardor of love toward you, regarding how much I might presume for myself about you.

For this reason, offering my greetings and beseeching intercession on behalf of the bearer of this letter, I render insufficient thanks. And because the labor of this poor unfortunate, on account of which he has been tossed about in exile through diverse regions for the sake of the release of his wife, was negated by her death immediately after her redemption, and now, again, his paternal anxiety is aroused for the sake of the redemption of his daughter, may you command that he be accompanied by your letters, for the sake of the accumulation of the richness of your reward.

May the dutiful Lord deign to endow Your Beatitude with both years and merits to the profit and ornament of His church, lord most blessed and reverend, and a patron in Christ to be respected singularly by me with fitting worship.[68]

Even though Victorinus had met Ruricius only once, he felt free to call upon him for assistance. Ruricius apparently was not being asked to do anything more than show hospitality and provide an additional letter of reference; but, such letters counted for a lot. They exhibit the operation of a "bishops' network" that provided a social safety net for persons in distress. This system was an expansion upon the Roman custom of great men doing favors for each other; and, if anything, episcopal participation was even more obligatory, for it was mandated by the Christian ethos. At the same time, moreover, the great number of refugees also provided bishops with a ready supply of messengers—as long as the bishops acceded to the travelers' appeals for assistance.

The Wandering Clerics

The dislocation of northern clerics also is attested, a result, in part, of the expansion of the Franks under Childeric and Clovis beginning in the 460s. Not only did Bishop Polychronius of Verdun choose to go

---

68. Like Faustus of Riez, Victorinus repeated his salutation in his very ornate farewell salutation.

into exile, perhaps in the 460s or 470s, but so did four of his clerics—
the priests Francus, Paulus, and Valerianus, and the archdeacon Sisinnius—who sought refuge with a Bishop Castor, apparently of
Chartres. In a letter to Polychronius, who was in exile elsewhere, they
described their misfortunes.[69]

4.11[70] The priests Francus, Paulus, Valerianus, the archdeacon Sisinnius, and
all the clerics, to the lord Polychronius, blessed and deserving in the
love of Christ.

We have been compelled by grave necessity to leave our homeland,
and the misfortune that has made you an exile from our homeland also
has compelled us to go into exile: but through your intercession we
have been tended to by the humanity of the blessed bishop Castor, who
through consideration of you, arranged a place in which we were able
to obtain rest. It is fitting that you, whom we know to have acted with
the fullest charity toward us, repay him for this kindness on behalf of
us, who are your people, because we believe that for us it is all too little unless the kindness of such a great man is in some way compensated
for by you, whom he esteems so greatly. Sanctified Lord, it is fitting
that you should think it proper to come to visit your people on the
blessed paschal day, because if they were soothed by the nourishment
of your benediction, they more easily would have faith that they could
sustain the necessity of travel, and at least your visit, with the help of
God, would be offered to those to whom your presence is denied for
long periods. We hope, with the prayer by which we trust that you are
well, that you do not have such great weariness of us that you will
refuse to travel all the way to us. We also think it proper to hint to the
aforementioned bishop, and to his other brothers as well, that however
much, in your absence, we know that they think it fitting to offer in
consideration of you, so much more, in your presence, anticipating our
journey, do we believe they ought to grant in consolation.

---

69. Polychronius presumably is the bishop of Verdun of that name who was a disciple of
Lupus of Troyes: *Vita Lupi* (Life of Lupus): *MGH SRM* 3:123; see Duchesne, *Fastes,*
3:69–70. The only Bishop Castor attested for the fifth century was at Chartres (*Fastes,* 2:424).

70. Francus, Paulus, Valerianus, Sisinnius, et al., *Epist.* "Patria gravi sumus": C. Turner,
Journal of Theological Studies 30 (1929): 27; G. Morin, "Castor et Polychronius: Un épisode
peu connu de l'histoire ecclésiastique des Gaules," *Revue bénédictine* 51 (1939): 31–36; and
PLS 3:831–32.

This plaintive missive suggests that the welcome of the refugee clerics was beginning to wear thin. Their host wanted not only some contribution, but also to rid himself of his guests. Polychronius was asked to come and get them—if he did so, perhaps past expenses would be waived, and additional contributions might even be forthcoming if he were to take them off Castor's hands. What may have happened, however, is that Polychronius not only came, but remained as well, for Castor's successor twice removed was named Polychronius.[71]

A Confrontation at Court

Those who did not flee or become refugees could have their personal security threatened in other ways. In the early phases of the barbarian settlement there were not yet any formal procedures by which Romans could obtain redress for grievances suffered under Germanic rule. A settlement often would turn upon a direct appeal to a barbarian king. One such case occurred circa 468, when the abbot Lupicinus of St-Claude was involved in a hearing before the Burgundian king Chilperic (ca. 458–ca. 480). Lupicinus was there on behalf of some Romans who, he asserted, had been wrongly enslaved by a member of the Burgundian court.

2[72] And, on a certain occasion, when the servant of God,[73] in the presence of that illustrious individual, then the patrician of Gaul, Chilperic (for the public law at that time was administered under royal jurisdiction), struggled with a most pious defense to speak out on behalf of the anguish of some paupers, whom a certain individual, bloated by the honor of his courtly dignity, had placed under the yoke of servitude by the force of an illegal assault, that nefarious oppressor, aroused by the fury of rage, belching forth a kind of froth of words full of rage and detrimental to the most blessed man, said, "Are you not that recent trickster of ours who, around ten years ago, while you were insolently denigrating the policies of the Roman government, asserted that even

---

71. See Duchesne, *Fastes,* 2:424–25. This would be analogous to the situation at Clermont, where the refugee Aprunculus succeeded Sidonius, and the refugee Quintianus succeeded Apollinaris (*Fastes,* 2.34–36).

72. *Vita Lupicini* (Life of Lupicinus), 10: F. Martine, ed. and trans., *SC* 142:336–40; *MGH SRM* 3:149.

73. That is, Lupicinus.

then ruin threatened this region and our families? I ask you, therefore, false prophet, to explain why the terrible portents of your prediction are confirmed by no evidence of woeful occurrence."

Extending his hand to the aforementioned Chilperic, a man singular for his talent and special goodness, Lupicinus boldly responded, "Behold, you perfidious and depraved man! Give heed to the wrath that I used to preach to you and those like you. Do you not see, degenerate and unfortunate one, that law and right have been disrupted, on account of the repeated attacks of you and yours upon the innocent, [and] that the purple fasces have been transformed under a skin-clad judge? Finally, come to your senses for a time and consider whether a new guest[74] might not appropriate and seize for himself your fields and acres by means of an unexpected application of the law. Moreover, just as I do not dispute that you know or perceive these matters, I likewise do not deny that you have decided to sully my little person by the mark of the stigma of a two-pronged dilemma—either to be made timid by the king or to be made fearful of the outcome."

What more? The aforementioned patrician was so enchanted by the audacity of truth that, by divine judgment, with his courtiers standing near, he confirmed, with many examples and a long discussion, that Lupicinus spoke the truth. Indeed, soon afterward, when his decision had been published with royal vigor, he restored those who were free to liberty, and he allowed the servant of Christ to return honorably to his monastery, with gifts provided for the needs of the monks and the monastery.

The incident to which Lupicinus's accuser referred would have occurred circa 457 or 458, in the troubled times immediately after the fall of the Gallic emperor Avitus (A.D. 455–56), when the Burgundians were extending their control into the area of Lupicinus's own monastery.[75] Presumably, Lupicinus had been speaking out on the failure of Roman policies, and his predictions of gloom and doom may have involved the catastrophe that he felt was sure to follow upon the Burgundian takeover. His accuser suggested that, in spite of Roman fears, the barbarian occupation had not, in fact, brought ruin and dis-

---

74. "Novus hospes": Roman landowners often were compelled to share their estates with barbarian settlers known as *hospites* (guests).

75. For these events, see Mathisen, "Resistance and Reconciliation."

aster. Lupicinus responded that if the law was not applied fairly, his accuser, who therefore would have been a Roman in the service of the king, ran the risk of losing his own land.

A Change in Management

Eventually, the relationship between Romans and barbarians became more and more regularized. On a formal and official level, individual Gallo-Roman potentates made their peace and learned to deal with the new Germanic rulers in much the same way they had related to the former Roman officials. Bishop Remigius of Reims, in a letter written during the 480s, not only portrayed the Frankish king Clovis in the role of a Roman administrator but also presumed to advise him on how to conduct himself:

[76]   Bishop Remigius to King Clovis, an outstanding lord, magnificent in merits.

The important report has come to us that you have undertaken the administration of Belgica Secunda. This is nothing new, for you begin to rule just as your ancestors always did. In the first place, this must be done, that you act in such a way that God's judgment will not abandon you and so that your merits will keep you at the eminence where you have arrived by your humility. You ought to choose advisers who will be able to augment your reputation. Your dealings should be righteous and honest. And you ought to defer to your bishops and often to have recourse to their advice, because if there is harmony between you and them, your province will be more effectively administered. Encourage your people, relieve the afflicted, shelter widows, nourish orphans, if you wish to provide an example, so that all may love and fear you. May justice come forth from your mouth. Ask nothing from the poor or from strangers. Let your tribunal be open to all, so that no one will depart from it in sorrow. Whatever paternal wealth you possess you furthermore should use to free captives and to liberate them from the

---

76. Remigius of Reims, *Epist.* "Rumor ad nos": *Epistulae Austrasicae,* 2: *MGH Epist.* 3:113; for a variant translation, see Hillgarth, *Conversion of Western Europe,* 74–75. The letter usually is dated to just after Clovis's defeat of Syagrius of Soissons in 486, although it in fact may have followed Clovis's succession to Childeric as king at Tournai and elsewhere ca. 481. Reims, Soissons, and Tournai all were situated in the Roman province of Belgica Secunda.

yoke of servitude. If any are admitted into your presence, let them not feel that they are strangers. Joke with the young men and deliberate with the elders if you wish to rule and judge as a noble.

By this time, Gallo-Roman potentates were struggling to make the best possible accommodation with the Germans. Remigius clearly has given up any hopes of a Roman restoration. His initiatives bore fruit in the late 490s, when he himself baptized Clovis as a Nicene Christian.

Too Little, Too Late

In the early sixth century, the dénouement of the assimilation issue can be seen in the diligent efforts of barbarian rulers to reach a rapproche-ment with the Gallo-Romans. In one such case, the Visigothic king Alaric II (484–507), faced with the threat of Frankish expansion, issued on 3 February 506 the *Lex Romana Visigothorum* (Roman Law of the Visigoths), a conflation of earlier Roman legislation now com-monly known as the *Breviarium Alarici* (Breviary [Abridgment] of Alaric). Alaric, an Arian, felt that this was one way to conciliate his Nicene subjects.[77] The code was distributed by two Gallo-Romans, the *vir spectabilis* Count Timotheus and the *vir spectabilis* Anianus, and was prefaced by instructions to the former:

4.14[78]   Instructions to Count Timotheus, a respectable gentleman.

Considering the best interests of our people, with the favor of God, it seemed that we should correct with a more careful deliberation what-ever seemed unjust in the laws, so that all the obscurity of Roman laws and ancient jurisprudence, led into the light of a better intelligence with the assistance of bishops and the nobility, might be made clear and so that nothing might remain in doubt that would result in the constant and varied objection of litigants assailing it. Now that all these matters have been gathered together by the selection of prudent men and col-lected into one book, the assent of our chosen provincials and venera-

---

77. In the same year, Alaric allowed the first synod of Nicene bishops to be assembled in the Visigothic kingdom, at Agde. For discussion, see Ralph W. Mathisen, "The 'Second Council of Arles' and the Spirit of Compilation and Codification in Late Roman Gaul," *Journal of Early Christian Studies* 5 (1997): 511–54.

78. *Breviarium Alarici,* preface: Th. Mommsen, P. M. Meyer, and P. Krüger, eds., *Theo-dosiani libri XVI* (Berlin, 1905), 1.xxxiii–xxxiv.

ble bishops has fortified these matters that were excerpted or arranged by more eminent interpretation. And therefore, according to the authorized text that was provided and we have in our treasury, Our Clemency commands this book to be sent to you for the settlement of issues, so that according to its arrangement all controversy of cases might be settled, nor is it permitted to anyone to put forward in a dispute anything regarding the laws or legal rights except for what is embraced by the organization of the book forwarded and authorized by the hand of the respectable man Anianus just as we ordered. It befits you, therefore, to see to it that in your forum no other law or formula of legal rights is put forth or accepted. But if by chance it should be clear that this has been done, be advised that you will be in danger of capital punishment or the confiscation of your property. Truly, we order this precept to accompany the forwarded books, so that the principles of our ordinance might hold and the punishments constrain everyone.

We have reviewed this.[79]

Given at Toulouse on the third day before the Nones of February in the twenty-second year of King Alaric.

In this manner, the promise of Athaulf made nearly a century before was brought to fruition, and the Visigoths did indeed become the supporters of Roman law.

This code, compiled by Gallo-Roman jurists and endorsed by secular and ecclesiastical notables, included an abridgment of the Theodosian Code, which had been issued in 438. In the Byzantine east, this code would soon be superseded in the 530s by the Code of Justinian. But in the west, the legacy of the Theodosian Code remained; indeed, its very survival was partly a result of its incorporation into barbarian law codes. The Germanic kingdoms preserved many other Roman practices and institutions as well, such as the dating formulas at the end of official documents with, in this case, the regnal year of the king replacing the Roman use of consular years (which continued in the Burgundian kingdom, as already seen).

Even though the Goths were defeated by the Franks at Vouillé in 507 and Alaric was killed, this lawcode, and others like it issued by other barbarian peoples (such as the Burgundians, the Franks, the Ala-

---

79. *Recognovimus:* the authorizing subscription of the king himself, in his own hand.

manni, and the Lombards), continued to protect the interests of the
Roman population. And such protection was certainly necessary, for
barbarians sometimes attempted to take advantage of their newly
acquired social and political status. In the Burgundian Code of 517, for
example, it was decreed, "If a man making a journey on private business comes to the house of a Burgundian and seeks hospitality and the
latter directs him to the house of a Roman . . . let the Burgundian pay
three solidi to him to whose house he directed the traveler."[80] Apparently, Burgundians had been foisting unwanted visitors upon their
Roman neighbors.

Germanic lawcodes attempted to promote harmony in other ways
as well. For example, the Frankish Salic Law, first promulgated in the
early sixth century, in the section entitled "Concerning Insults" established a penalty of three solidi for calling a man a "fox" or a "hare," or
for falsely claiming that someone had thrown away his shield. For
falsely accusing someone of being a spy or perjurer, the fine was fifteen
solidi, and the penalty for wrongly calling a woman a harlot was forty-
five solidi.[81]

Legal Redress

Romans eventually gained access to even more formal means of
redress in barbarian-ruled Gaul; indeed, at Clermont there was a standard formula that came into use by the mid–sixth century for the
recovery of property that had been lost through hostile activity:

4.15[82]   [Declaration or Grievance].
    . . . For this reason, therefore, I (name) and my wife (name), dwelling
in the city of the Arverni, in the hamlet (name), on the estate (name),
just as it is common knowledge that because of the belligerence of the
Franks[83] we lost our property records for our lodging on the same

---

80. *Lex Burgundionum,* 38.7; for translation, see Drew, *Burgundian Code,* 48.

81. *Lex Salica* (Salic Law), title 30, "Concerning Insults." For Roman legislation on false
accusations in late Roman Gaul, see Alberto de la Hera, "'Falsus testis' y 'delator,'" *Anuario
de Historia del Derecho Espanol* 33 (1963): 365–73.

82. *Formulae Arvernenses* (Arvernian formulas), 1.a: K. Zeumer, ed., *MGH Leg., Sectio
V, Formulae,* 28. The heading is missing and has been restored based on the contents. The
document would have been addressed to a chief municipal official, either the *comes* (count)
or the *defensor* (defender).

83. Probably a reference to a Frankish attack upon Clermont ca. 532: see Greg.Tur. *Hist.*
3.12, *Glor.mart.* 1.52, *Vit.pat.* 4.1–2, *Virtutes s. Iuliani* (Virtues of St. Julian), 13.

estate (name), where we are known to dwell, we likewise petition and will make it known that, because of this incident, our ownership not be invalidated with respect to whatever we are known to possess at this time on the authority of documents themselves. Among the letters (named) regarding the lodgings on the same estate (name), concerning which we have reconstructed the original condition, we likewise have lost everything previously written, either that which we are not at all able to remember—in judgments, summaries, notices, promises, petitions—or other documents, whether ours or also those that were entrusted to us: this we have lost among the same estates cited above and in the same turmoil. And we petition to be allowed to compile and certify this little declaration or grievance in our name by means of this *charta*,[84] wherefore we have acted as follows: according to the decree of the emperors, when Honorius and Theodosius were consuls, we posted and safeguarded it at the citadel of Clermont[85] for three days,[86] either at the sanctified altar (name) or in the public market, where the business of the town council, or of the record keeper (either the king's or yours), or of the persons of that same citadel, is conducted, so that when this little declaration or grievance has been read in your presence according to standard legal practice, you will proceed to endorse [it] with your signed subscription, so that through your declaration a remedy for our misfortune as described above might be obtained in some manner according to the legal authority, so that they might reinstate our ownership by the authority of the laws.[87]

The recourse to a law of Honorius and Theodosius demonstrates, again, the continued validity of Roman law in early medieval Europe, as also attested by the slave Andarchius's study of the Theodosian Code in chapter 2.

---

84. Technically, a papyrus document.

85. *Castro Claromonte:* the more medieval appellation of the "Civitas Arvernorum" (City of the Arvernians), that is, Clermont.

86. It is unclear whether the law issued during one of the years (407, 409, 412, 415, 418, 422) when Honorius (395–423) and Theodosius II (402–50) shared the consulate refers to property claims or the three-day waiting period. If the former, the only relevant law seems to be *CTh* 10.10.27 (11 October 415), which restricts to one year claims against vacant property. The only ruling relating to a *triduum* was issued by Arcadius and Honorius, *CTh* 11.30.56 (22 July 396). Of course, the law cited here might have been in a lost section of the Theodosian Code, or never have made it into the code at all. For another example of a three-day waiting period, note Greg.Tur. *Hist.* 10.19, a three-day grace period for appealing a conviction.

87. There then follows the *gesta,* that is, the words of the proceedings that the magistrate would oversee.

The preceding chapters have illustrated how individuals, families, and society as a whole functioned and were affected by the changes that were occurring during Late Antiquity. As has been seen, some old customs were being replaced by the new. As a consequence of political and religious upheaval, old kinds of social distinctions had lost some of their validity. And violence, in spite of efforts to restrain it, became endemic as a means of self-expression. The next section will look at ways in which some individuals were able to take advantage of new opportunities that were available during Late Antiquity.

CHAPTER 5

The Triumph of Christianity and Life in the Church

The religious revolution of Late Antiquity, fueled by the spread of Nicene Christianity and the adoption of the Christian ethos, had repercussions in every corner of society and touched different individuals in different ways. Its ramifications surmounted social and cultural boundaries. Intellectual attitudes, aristocratic careers, social relations, family life, and gender roles all were affected. If the secular milieu of the Roman Empire represented the ancient past, the ecclesiastical world of the Christian Church symbolized the medieval future. Roman aristocrats moved in both worlds. At the same time that they perpetuated classical literary practices, they also adopted a new ecclesiastical ideology that, according to some, necessitated a rejection of the classical past. Of course, such significant social and cultural transformations did not occur without some discord and disruption. Not everyone welcomed them. The process by which Nicene Christianity supplanted not only classical paganism but also other forms of Christianity entailed a certain amount of conflict.

Conversion

One encounters many descriptions of the conversion of the "pagan"[1] Roman population. On occasion, this process involved confrontation. Sometimes non-Christians emerged victorious, although even these occurrences could provide the Christian establishment with a new

---

1. Traditionally, a word derived from *paganus,* an inhabitant of the countryside. Generally, Christianity made inroads into urban more quickly and easily than into rural society.

source of martyrs, who had been in short supply after the cessation in the early fourth century of "persecutions" by the Roman government.

Instant Martyrs

One case was reported by Bishop Vigilius of Trent.[2] In A.D. 397 three of his clerics established a church in a secluded rural area of the Val di Non in northern Italy. On 29 May, the locals, still fancying their old gods, made their own preferences known in a particularly emphatic manner. Vigilius described what happened in an elaborately stylized letter to John Chrysostom, bishop of Constantinople:

5.1[3]   (1) A guest of charity should not otherwise approach sanctified ears, nor, when called forth, bring shame upon a primacy,[4] or as an unknown person initiate discourse, unless at the same time he calls forth recompense. Therefore, dearest brother, let my position of petitioner and the fulsomeness of my letter take their lead from the apostolic man,[5] so that you might understand in a straightforward context that eulogies of martyrs ensue. For Jacobus, a man steadfast in heavenly aspirations, on the verge of retiring from the position of count[6] in the midst of the comrades of Christ, has demanded relics, newly made and still smoldering with smoke. On the verge of retirement, I said, because one cannot put aside the rank that has been accumulated in the Lord. Amply apprehensive of him, and not a little concerned, I wrestled with myself regarding an appropriate apportionment, with the result that I did not act as a suitable distributor, and in my fear I

---

2. See Dennis Trout, "Town, Countryside, and Christianization at Paulinus' Nola," in Mathisen and Sivan, *Shifting Frontiers,* 175–86; note also Maximus of Turin, *Sermons,* 105–6 (*CCL* 23:413–18); and C. E. Chaffin, "The Martyrs of the Val di Non: An Examination of Contemporary Reactions," *Studia patristica* 10 (1970): 263–69.

3. Vigilius of Trent, *Epist.* 2, "Ad sanctas aures": *PL* 13:552–58; Enrico Menestò, "Le lettere di S. Vigilio," in *I martiri della Val di Non e la reazione pagana alle fine del IV secolo,* ed. A. Quacquarelli and I. Rogger (Trent: Istituto Trentino di Cultura 1985), 151–70. The surviving text lacks both introductory and concluding salutations.

4. *Primatus:* in this case, the see of Constantinople, which ranked as the "first see" of the East.

5. That is, the apostle Matthew: see Matt. 10.41, "He that receiveth a righteous man in the name of a righteous man shall receive a righteous reward."

6. Jacobus served as *comes et magister equitum* ("count and master of horse," the second-ranking master of soldiers) in the West ca. 401–2 and was a great believer in the efficacy of saints' relics (see *PLRE* 2:581–82).

nearly denied what always ought to be expended so that someone might profit. I confess to a personal fear of many things, until I looked again to Jacobus, who, through certain nourishments of reverence, was going to transport [my gift] to the sanctified John, so that the martyrs would be delivered by means of a delegated love with religious words, and so that again an unforeign brotherhood would be linked through their blood. Accepting freely, among other things as well, this presumption of faith,[7] which rightly ridiculed my anguish, I delayed nonetheless, but I did not deny. I delayed, so that again my procrastination might be clearly betrayed, I who least of all deserved to follow in the footsteps of my comrades. I confess, I would have chosen to do so, but the crown of justice does not lie solely in desire.[8]

Now, however, if a gradual progression is not onerous to your thirsting ears, following the most significant traces of the events without squeamishness, I shall commence with the character of the region and their route, so that the flood of their merits might gush forth more precipitously if, with capacious love, you go all the way to the source of the spring. (2) Now, the place, for which the local name is Anagnia, is located twenty-five stades[9] away from the city [of Trent], isolated as much by its treacherousness as by its geography on account of the narrow passes. It is accessible through only one entrance (the path of the three martyrs, you might say), which is arched on a gently sloping ridge with the valley falling away on each side; there are little forts situated all around in the heights, as the neighboring places conspired among themselves in their treacherousness, and nature's stage[10] provided a kind of amphitheater.[11] A purpose[12] was lacking for this place, but Christ provided a fitting purpose, with the result that the sport[13] of the devil would provide the ceremony[14] for a martyrdom. Let not a description of the geography be tedious to the ears of the listener. Indeed, this consonant location, a hollow in the mountains, wickedly was always an ally to itself. When the service of Christ first clambered

---

7. That is, that his gifts would be welcome.

8. Vigilius seems to be apologizing for not having been martyred himself.

9. Furlongs.

10. *Scena:* as in a theater.

11. *Spectaculum:* here as an allusion to past martyrdoms that occurred in the arena.

12. *Causa,* which also could refer to a court case, or trial, i.e., an allusion to the coming ordeals of the martyrs.

13. *Ludus:* an allusion to the spectacles of the arena.

14. *Pompa:* a solemn procession, as at a Roman triumph.

up to it, a truculent paganism, often aroused by trumpets, was inflamed with a jealous fury by the clamor of war. Truly, one kind of fray was appropriate for saints: to undergo all things, to yield when provoked, to endure while suffering, to restrain those about to reveal public fury with a private gentleness, to vanquish by refusing. But the predestined[15] glory of a timely death pressed upon them with testimonies that the fitting order of things had engendered. For, when prolixity is omitted and long digressions are cut off (I refer only to things that were done) with which the virtue of the martyrs is nourished, [there is] a loss of the praise when careful consideration is swept away.

(3) Because the name of the Lord was still unknown in the aforementioned neighborhood, and there was no indication that demonstrated even a little sign of faith, these men, singular then in their number and now in their merit, were newcomers as much by their religion as by their ethnicity. God—unknown during the peaceful interchange of a calm and lengthy time during which no utility of faith stimulated—was proclaimed by them in a not unworthy manner. But now, should a cause for the rising hatred against the Lord be sought, it comes under the heading of violated peace, because one of these men, Sisinnius by name, more elderly than the others, in whom alone, in fact, there was venerable elderliness, built a church at his own expense. Richer in faith than in property, wealthy in spirit but a pauper in fortune,[16] he handed the sheepfold over to the shepherd. It was built; he was the founder, the sentinel. But this was a sheepfold opposed to wolves. Devilish ruin was resentful of the lofty steeple. This was the first apportionment of martyrdom: that while the sheep pursued the lamb, they perished. It was added like a sacrifice, that purpose more just to God, for when, in a wild display, the people wished to carry out the lustral wickedness[17] around the boundaries of the fields, they trampled the sprouts as much as they defiled them.[18] Likewise intending to trample the seeds of

---

15. *Praedestinata:* in the fifth century, Augustine's theory of "predestination" was to become a cause celèbre, and to be condemned as heresy in Gaul. But in Italy it faced no such opposition.

16. A claim seemingly belied by his ability to fund the construction of a church.

17. *Lustrale malum:* a purification ceremony; a *lustrum* was a period of five years. A similar ceremony is reported as occurring in Gaul at about the same time in the *Life of St. Martin* 12: "This was the custom of the Gallic rustics, to carry statues of demons, covered by a white veil, around their fields with a pitiful madness."

18. Vigilius argues that the purification rite had the contrary effect, for it resulted in the trampling of the crops whose growth it was intended to encourage.

Christ, crowned with baleful ornamentation and with the ululating song of the devil, in processions with diverse animals and with banners erected within the house of the Lord, they compelled one of their own people, who recently had been converted [to Christianity], to make sacrifices to the undertakings of the shades.[19] Because the ministers of the Lord could scarcely observe this happening without culpability on their part, because they, standing nearby, also seemed to be partaking[20] in these misconceived activities, the bodies of the saints on that day were pledged to a calamitous slaughter, but one in which the palm of victory was borne aloft. . . . (5) For subsequent to the display of the dia-bolical festivals, which, as I said, was an indication of glory soon to come, they ascended to the crown that had been delayed for one night. For in the morning hours when the dawn was breaking as the shadows of the sky withdrew, an unanticipated but conspiratorial crowd col-lected, armed with fire-hardened stakes and axes, because devilish anger had created a spear for these searchers. And after several deacons who were singing the morning hymn there in the church were seized, there occurred a great pillaging, a savage plundering. All the mysteries, as secret as they were divine, were profaned; ultimately, religion itself became plunder. Let no one think that this was a common sort of conflict, as when insensible idols are overturned by sensible people, or when buildings of stone are disturbed along with their builders, so that regarding the worshipper and the object of worship you would consider it to be unclear which you would judge to be more disagreeable. Christ tried Peter in everything, and this craggy rock was repeatedly put to the test by the nations and again had to be proven to the world when he strove to rebuild its ruins from his gushing blood.

In the midst of this, faith provided its own spectacle. The body of the deacon Sisinnius then was confined in his cot, stabbed and smitten also by previous wounds, when he was ordered either to bring a sheep to the sacrifice or to become the sacrifice himself if he did not partici-pate in these feral sacrifices. The trumpet was sounded with which they manifested the song of the devil; not unworthily he who first intro-duced the sound of faith, he who had withheld his own ax from the sterile tree of paganism, was hacked by axes.[21] And, lest I draw out any

---

19. The pagan sacrifices would seem, therefore, to have been carried out inside the church.

20. The word is *communicare,* the word used for Christian Communion.

21. Meaning, perhaps, that he, unlike some Christian zealots, had not openly antagonized the locals by chopping down any sacred trees.

longer the conclusion, he is apprehended, as I said, in the deserved peace of his cot. Having confessed [his faith], I believe, so that in a private rite he quickly would attain the cross, with the intention of redeeming a paralytic people, (6) he is bound to a stake with cords.

The lector Martyrius, likewise a confessor and assertor of His name, who then first and now alone had sung a new song in an alien land, in the midst of the howling and hideous pastoral shouts, with the praises of a gentle address already rendered to God, as I recalled above, also had conveyed medication and relief to the deacon Sisinnius, intending to salve his hurts, even though doing so meant that he was going to receive wounds, summoning back with exquisite draughts the spirit departing not from its body but from suffering. Truly, the saint,[22] with the journey of martyrdom to Christ already ordained, refused the drink of water because the wine of suffering had come, which was mixed in the quaffed chalice of a flowing, truer life. In the midst of this caring, therefore, he was discovered, he who always had been concerned for the health of souls, born not for himself alone nor about to be victorious, surely, for himself alone. He withdrew into the recesses of the garden which is joined alongside, that is, he did not leave the grounds of the church. This, as you well know, is the garden in the church, planted with screens of the living commandments.[23] He did not offer his body, which he did not wish to refuse, nor did the confidence of piety espouse the rashness of temerity—just as in the African regions it is said, "Those who prepare for funerals voluntarily, because they do so without fear, are soliciting them out of pride."[24] Moreover, the martyr-to-be stood free as a captive, fearless having confessed, giving thanks as he was wounded, injured in body but secure in spirit, with his head smitten he was bathed in blood in a personalized baptism. . . . Martyrius is brought forth from the garden where he had withdrawn . . . . Bound to stakes, he was led to the idol, but he merited becoming a sacrifice before he arrived at the altar of the devil.

(7) The third crown of the Lord, to be in honor of Alexander, also is manifested. . . . Alexander, alive in the midst of them, was led out with his feet bound, about to send forth through the crags part of his palpi-

---

22. I.e., Sisinnius.

23. Vigilius takes pains to establish that Martyrius did not try to flee.

24. For this African practice, see J. E. Merdinger, *Rome and the African Church in the Time of Augustine* (New Haven: Yale University Press, 1997), 10: "Baiting the authorities in hopes of getting arrested was frowned upon."

tating members until he was led to the boundary, I say, of the realm of life. Subsequently, they went to religious heights, that is, to the tall temple of the god, beyond the corpses, pinnacles strewn on the ground, after a pyre had been made from the sanctified beams in the sight of Saturn, an ancient idol from a long-ago time. After the twin brotherly bodies had first been thrown into the fire, Alexander stood, wounded, about to confess again. The reward of life was offered to him, with the result that he could lose his life: he might say that he surrendered to their shades if he wished to escape the present flames. . . . The fervor of faith repelled the flame, the degree of his suffering also upheld the reverence of his station. The last one is received, but he is crowned not the least among his brothers. . . .

(11) Accept now, brother, the gift of these three lads, or rather the three lads from the furnace,[25] still, almost, traversing the flames of the blustering fire, and if the envious furor of the flame had not accepted the half-dead bodies, the example of history would have lived again. All three portrayed themselves with a nearly similar honor: their voice, the moisture, the number, the furnace. Their voice [represented] their consonant faith, the moisture the rain, the furnace the pyre, and the number the Trinity.[26]

This account is noteworthy for both its detail and its immediacy. It shows that the Christianization of the countryside sometimes met serious resistance from the pagan rustics, who even at this early period could be classified as "barbarians."[27]

Eutropius Confounds a Pagan

In most accounts of such confrontations, of courses, the Christian participants prevailed. Bishops played a much ballyhooed role. One incident was reported in the life of Bishop Eutropius of Orange (ca. 450–75), composed circa 495 by his successor, Verus. It skillfully inter-

---

25. For Shadrach, Meshach, and Abednego in the furnace of Babylon, see Daniel 3.

26. Apparently Vigilius felt he had to spell it out in case John did not get it.

27. Vigilius's other surviving letter, on the same topic, was sent to Bishop Simplicianus of Milan: *Epist.* 1, "Quamvis facta": *PL* 13:550, "Sisinnius novam Christiani nominis pacem intulit barbarae nationi." It dates the martyrdom to "quarto Kalendas Junias, sexta feria," that is, to Saturday, May 28. The festival therefore occurred on Saturn's own day. See also Gennad. *Vir.ill.* 37.

twined into a single narrative several aspects of late Roman social relations.

5.2[28] Moreover, I must not omit what he did on a particular occasion. A certain old man, devoted to the worship of idols, was deformed in his entire body as a result of being struck by lightning, and like a wild beast, with the function of his hands changed into that of feet, he went about like a quadruped. He was so befouled by a disfigurement of the normal kind of intact skin that he was defiled, afflicted by an unspeakable kind of infirmity. Furthermore, seeking the secluded places of the city, he concealed himself without the knowledge of St. Eutropius. It came about that on a certain summer day, as often happens at the noontime hour, an atmospheric disturbance discharged violent storms.[29] With fearful tempests and hail, a billow of rain pelted the terrain here and there with a violent impact. The aforementioned pagan said to someone, "I am confident that I can end the coming storm with my word."[30] This vain promise of the madman was reported to St. Eutropius. He, because he was a man who had the right to say, "The zeal of your house torments me,"[31] burned with fury and with a brisk precipitousness commanded that the old man be thrown out of the city. But at once the finality of his command assailed the commander, and he ordered him whom he had commanded to be expelled to be presented to him. The man was displayed, with his hands more bizarre than his feet, a deformed and scarcely mobile creature. The saintly man shrank from the sight of his presence, and wept, professing that this was a worthy dwelling place of the devil. And he said to him, "Tell me, unhappy creature, what sort of citizen are you? Where are you from?" He responded that he was Italian, and that he had been struck by a lightning bolt, and thus he appeared to be miserably injured. St.

---

28. Verus of Orange, *Vita Eutropii* (Life of Eutropius): P. Varin, ed., *Bulletin du Comité Historique des Monuments Ecrits de l'Histoire de France* 1 (1849): 59–60.

29. Derived, perhaps, from Ps. 90:6, "non timebis . . . a pernicie quae vastat meridie" [you will not fear . . . the destruction that destroys at noon]; and for the *daemonium meridianum* (noonday demon), see Rudolf Arbesmann, "The 'Daemonium meridianum' and Greek and Latin Patristic Exegesis," *Traditio* 14 (1958): 17–32.

30. *CTh* 9.13.3, in the section "On Sorcerers, Numerologists, and Other Similar Persons," makes it is permissible to halt storms using magic, but it also has an interpretation, issued in Gaul in A.D. 506, stating that the "summoners of storms" [*immissores tempestatum*] are to be "punished with every kind of punishment."

31. "Zelus domus tuae comedit me": see Psalms 68 (69): 10 and John 2:17, where the phrase is associated with Christ's expulsion of the moneylenders from the Temple.

Eutropius replied to him, "How can you remove a tempest from others when you are unable to ward it off from yourself?"[32] And he added, "Have you not been baptized?" He responded that he was a pagan, following the religion of his parents. St. Eutropius said to him, "Do you wish to be made whole?" The afflicted man responded, "I would if I could, but many things already have been done that have had no effect regarding a remedy for me." The man of God countered, "I promise you your health in the sign of Christ if you come to my faith, and if from your heart you promise to me your belief." To whom the afflicted man replied, "Thank you, most hallowed lord; should you free me from such an unspeakable infirmity in any way at all, you also shall acquire me for the God in whom you believe." Self-assured, St. Eutropius, not as if for one about to be cured but as for one already cured, ordered him to be enrolled,[33] and at the order of the bishop a certain priest confidently immersed in the baptismal font the man who had been presented and could scarcely be touched. The infirmity was put to flight with the great clamor of a rattling rupture; health was everywhere reinfused, debility was put to flight. And immediately the restored connection among the joints of his spine constructed itself as a framework at the site of his ribs. His skin cleansed, the old man arose in juvenile splendor, like a living tidal wave at birth, like a new man.

This account has several interesting elements. For one thing, the old man was an outsider in ways other than his Italian origin and religious orientation. He had been hiding out in the city—apparently a fifth-century version of a homeless person. His other infirmities would have set him apart as well. And he also claimed to have magical powers, which perhaps arose from his having been struck by lightning, one of the traditional methods the pagan gods used to communicate with humans.

There also is no hint of any secular magistrates in the city. The bishop was the chief municipal official, and it was he who, angry over the challenge to his authority, ordered the expulsion of the pagan. The confrontation between Christian and pagan also is used to introduce another element common to the Christian literature of the period: the miraculous cure of paralysis. In this way, the bishop effectively demonstrated that his magic was more effective than the magic the pagan

---

32. A rhetorician's argument.
33. That is, as a member of the church.

offered to use to control the weather. And once the pagan had acknowledged the bishop's authority, he was effortlessly integrated into the community.

The Compleat Bishop

As for Eutropius, there survives a fragmentary (and therefore heavily restored) elegaic epitaph that attributes to Eutropius some conventional Christian virtues:

5.3[34]   Here, Christ, this noble urn protects, embraced in body,
Your Eutropius, approved[35] in virtue,
Although he manifested the greatest things by repeated
    demonstrations,
It is yet fitting to divulge a few things upon his grave with this
    poem.
I speak not of doubtful matters but of distinguished achievements,
To which the eyewitness accounts of the people of Orange attest.
Although he would have sublimely augmented the distinction and
    splendor of
His family, he chose to seek Christ with a dutiful spirit.
For him, a scant diet; austere accommodations for his limbs,
And as a garment for them, there was the covering of the tunic of
    faith.[36]

Scarcely anything here, save the city name, was unique to Eutropius. His epitaph rather manifests the qualities that any bishop worthy of admiration was said to possess.

Cerasia's Ministry

Along with dividing pagans from Christians, religious differences also separated Romans from barbarians, who, from the Roman perspective, could be either ignorant pagans or Arian heretics. Prior to the late fifth century, few accounts survive of attempts to expose pagan barbarians to Christianity. Those that were often were attributed to

---

34. *CIL* 12:1272 = Heinzelmann, *Bischofsherrschaft in Gallien,* 94ff.
35. Cf. the epitaph of Proba in chapter 3.
36. The remainder, consisting of a second column of equal length, is lost.

women. The efforts of the Roman Cerasia were recounted by the Aquitanian (or Spanish) priest Eutropius[37] in a lengthy tract (transmitted under the name of the apostle John) that he addressed to her when she became ill during a plague and famine:

5.4[38] Here begins the book of the blessed John, "On the Likeness of Carnal Sin."

Has the spirit of sickness dared to afflict even you? Has the force of the fever driven even you nearly to the gates of death? Has the blazing of this unpleasantness, which the entire province unhappily experiences in the blighted character of the weather, attempted to infect even your spirit? Do not the merits of your faithfulness withstand it? As these evils threaten, do not the activities of your justice array themselves in opposition, and do not the very mandates of mortality fear you as you live in the Lord? O miserable me! O unhappy me! "For if they do these things in a green tree, what shall be done in the dry?"[39] "And if the righteous scarcely will be saved, where shall the ungodly and the sinner appear?"[40] I was dismayed by your letter, which reports that you have lain lifeless for two days. After reading it, or rather nearly erasing it with my tears, for they were well deserved, I also bemoaned the state of my own condition. . . .

[There intervenes here a lengthy generalized hortatory statement.]

Likewise, you nightly delivered food to those worn out from hunger; you, as you yourself were about to lie on the ground, smoothed with your own hand the straw of their beds, and for those who could not sleep you sleeplessly spent the nights in prayer, and in this way you alone rendered to all the disbursement of a gentlewoman, the affection of a mother, the attentiveness of a servant, the scrutiny of a physician, and the visitation of the church. These benefactions you gave in common to all. But you particularly provided them both to pagans and to those barbarians—no less in spirit than in language—of yours, who believe that their idols do not experience death: you disclosed the

---

37. Not the same person as Bishop Eutropius of Orange. For this Eutropius, see Gennad. *Vir. ill.* 49; and F. Cavallera, "L'héritage littéraire et spirituel du prêtre Eutrope (IVᵉ–Vᵉ s.)," *Revue d'ascétique et de mystique* 24 (1948): 60–71.

38. Eutropius, *Liber de similitudine carnis peccati* (Book on the likeness of carnal sin): *PLS* 1:529–56; it survives only in a ninth-century Paris manuscript, BN 13344.

39. Luke 23:31.

40. 1 Pet. 4:18; cf. Prov. 11:31.

knowledge of our God in winsome speech, to each in his own tongue, and you professed Hebrew doctrine in a barbarian language,[41] as you were about to say, along with the apostle, "It is fitting that I speak in the language of all of you."[42] You demonstrated that an idol is not God, that the true God is not on an altar in the woods but in the mind of His saints; and thus, if they wish to be saved, they must believe in the savior. And you immediately procured the assistance of clerics for those who were desirous and already had made their choice. And then, truly, with wine and unguents you tended those who had been injured by bandits;[43] amid the augmentation of your own tribulation you were about to sing, "From this time their grain and wine and oil have been multiplied."[44] Thus, by human and divine art you saved some from the fever, others from perdition. Provoked by your achievements, that force, contrary to the one through which the bodies and souls of mortals were uplifted by your intercession, attempted to fetter the strong house so that it might shatter the vessel[45] that it was unable, repelled at every opportunity, to bring under its control. So it finally directed at you an arrow, secretly and from a gloomy place but without danger to your soul, over which it had no power. It therefore straightaway attacked your entire family more maniacally, wishing to satiate the depravity of an extended accumulation of hunger with funeral rites. And what must be lamented is that it killed many of its own people when they lost your protection.[46] For while a mother, while a sister, while servants and those who through you already had trampled upon what they feared, occupied you, that infirmity, overpowered by gold and silver vessels,[47] shattered any that were common and earthen[48] by snatching some of them who lacked the protection of baptism because

---

41. For a complementary example, see Jerome, *Epist.* 106.1, to the Gothic priests Sunnias and Fretela, "quis hoc crederet, ut barbara Getarum lingua Hebraicam quaereret veritatem?" [who would believe this, that the barbaric tongue of the Goths would seek Hebrew truth?]; on which see M. Metlen, "The Letter of St. Jerome to the Gothic Clergymen Sunnia and Friþila concerning Places in Their Copy of the Psalter," *Journal of English and Germanic Philology* 36 (1937): 515–42.

42. Cf. 1 Cor. 14:18.

43. For disruption caused by bandits, note the examples of the Vargi in chapter 2 and of Coroticus in chapter 4.

44. Ps. 4:8.

45. Cf. Ps. 31:12.

46. That is, the demon-induced plague killed pagans who would have been saved through Cerasia's ministrations had she not fallen ill.

47. That is, those individuals who had been baptized.

48. Cf. 2 Cor. 4.7.

they previously had been unable to come into your presence. . . . For you are a defense for the guilty and a model for the innocent, so that a faithful person cannot gain glory without imitating you, and an unfaithful one will not obtain pardon without your prayers. Moreover, what other person can be so easily found who is so much a leader of the good people or a patron of the wretched?[49] For those you inspire, these you cherish; you live with those, you pray for these. Thus you already are established as an model of virtue, because you do not fail in your duty toward the fallen.

This eulogy portrays Cerasia not only doing charitable work in the church, but also undertaking the responsibility of converting pagan Romans and barbarians to the Christian faith, although in these instances she could not, of course, perform the actual baptisms herself, but had to call upon male Christian clerics. Furthermore, Eutropius's reference to "those barbarians of yours" [*barbaris vestris*] indicates that Cerasia had some particular personal concern for them. Perhaps they were barbarian *hospites* (guests) who had been settled on her own property.

As for the plague and famine, this report has striking similarities to the Spanish chronicler Hydatius's account of the year 410:

While the barbarians were rampaging through Spain and the evil of pestilence ravaged no less . . . a dire famine prowled; such was the force of hunger that human flesh was devoured by humankind, and mothers feasted on the bodies of their own children, who had been butchered and roasted. Wild beasts, accustomed to eating those killed by sword, famine, and plague, killed even the stronger men.[50]

---

49. *Dux . . . patrona:* customarily epithets of aristocrats.

50. Hydatius, *Chron.* 48, "Debacchantibus per Hispanias barbaris et saeviente nihilominus pestilentiae malo . . . fames dira grassatur adeo ut humanae carnes ab humano genere vi famis fuerint devoratae: matres quoque necatis vel coctis per se natorum suorum sint pastae corporibus. bestiae, occisorum gladio fame pestilentia cadaveribus adsuetae, quosque hominum fortiores interimunt . . ." For plagues, see J.-N. Biraben and J. Le Goff, "The Plague in the Early Middle Ages," in *Biology of Man in History,* ed. R. Forster and O. Ranum (Baltimore: Johns Hopkins University Press, 1975), 48–80. For famine in the later fifth century, period, see Ralph W. Mathisen, "Nature or Nurture—Some Perspectives on the Gallic Famine of Circa A.D. 470," *Ancient World* 24 (1993): 91–105.

Rhetoric aside, Cerasia's activities therefore may belong in the context of the barbarian arrival in Spain as of 409, and the barbarians in question therefore perhaps were the pagan Alans or Suevi, rather than the Arian Vandals.[51]

The Conversion of Clovis

The conversion to Nicene Christianity of the pagan Frankish king Clovis in the late 490s, meanwhile, represented a recognition of political reality for him, and resulted in a public-relations windfall for Gallic bishops.[52] Shortly thereafter, Bishop Avitus of Vienne wrote to congratulate him on his acceptance of the Nicene faith, and to exhort him to promote its spread.

5.5[53]   Avitus, bishop of Vienne, to King Clovis.

The adherents of certain heresies seemed to enveloped the sharpness of Your Subtlety by a darkening of the Christian name with their beliefs, which were varied in opinion, diverse in their multitude, empty of truth. But whereas we commit these issues to eternity and whereas we trust that the truth of each man's belief will appear at the future judgment, even in the present the gleaming ray of truth has shone forth. Divine foresight has found an arbiter for our times. When you made your choice, you decided for us all. Your faith is our victory. Many people, in this same situation, if for the sake of seeking safety of belief they are advised either by the exhortation of bishops or by the suggestions of certain of their friends, are accustomed to raise in objection the traditions of their people and the customs of their ancestral practices, thus preferring injurious propriety to salvation. At the same time that they observe a futile reverence for their ancestors through their adherence to their incredulity they confess, in some manner, that they do not know what choice they should make. After the miracle of your action, therefore, harmful seemliness can abandon this excuse. Content to retain your nobility alone from all your lineage of ancient origin, you wanted to generate for your people on your account what-

---

51. See P. Courcelle, "Sur quelques textes littéraires relatifs aux grandes invasions," *Revue belge* 13 (1953): 21.

52. For the role of Clovis's wife Clotilde in his conversion, see the following chapter.

53. Avit. *Epist.* 46: *MGH AA* 6.2.75–76; for another translation, see Hillgarth, *Conversion of Western Europe,* 75–77.

ever can embellish the height of complete nobility. You have [as ancestors] the creators of good things, you wanted yourself to be better. You resemble your ancestors in that you reign in this world; you instruct your descendents in that you reign in heaven. Let Greece therefore rejoice that it has a ruler of our faith,[54] but no longer does Greece alone merit being ennobled by the gift of such a great service, because the faith's brilliance also is not lacking in the rest of the world, inasmuch as, in the person of a king who is not new, the light of a new sun shines in western regions. Fittingly, the birthday of our redeemer inaugurated its splendor, so that the rejuvenating waters correspondingly brought you forth to salvation on the very day when the world received the Lord of heaven, born for its redemption.[55] Therefore, the [day] that is celebrated as the Lord's birthday also is yours,[56] on which you certainly were born to Christ, as Christ likewise was born to the world; on it you consecrated your soul to God, your life to your contemporaries, and your glory to your descendents.

What can be said about the glorious solemnity of your regeneration? Even if I was not present corporally among its ministers, I nevertheless was not absent from the sharing of its joy, inasmuch as the divine piety also added this degree of rejoicing from our territories, in that before your baptism a messenger of Your Most Sublime Humility came to us announcing that you were seeking baptism. Whence, after this anticipation, the sacred night found us already confident in you. We conferred and considered among ourselves regarding what it was like when the crowd of assembled bishops, in their pursuit of holy servitude, bathed your royal limbs in the life-giving waters when that head, feared by barbarian peoples, bowed itself before the servants of God; when the salutary protection of the holy oil enveloped the flowing hair under your helmet; when, with the covering of your breastplate removed, your immaculate limbs gleamed with a whiteness like that of your vestments. That soft raiment will cause, if you have any faith, most flourishing of kings, it will cause, I say, the force of your arms in turn to be stronger, and whatever good fortune has provided up to now, sanctity will augment in the future.

But I would like to add some sort of advice to your praises in case

---

54. The Byzantine emperor Anastasius (491–518), suspected of having Monophysite sympathies, had been compelled to support the Nicene Creed.

55. Clovis was baptized at Reims on Christmas Day.

56. I.e., Christmas, the day Clovis was baptized.

anything has escaped either your knowledge or your attention. Should I preach to a purified one a faith that you perceived without a preacher before your purification? Or, perhaps, a humility that you, who only now owe it through your confession, already have devotedly expended upon us for a long time? Or a mercy that a captive people, recently freed by you, makes known with delight to the world and with tears to God? There thus is one thing that I would want to be amplified: that, because God will make your people totally his through you, you extend to the foreign nations,[57] which, living hitherto in a natural state of ignorance, no seeds of depraved teachings[58] have corrupted, sprouts of faith from the righteous treasure of your heart. Nor should it be irksome or embarrassing for you, having sent delegations[59] to them, to expand the realm of God, who has so greatly supported your realm, inasmuch as foreign pagan peoples, too, for the first time on the verge of serving, through you, the power of religion whereas hitherto they seem to have had a different disposition, notice the nation rather than the ruler.[60]

Clovis's subsequent actions were consistent with this advice. In 507 he defeated the Arian Visigoths and fostered the spread of Nicene Christianity throughout most of Gaul.

Guess Who's Coming to Dinner

Of course, Nicene ecclesiastics still had to deal with heterodox Christians, both Romans and barbarians, on an individual basis. In spite of some conventional disapprobation of "heretics," it seems that heresy, such as Arianism, often was not perceived as posing a great threat to the Nicene majority. Gregory of Tours provides an anecdote about a dinner party, perhaps dating to the first half of the sixth century, that united a Nicene woman, her Arian husband, and priests of both faiths:

---

57. Not only other bands of Franks, not yet assimilated by Clovis, but also other peoples, such as the Thuringians.

58. That is, they were still pagan and had not been converted to heterodox Christianity, presumably Arianism.

59. For later Frankish missionary work, see William H. C. Frend, "The Missions of the Early Church, 180–700 A.D.," in *Miscellanea historiae ecclesiasticae III. Colloque de Cambridge 24–28 septembre 1968,* ed. Derek Baker (Louvain: University of Louvain, 1970), 3–23.

60. The remainder of the letter is lost.

5.6[61] Heresy, in fact, is always inimical to Catholics, and it does not neglect to extend its intrigues wherever it can, just as in this case, which a tale commonly reports[62] occurred in a certain place. There was a certain Catholic woman who had a heretic[63] as a husband. When an exceptionally Catholic priest of our religion came to her, the woman said to her husband, "I pray Your Charity that because of the arrival of this prelate, who deigned to visit me, we have a celebration in the house, and that we eat with him a meal prepared with appropriate outlay." Furthermore, after her husband promised that he would do just as she had asked, there arrived another priest, of the heretics, and the man said to his wife, "Today the celebration is doubled because priests of both religions are in our home." Then, when they reclined for dinner, the husband and his priest occupied the right cusp of the table, placing the Catholic priest at the left, with a chair placed at his left in which his wife sat. The husband said to the heretical priest, "If you concur with my idea, let's have a good laugh[64] today at the expense of this Roman priest, so that when each course is laid down, you quickly hasten to bless it, and when he does not put out his hand, we shall eat the food with pleasure while he laments." He replied to him, "I will do as you request." Then, when the plate with the vegetables[65] arrived, the heretic blessed it and placed his hand upon it first. When the wife saw this, she said, "Don't do that, because I resent this offense to my prelate." And then another dish was brought out and the Catholic ate it. But the heretic did the same to the second and the third course. Moreover, when the fourth was brought out, in the midst of which lay a steaming frying-pan in which the food was arranged, which consisted of flour mixed a bit with beaten eggs, garnished in the usual way with sliced dates and round olives,[66] the heretic blocked the dish with his raised hand and hastily blessed it before it even touched the table. He

61. Greg.Tur. *Glor.mart.* 79; for another translation, see *Glory of the Martyrs,* trans. Raymond Van Dam (Liverpool: Liverpool University Press, 1988), 101–3.

62. *Fama refert;* the story even then may have been apocryphal.

63. That is, an Arian. This could suggest that the husband was a barbarian (of uncertain ethnicity, as the provenance of this tale is unknown).

64. *Cachinnum,* a rare word. It would seem that Gregory had before him Sidonius Apollinaris's *Epist.* 1.11.10–12, which not only discussed seating arrangements at dinner parties (the consul lay "first on the left cusp," and the emperor reclined "on the right"), but also had this uncommon word in the very next sentence.

65. *Holeribus,* perhaps cabbage, i.e., a salad.

66. The ingredients—eggs, flour, and various additions—and the need to eat quickly suggest that the dish was a soufflé.

immediately picked up the spoon, not knowing whether it was hot, and speedily swallowed the steaming food. Immediately, with his chest burning, he began to boil, and after letting out a groan with a great belch from his stomach, he breathed out his worthless spirit. Taken from the banquet and placed in the grave, he was covered up with the mass of a mound of earth. Then, gloating, the priest of our religion said, "Truly, God has avenged his servants." And turning to the man whose banquet this was, he said, "His memory perished with that sound,[67] and 'the Lord shall endure forever.'[68] Now then, serve something I can eat." Then that man was terrified, and when the banquet was finished, he threw himself at the feet of the priest. Having converted to the Nicene faith, he and his household, which had been gripped by that perfidy, believed, and the celebration was multiplied, just as his wife had entreated earlier.

Parts of this account are a bit ludicrous, such as burying the Arian priest and then heading right back to dinner, but other elements ring true, such as the matter-of-fact manner in which interactions among Nicenes and Arians are portrayed. Apparently there was nothing unseemly about members of the two faiths, and even clerics, not only fraternizing but even having dinner together. And in this regard, this account also gives a quite proper account of seating arrangements at Roman dinner parties. The men reclined on a couch or couches arranged in semicircular fashion. The host was placed on the right cusp, as here, and the guest of honor on the left. This indicates that the Nicene priest, not the Arian, was favored, although whether because of his age, because he had arrived first, or for some other reason, one cannot say. Women, at least in this case, were seated.

The Christian Way of Life

Culture Shock

The comprehensive adoption of a Christian lifestyle entailed, at least overtly, a change in intellectual attitude. Some zealous Christian intel-

---

67. Cf. the sound associated with the healing of the pagan by Eutropius above.
68. Ps. 9:7.

lectuals purported to abandon classical learning altogether. In a letter to Eustochium, a virgin of Rome, St. Jerome told of having a dream in which he was rebuked for not having done so fervently enough:

.7[69] (30) Many years ago, when for the kingdom of heaven's sake I had cut myself off[70] from home, parents, sister, relations, and—more difficult still—from the dainty food to which I had been accustomed, and when I was on my way to Jerusalem to wage my warfare, I still could not bring myself to forego the library that I had formed for myself at Rome with great care and toil. And so, miserable man that I was, I would fast only that I might afterward read Cicero. After many nights spent in vigil, after the tears that the recollection of my past sins called from my inmost heart, I would once more take up Plautus in my hands. And when at times I returned to my right mind, and began to read the prophets, their style seemed rude. I failed to see the light with my blinded eyes; but I attributed the fault not to them, but to the sun. While the old serpent was thus making me his plaything, about the middle of Lent a fever deep in my marrow fell upon my weakened body, and as it destroyed my rest—the story seems hardly credible—it so wasted my unhappy frame that scarcely anything was left of me but bone. Meanwhile, preparations for my funeral went on. As my whole body cooled, the warmth of life beat only in my throbbing breast. Suddenly I was caught up in the spirit and dragged before the tribunal of a judge, and here the light was so bright, and those who stood around were so radiant, that I cast myself upon the ground and did not dare to look up. Asked about my status, I replied, "I am a Christian." But He who presided said, "You lie, you are a follower of Cicero and not of Christ. For 'where thy treasure is, there will thy heart be also.'"[71] Instantly I became dumb, and amid the strokes of the lash—for he had ordered me to be scourged—I was tortured more severely still by the fire of conscience, considering with myself that verse, "In Hell who shall give thee thanks?"[72] Yet for all that I began to cry and to bewail

---

69. Jerome, *Epist.* 22: *CSEL* 54:143–200; translation based on W. H. Fremantle, *Jerome, Library of the Nicene and Post-Nicene Fathers*, vol. 6 (New York, 1893), 35–36.

70. The verb *castrare* is particularly graphic and underscores the irrevocability of Jerome's decision.

71. Matt. 6:21.

72. Ps. 6:6.

myself, saying, "Have mercy upon me, O Lord, have mercy upon me."[73] Amid the sound of the scourges this cry still echoed. At last, the bystanders, falling down before the knees of Him who presided, prayed that He would have pity on my youth, and that He would give me space to repent of my error. He might still, they urged, inflict torture should I ever again read the works of the Gentiles.[74] Under the stress of that moment I was ready to make even greater promises. Accordingly, I made an oath and called upon His name, saying, "Lord, if ever again I possess worldly books, or if ever again I read such, I have denied Thee." Dismissed, then, on taking this oath, I returned to the upper world, and, to the surprise of all, I opened upon them eyes so drenched with tears that my distress served to convince even the incredulous. And that this was no sleep nor idle dream, such as those by which we are often mocked, I call to witness the tribunal before which I lay, and the terrible judgment that I feared. May it never, hereafter, be my lot to fall under such an inquisition! I profess that my shoulders were black and blue, that I felt the bruises long after I awoke from my sleep, and that thenceforth I read the books of God with a zeal greater than I had previously given to the books of men.

Yet, in spite of his dream, Jerome, like all educated Christian writers, found it quite impossible to abandon his literary models.

A Woman's Perspective

From approximately the same time, place, and social milieu as the letter to Cerasia comes an enigmatic letter (which survives only in one manuscript, the Codex Sangallensis 190 of ca. 800) addressed by one aristocratic woman, otherwise unknown,[75] to another. The author of the letter, replying to a previous equally laudatory letter, provides a uniquely feminine perspective on the significance of the adoption of the Christian lifestyle, an ideology for which nearly all of the attestations are male.

---

73. Ps. 56:2.

74. That is, pagans.

75. The suggestion of Egeria, the Spanish or Gallic author of a late-fourth-century *Itinerary,* as the author has been made, but this is the sheerest of speculation made in virtually total ignorance about female literary circles in Late Antiquity.

§.8[76] Unless you had interpreted my silence, from such a source,[77] as an injury to yourself, I would have thought that the prophetic sentiment applied to me, which says, "If you have something to say, respond at the first opportunity; but if not, keep your hand over your mouth."[78] Indeed, how can I answer you, or, whence can I grasp the words to speak? For in the discourse of your letter you have embraced in such a manner the total body of Scripture[79] that you have left nothing for me to say. Until now, the treasury of the Testament—that is,[80] the binding of your heart, in which an entire library of books is amassed—has been hidden from me. It truly deserved to be gilded both inside and out with the exquisite material that protects so faithfully the words written by the finger of God. Indeed, the prophetic testimony was merited by that bride-to-be in the mystery of Christ who satiated the thirsting servant of Abraham with the water of the ewer that she lowered from her shoulders.[81] But you, no less than she, must be endowed with praises and sanctified by sentiments, you who have satiated me, a servant of Abraham (because each one who sins is a servant), from the ewer of your heart—that is, from "the treasure of an earthen vessel."[82] Certainly, I have drunk from the words you have written, and I have watered my camels[83]—that is, I recognized all my sins, because I have found none of those things that you thought were in me. But it is remarkably clear that you have compensated for my infelicity and ignorance in your writing, and that whatever the care of daily labor imposes upon you, you have put all this in support of me. Indeed, I

---

76. *Epist.* "Nisi tanti seminis": G. Caspari, ed., *Briefe, Abhandlungen, und Predigten* (Christiania, 1890), 398–404 (placed in Gaul); *MGH Epist.* 3:716–18 (dated to A.D. 500/600); G. Morin, "Pages inédites de deux pseudo-Jérômes des environs de l'an 400," *Revue bénédictine* 40 (1928): 289–318 (dated to ca. A.D. 400, from the region of the Pyrenees). For another translation, see M. Thiébaux, *The Writings of Medieval Women* (New York: Garland, 1987), 57–62.

77. The words "tanti seminis" are difficult; Morin emends to "tantis minis" (with such threats).

78. The Wisdom of ben Sirah 5:12 (an apocryphal book of scripture).

79. "Canonis": in this context, *canon* could refer either to the canonical books of the Bible or to the "rule" for leading a Christian life. If the former, it is ironic that the preceding sentence quotes from an apocryphal work.

80. *Hoc est:* a favorite locution of the author.

81. Rebecca: Gen. 24:45–46.

82. 2 Cor. 4:7.

83. Again, Gen. 24:46: "And she made haste, and let down her pitcher from her shoulder, and said, 'Drink, and I will give thy camels drink also': so I drank, and she made the camels drink also."

ought to be such a one as you think that I am, because "All things are possible to him that believeth."[84] But, whereas I can come near to desiring this, it is straightway impossible to accomplish it. But both things exist in you, and both prosper. I certainly know why the prophet said, "Behold, a virgin shall conceive in her womb and bear a son."[85] You can freely proclaim, "I have conceived in my womb, Lord, and I have given birth to the spirit of your salvation that you have made over the earth."[86] You have given birth to the word of God, you have delivered His discourse, thus you are in labor with the knowledge of God for us, so that you are always magnified and pregnant in yourself. Let them know, those who doubt, how a virgin can conceive and how she can give birth. And let them read your writings, because here is the undefiled fecundity of the virgin birth. For you, truly, is the example of Sarah: after seven husbands—that is, spirits of the world—had died, when she married Christ with an angel serving as bridesmaid, the enemy then succumbed.[87] For my unworthy self, however, it is necessary to pray to my father that I might lament my virginity before I can discharge the promises of the paternal lips, because until now I display no fruit of my virtue in the sight of the Lord.[88] Indeed, my father slew the Moabites and Ammonites—that is, he destroyed the nature of drunkenness and fornication in me. But what does it profit me if I do not have the word of God in my womb—that is, in my heart? And I know that virginity alone, without knowledge, walks in shadow and does not know the light. And one possessing the name only without the deeds in no way crosses the threshold of the betrothal canopy. Drained by the dryness of my wick, I bear the oil lamp of my throat—that is, it is filled by the frivolity of empty words, with regard to which I know that I am unworthy, because the richness of knowledge does not anoint it. I even implore you, who are rich in oil, to point out from whom I ought to acquire it. But sometimes now I will say what Job said to the

---

84. Mark 9:23.

85. Isa. 7:14.

86. A variation on Isa. 26:18.

87. See Tob. 3:7–17. The canonicity of the book of Tobit was denied in the east but accepted in the west. The first seven husbands of the Mede Sarah had been killed on their wedding night by the demon Asmodaeus, who later was overcome by the angel Raphael. See Judg. 11:29–40. The Israelite Jephthah promised God to sacrifice the first thing he saw at home if he could defeat the Ammonites: it was his virgin daughter.

88. Cf. Matt. 25:8–9.

Lord, "What can I say when I hear such words, or what can I reply when I am nothing? But once I have spoken, I will not add anything again."[89] I certainly acknowledge that I am dust and ash because I see that the work of others is so great; I feel that there is nothing of them in me. In the example of the blessed Mary, the angel, that is, the spirit, appears to speak with you because you are learned in such language. Watch over, indeed, watch over, you who must be called not sister but lady, that which the shrine of your heart has conceived, and the fruit of your womb has poured forth, so that you might parade and display your son in Egypt—that is, you display the fruit of your teaching to us living in the darkness of the secular world. Have no doubt, I would say that you are one of the four prophesizing maidens[90] whom the author of the Acts of the Apostles discussed. Absolutely, you are indeed that one about whom the sacred singers have sung: you are "garbed with diversity in golden fringes."[91] In fact, what would I interpret as the golden fringes if not the beautiful and faithful writings of your perception, which gush and descend from each side of your mouth? There is in them a beautiful diversity because you paint the text of your letter in the manifold color of citations from the law, the prophets, and the evangelists. Certainly, it appears that you do not eat food at your ease, and inasmuch as that consort of yours, who was said to be the son of a carpenter, constructed a spindle for you from the wood of learning, with which you create from the plentiful wool of history a thread of spiritual words, I confess to you, venerable sister, that I would not have comprehended that prophetic dictum where it is said, "Grain for the youths, and sweet-smelling wine for the maidens,"[92] if I had not understood it from the virtue of your writings. You, indeed, are the one who has the sweet-smelling wine—that is, from the fruits of Christ, who is the true vine. You are exuberant in the joy of spiritual knowledge, which animates the interior of your innards with the juice of its sweetness and virtue. You emulate well that Shunammite maiden, the minister and guardian of the body of David,[93] you who by the insight

---

89. Cf. Job 40:4.
90. Acts 21:9.
91. Cf. Ps. 44:10.
92. Zech. 9:17.
93. 1 Kings 1:15: "And Bathsheba went in unto the king into the chamber: and the king was very old; and Abishag the Shunammite ministered unto the king."

of your intellect did not cease to warm and shelter the mature and perfected royal knowledge. Already you have attained a reward for this attentiveness by receiving his keys, with which you open that which no one closes, and close that which no one opens. In you, the son of Bathsheba—that is, of wisdom—has that which he greatly desires, that a false brother neither desire nor touch you. Truly, your venerable sanctity writes this to me because I have hidden the garment that girded my loins in a hollow of the rock above the river Euphrates.[94] I recognize this: that as a result of the worldly precipice and the hardness of my heart, the coverings of my virtue have been torn away, and now, denuded of the protection of wisdom, I am not seen to be despoiled of the ancient man.[95] But because both the ignorance of my heart and the grief of maternal suffering now hinder my tongue, and the sadness of my heart scarcely permits this little bit to be said, I ask that you frequently apply to the dry roots of my perception a basket of manure—that is, the richness of your words—so that when you visit me, as is your custom, you will find in me the fruit of your good work.

This letter by a woman learned in Scripture brings a woman's perspective to the religious life, not only by employing the examples of Mary, Rebecca, Sarah, Abishag, and Bathsheba, but also by seeing virginity as a form of fruitfulness, and looking at conception and birth from a metaphorical rather than a physical point of view.

The Making of a Bishop

The adoption of Christian mores had a significant effect not only on one's lifestyle, but also on one's professional opportunities. A career in the church became just as desirable as a secular one, if not even more so, and it was not uncommon for high-ranking government officials to transfer directly to church office *per saltum* (by a leap). The life of Bishop Germanus of Auxerre (ca. 418–46), written ca. 480 by the priest Constantius of Lyon, outlines some of the standard elements of an ecclesiastical career.

---

94. See Jer. 13:4, "Take the girdle that thou hast got, which is upon thy loins, and arise, go to Euphrates, and hide it there in a hole of the rock."

95. That is, she still bears the sin of Adam.

9[96] (1) Germanus, therefore, was a native of the town of Auxerre. He was born of parents of most exalted rank, and from his very earliest infancy he was instructed in liberal studies. In him the conferral of teaching, consistent with the abundance of his talent, rendered him learned with a double benefit, that is, of nature and of industry. And so that there would coalesce in him a full perfection of knowledge, after he was finished with the Gallic lecture halls he added to the fullness of his perfection the knowledge of law in the city of Rome. Subsequently, serving as an advocate, he adorned the tribunals of the prefecture.[97] In this capacity, while he was shining with the light of multifarious praise, he obtained a wife who was outstanding in family background, wealth, and character.[98] Forthwith, the Republic promoted him, as he excelled in civil service, to the insignia of office by conferring upon him the eminence of a dukedom and authority over several provinces.[99] He truly was being trained by the hidden judgment of the divinity, so that no element of perfection would be lacking for this apostolic bishop-to-be. Eloquence was provided for his sermons, knowledge of law for his justice, and the company of a wife as a testimony to his chastity. (2) Then, suddenly, the divine authority, which the consensus of all put into effect, sprang forth, for all the clerics and the entire nobility, the plebs both urban and rustic, were united in one opinion: the united voice of all demanded Germanus as bishop. War was declared on the state official, whom it was easy to subdue, because he was assaulted even by those who had supported him. He assumed the pontificate unwilling, compelled, appointed; and suddenly he was changed in all regards. The service of the world is abandoned, that of heaven is assumed. Secular ceremony is despised, the humility of conversion is embraced. His wife is transformed from a spouse into a sister, his wealth is dispensed to the poor, poverty is pursued. (3) Now, truly, it is impossible to describe the

---

96. *Vita Germani Autissiodorensis* (Life of Germanus of Auxerre), 1: *MGH SRM* 7:225–83; R. Borius, ed., *SC* 112 (Paris, 1965); for another translation, see Hoare, *The Western Fathers,* 281–320.

97. That is, he served as a legal specialist on the staff of the praetorian prefect, presumably of Gaul. The post of *advocatus* was a first rung on the ladder of advancement in the civil service.

98. This sounds like a typical sort of aristocratic marriage; his wife, according to a late source, was named Rustica.

99. Germanus probably was made "duke of the Armorican and Nervican Region," a military official who was in charge of the local militia in Brittany and Belgium and whose authority also was extended over several provinces of Aquitania and Lugdunensis.

force of the hostility that he inflicted upon himself; what crosses and what punishments this persecutor of his own body endured.

Along with the life of St. Martin of Tours, the life of Germanus went on to become a model for how to write a saint's life.

Remigius Vents His Spleen

Under barbarian rule, the process for choosing clerics sometimes had an extra step, for kings could take it upon themselves to recommend individuals for clerical posts, even for bishoprics. The case of the priest Claudius, whose name, at least, would suggest that he was a Roman, is instructive. Apparently, the Frankish king Clovis had prevailed upon his particular friend Bishop Remigius of Reims (ca. 480–533) to make Claudius a priest. The bishops Heraclius, Leo, and Theodosius objected, claiming that the appointment was scandalous. They further charged that Claudius had been involved in the abduction of a certain Celsus, whose property had been ransacked. They demanded that Remigius look into the matter. Remigius, meanwhile, already had assigned a penance to Claudius and had assumed that the matter was closed. In his reply, Remigius bitterly complained about colleagues whom he considered to be meddling busybodies.

5.10[100]   Bishop Remigius to his brothers Heraclius, Leo, and Theodosius, lords truly sanctified and meritorious, and most blessed in Christ.

The apostle Paul says in his letter, "Nothing surpasses charity."[101] This sentiment does not reside in your feelings, given that you send to me such a letter. For I uttered a simple plea on behalf of Claudius, whom you claim is no priest and as a result produce the indignation of your heart against me. I do not deny that he has sinned gravely, but it would have been fitting for you to respect my age, even if not my attainments, because, with the favor of God it might be said, "For fifty-three years I preside over an episcopal see,[102] and no one ever has addressed me so insolently." You say, "It would have been better had

---

100. Remigius of Reims, *Epist.* "Paulus apostolus" = *Epistulae Austrasicae* 3: *MGH Epist.* 3:114; Malaspina, *Liber epistolarum,* 64–65; *PL* 65:966–68.

101. 1 Cor. 13:8.

102. "Quinquaginta et tribus annis episcopali sede praesedeo": one would expect the verb "praesedi," "I have presided." If Remigius's tenure in office is in fact meant, then the letter would have been written ca. 533, at the very end of Remigius's life.

you not been born." This would have been a good thing for me, for I would not have heard the abuse of a transgressor. I made Claudius a priest, not having been corrupted by a bribe, but on the recommendation of our most excellent king, who was[103] not only the promulgator but also the defender of the Catholic faith. You write, "What you ordered was not canonical; we bishops exercise the greatest priesthood." But it was the ruler of the regions, the guardian of the homeland, the victor over barbarians who ordered it. Have you attacked me incited by such great spleen that you have no respect for the initiator of your own episcopates? I asked that Claudius, the perpetrator of sacrilege, be redeemed through penitence. For we read, we read, that the Ninevites evaded the destruction prophesied by celestial threat through penitence, about which John, the precursor of the Lord, spoke in his Gospel,[104] so that as the kingdom of heaven drew near, the people might perform it and not perish. In the Apocalypse to the messengers of the churches it is written at the command of the Lord Savior that the things they do that are unfitting they may correct through penitence.[105] I understand from the furious statements of Your Sanctity that you have no sympathy for a sinner after his disgrace, but I see that you rather wish that he not reform and find life, even though the Lord said, "I do not wish the death of one who is dying, but that he reform and find life."[106] It profits us to follow this teaching, and not to ignore the will of the Lord, but to grasp it, because he has placed us here not for fury but for the care of humanity and to serve piety rather than rage. You charge in your letter that a certain Celsus, who trusted Claudius, has been kidnapped and that you are unaware whether he is living or dead, and you demand that I investigate this matter. You do not know whether he is to be sought in this world or in the underworld, and you desire me to restore his property, which I did not even know had been taken away. You demand the impossible, to the extent that you commit impiety. You write that my number of years is "jubilant,"[107] making fun rather than affectionately rejoicing. With the

103. *Erat:* because Remigius spoke of the king in the past tense, he must have meant Clovis (481–511); Clovis's son Theoderic I lived until 534.

104. Jon. 3.

105. Rev. 2:22.

106. Ezek. 18:23, 33:11.

107. *Iubeleus:* an insulting reference to either to Remigius's age or his tenure in office: *iubileus annus* also refers to the year of Jubilee among the Israelites; a jubilee was a period of fifty years.

bond of charity unscrupulously shattered, you neither spare me nor respect me.

It is finished.

Remigius's position represented one of the realities of the ecclesiastical world of Late Antiquity: secular rulers, be they Romans or barbarians, had oversight of the Christian Church. Some might be more benign than others, or more circumspect, but when they made a request such as Clovis had made of Remigius, it behooved the bishop to consider it very carefully, especially given that the Council of Orléans, convened by Clovis in 511, had specified that royal approval was needed before a layman could be ordained as a cleric.[108] Moreover, even metropolitans like Remigius faced the possibility of second-guessing and trouble-making by their suffragans in the same way that, like Sidonius in chapter 4, bishops encountered opposition from their own clergy.

Life in the Wilderness

Clerics such as bishops and priests remained "in the world," so to speak. Other religious, however, withdrew into the monastic life. Doing so was a portentous step. A whole ethos accompanied it. A description of what becoming a monk meant on a personal level—both intellectually and socially—is found in the *De laude eremi* (In praise of the wilderness), written in 427 by the monk Eucherius, later bishop of Lyon (ca. 430–50) and dedicated to his friend Hilary. Hilary had followed his countryman Honoratus when the latter founded the monastery at Lérins in the early fifth century. Honoratus became bishop of Arles in 426, and Hilary accompanied him there, only to return to the monastery in 427 for a while (the occasion of this tract) before ultimately succeeding Honoratus at Arles in 429.

5.11[109]   (1) Recently, having departed in high spirits from your home and your family, you penetrated all the way to the outlying places in the great sea;[110] you now have sought the wilderness again with an even greater

---

108. *Corp. chr. lat.* 148A.6.

109. Eucherius, *De laude eremi* (In praise of the wilderness): S. Pricoco, ed., *Eucherii. De laude eremi* (Catania: University of Catania, 1965); for French translation, see L. Cristiani, *Saint Eucher de Lyon: Du mépris du monde* (Paris: Nouvelles éditions latines, 1950), 67–89.

110. The islands of Lero (Ste-Marguerite) and Lerinum (Lérins or St-Honorat), upon which the monastery was established, lie off the coast of southern France near Fréjus.

virtue. When you first entered it as a stranger, you had a leader and so-to-speak guide for your journey whom, as a master of the celestial service, you then followed, and even if you left your parents behind, you nonetheless followed a parent. Now, indeed, after you thought that the same adoptive parent had to be followed to the pontifical dignity, love of the wilderness recalls you to the familiar isolation. Therefore, you now are greater and nobler in this manner: indeed, when you initially sought the desert, you seemed in fact to accompany a brother; now, when you return to the desert, you have in fact left behind a brother. And what and how great a brother! One always honored by you with such great cherishing of esteem! One attached to you by such a singular affection! And one whose love you prefer over everything except perhaps only the love of the wilderness! Although you prefer this to him with a thoughtful rationale, you assert that you do not love him too little, but that you love the wilderness in some way more. You have shown how great that love of isolation is in you, to which even the greatest person yields. Indeed, what must this love of the wilderness in you be called if not the love of God? You therefore have preserved the rule of love prescribed by law by esteeming God first, then your kinsman. . . . (3) And although, rich in Christ, you long since poured forth your wealth on behalf of the poor of Christ, then, too, you reveal yourself to be elderly in character even if youthful in years. Indeed, you may be in talent distinguished and distinguished in eloquence, but I admire and love in you in the first place nothing more than that you yearn for the place of solitude. Therefore, because you repeatedly demand that I respond most fulsomely to your most lengthy and erudite letters, it is necessary that you, in your wisdom, endure my foolishness for a little while as I recollect the multifaceted favor of the Lord toward this beloved wilderness of yours. . . .[111]

(31) Who, indeed, can fittingly enumerate the benefits of the wilderness, and the advantages of the virtue of those residing within it? Dwelling in the world, in some way they withdraw from the world: "They wander in deserts," as the apostle says, "and in mountains, and in dens and caves of the earth."[112] Not inappropriately does this apostle deny that the world is suitable for such men, who are alien from that tumult of the human republic: withdrawn, tranquil, silent, they are no

---

111. There follow many biblical examples before Eucherius finally gets down to the business of describing Lérins itself.

112. Heb. 11:38, by the apostle Paul.

more removed from the ability than from the will to sin. (32) In the past, the distinguished men of this world, worn out by the labors of their occupations, used to retire to philosophy as if to their own home.[113] How much more splendidly do they now turn to these studies of the most manifest wisdom and withdraw more magnificently to the freedom of solitude and the isolation of deserts, so that, taking their ease only in philosophy, they are exercised in the corridors of this wilderness just as if they were in their academies? . . . (35) The salubriously engraved precepts of the interior man blaze there, as do, more subtly, the laws of the eternal age. There the human ordinances of accusations and crimes do not transmit their force and assert avenging laws concerning capital crimes. . . .[114]

(41) You rightly stand out, therefore, most revered terrain, recently become habitable and desirable to saints either stationed upon you or not far removed from you, because you are fertile with regard to the universal benefits of Him in whom all things are encompassed. . . . (42) Truly, I owe reverence to all the deserted places that are illumined by the withdrawal of pious persons, but I embrace my Lérins with particular esteem. At a time when the shipwrecks of a stormy world are poured forth, she receives in most conscientious arms those coming from it. Those burning in the heat of the world she gently guides into her shade, so that there those who are gasping can restore their spirits in that interior shade of the Lord. Bubbling with brooks, verdant with foliage, blooming with blossoms, pleasing with sights and smells, she shows herself to those in possession of her to be the paradise that they will possess. Deserving, she who was established in the celestial disciplines by the founder Honoratus; she who, after such a great beginning, obtained such a great father, who blazed forth with the vigor of an apostolic mien and spirit. Deserving, she who after receiving him sent him forth in such a way.[115] Deserving, she who both nourishes the most outstanding monks and produces the most coveted bishops. She now embraces by name his successor, Maximus,[116] distinguished because he merited being appointed after him. She held Lupus of the

---

113. For the aristocratic withdrawal to the philosophic life, see chapter 1.

114. A hint here that some of those who took refuge in the monastery might have been escaping criminal charges, which may have accrued as a result of the Gallic usurpations of Constantine III (407–11) and Jovinus (411–13).

115. That is, to be bishop of Arles.

116. A native of Riez who entered the monastery after a secular, possibly legal, career.

revered name, who rendered to us that wolf from the tribe of Benjamin.[117] She had his brother Vicentius,[118] a brilliant gem with an internal splendor. She now possesses Caprasius,[119] venerable in gravity and the equal of the ancient saints. She has now those saintly elders, who in their separate cells have imported the Egyptian fathers[120] to our Gaul. (43) Good Jesus, I saw them there, a gathering and congregation of saints! . . . (44) Returned and inserted into the fellowship of these persons, my dearest Hilary, you have bestowed more upon yourself, and even more upon those who now rejoice with a ready exultation because of your return. Along with them, I beg you, do not erase the memory of my sins and of intercession for them; along with them, I say, among whom I do not know whether you yourself bestow or obtain more joy. You, who behold God in your heart, now are a truer Israel; recently vouchsafed from the shadows of the world in Egypt, having crossed the health-giving waters with the enemy submerged, having followed the fire of faith ignited in the desert, you now experience pleasures through the wood of the cross; you draw the waters springing from Christ for eternal life, you nourish the internal man with the heavenly bread, you receive the divine voice of thunder in the gospel; you who are confined with Israel in the wilderness will enter the promised land with Jesus.
Farewell in Christ Jesus our Lord.

For these aristocrats, life in the monastery meant not only the adoption of a new Christian ideology but also a continuation of the comradeship, opportunity for advancement, and sense of elitism that they had shared in secular life.

Amanda Shoulders the Load

Sometimes adopting the ecclesiastical, and especially the monastic, life could have consequences on one's familial relationships. As seen

---

117. The word *lupus* means "wolf": see Gen. 49:27, "Benjamin shall raven as a wolf." Lupus came to Lérins from Troyes in 425 and returned home two years later to become bishop; he was married to Hilary's sister Pimeniola.

118. Another former secular official, he had come to Lérins with Lupus. He later wrote the *Commonitorium* (Reminder), a handbook on how to distinguish orthodoxy from heresy.

119. Cofounder of the monastery along with Honoratus.

120. *Patres:* their identity is unknown.

above, Salvian of Marseille became estranged from his in-laws, and the wife of Germanus of Auxerre became his "sister." Other cases could involve some role reversal. One such concerned Amanda, the wife of the ex-advocate and ex-governor Aper.[121]

The two wrote several letters regarding their situation to the expatriate Gaul Pontius Meropius Paulinus, who ca. 395 had become bishop of Nola in Italy. Paulinus's responses give additional insight into the give-and-take that went on between married persons. Even though they reflect many of the paternalistic and chauvinistic attitudes of the age, they also demonstrate that it was Amanda who was doing the work while Aper took his monastic leisure.

Paulinus's reply to their first letter outlines their problem: "You write that you are hindered from achieving your vocation through looking after your possessions and your sons. They make it essential for you to devote your attention to worldly matters when you long for heavenly ones."[122] Apparently, Aper and Amanda had intended to enter the religious life jointly, like Paulinus and his own wife Therasia had done, but their secular concerns inhibited them from doing so. Paulinus's second letter suggests a solution:

5.12[123]   The sinners Paulinus and Therasia greet their holy, rightly revered, and dearly beloved brethren Aper and Amanda.

(1) O that someone would give me literary resources like yours, so that I could adequately reply to your letter! Interwoven with the diverse blooms of spiritual graces, eloquent with the language not of secular learning but of God, it flowed with the milk of God's love and the honey of wisdom as though coming from the land of promise. . . .[124]

(3) . . . In your letter, too, your wife, who does not lead her husband to effeminacy or greed, but brings you back to self-discipline and courage to become the bones of her husband,[125] is worthy of admiration because of her great emulation of God's marriage with the church.

---

121. Note the similarity of Aper's early career path to that of Germanus above.

122. "Nam quod scribitis inpedimenta vestri esse propositi possessionis et filiorum curam, qui causa sint necessitatis istius qua terrena curatis, cum caelestia desideretis" (Paulinus of Nola, *Epist.* 39: *CSEL* 29:334); for translation, see *The Letters of St. Paulinus of Nola,* trans. P. G. Walsh, vol. 2 (Westminster, Md.: Newmann, 1967), 196.

123. Paulinus of Nola, *Epist.* 44: *CSEL* 29:369–78; translation from *Letters of St. Paulinus of Nola,* 2.234–43.

124. There then follow four pages of ecclesiastical boilerplate.

125. From Augustine, *Epist.* 27.2; cf. Gen. 2:23.

She is restored and reinstated into unity with you, for Christ's love joins you with spiritual bonds that are all the stronger for being more chaste. You have passed from your own bodies into Christ's. . . .

(4) . . . See how you remain the married couple you were, yet not coupled as you were. You are yourselves yet not yourselves. Now you know each other, as you know Christ, apart from the flesh. . . .[126] Blessed is [Amanda] among women, faithful and most acceptable to the Lord by reason of that further dedication with which on your behalf she has confronted worldly needs as a tower founded on unbudging rock confronts storms. Established on that rock, on which a house once built shall not fall, with the steady immobility of her unremitting mind, she has become your "tower of strength against the face of the enemy";[127] she breaks the force of the worldly waves and whirlpools by interposing her holy slavery, so that you may be shielded from the sea and preserve your mind unshaken like a ship safe in the harbor of the church, plying the oars of salvation which are persistent meditation on studies and works of godliness. For "bodily exercise," says Scripture, "is profitable to little, whereas godliness is profitable to all things."[128] This godliness made you submit to Christ, for you preferred even to "lie abject in the house of the Lord rather than be prominent in the tabernacles of sinners,"[129] and bound your fellow servant Amanda to physical labors on behalf of your soul out of spiritual love for you, so that she might make her service the price of your freedom. In the transactions of the world she serves not the world but Christ, for whose sake she endures the world that you may avoid enduring it. Truly she has become the help to you that God's work and word prescribes. To you she turns, hanging on your nod,[130] standing where you stand, walking in your footsteps, enlivened by your spirit. She suffers need on behalf of your life, that she may be refashioned by it. She takes charge of secular business so that you may forget it; she handles it so that you may handle God's. She gives the appearance of having possessions[131] so

126. This is the same altered relation experienced by Germanus and his wife Rustica.

127. Ps. 60:4; also Matt. 7:24.

128. 1 Tim. 4:8.

129. Ps. 83:11.

130. Paulinus bolsters Aper's male pride.

131. Clearly, Aper and Amanda continued to possess property, an apparent violation of the topos that those truly dedicated to the religious life should divest themselves of their possessions. Few actually did.

that you may be possessed not by the world but by Christ. No discordant will severs her from your committed life; more remarkable, harmonious faith keeps her apart from your work but joins her to you in will. Uncaptured in mind, she carries out the tasks of captivity with freedom of spirit. . . . She makes the necessary division; through her own person she "renders to Caesar the things that are Caesar's," so that through you she may "provide God with the things that are God's."[132] For when, as scripture says, she has paid "tribute to whom tribute is due,"[133] then she "opens her hands to the needy."[134] By proffering the fruits of her work to the poor, she pays spiritual taxes and devotes the revenue from her possessions to your salary[135] as a soldier; for she is more greedy for the loss that brings salvation than for the gain that brings death. . . . You are her head in Christ, and she is your foundation. By her work, your foot stands on the Lord's path; and she will share your head because you are one framework of faith united in the body of the Lord. For although her preoccupations are different from yours, she keeps unaffected her mind in compliance and harmony with yours, agreeing with your decision to follow your vocation.

Paulinus's letter, larded with biblical citations and allusions (many of which are omitted in the above extract) so as to give it even greater authority, subordinates the aspirations of Amanda to those of her husband. However much he lauds her devotion to duty, it is still Aper who gets to be the monk, and she who gets to do the work. One wonders whether this settlement was as amicable as Paulinus portrays it. Or was his letter actually intended to respond to Amanda's objections?

Another consideration in a decision to adopt the religious life could be the nature of the barbarian settlement. This could be of particular concern in the north, where the barbarian impact had its initial and most devastating effect. Roman centers such as Trier and Cologne were occupied, and Roman society was terrifically disrupted. Most of those who could do so left; those who remained were compelled to fend for themselves.

An example of both eventualities is found in another letter of Sal-

---

132. Matt. 22:21.
133. Rom. 13:7.
134. Prov. 31:20.
135. *Stipendium:* this may mean that Amanda's income replaced Aper's state salary, or that it had to be repaid because Aper was no longer doing his military duty.

vian, himself a refugee from the north in the early fifth century. After a
stay at the monastery of Lérins he moved to Marseille. Later, perhaps
in the 430s, he wrote to his erstwhile brethren to ask a favor. And
because Salvian, whose haughtiness already has been portrayed above,
apparently had not left Lérins on the best of terms, going back hat in
hand seems to have stuck in his craw. The letter lacks a surviving salutation; it probably was addressed something like, "To the brethren of
Lérins."

3[136] (1) O Love, I know not what to call you, good or evil, sweet or bitter,
pleasant or unpleasant, for you are so filled with both qualities that
you seem to be both. It is proper to love our friends; it is bitter to
offend them. Yet there are times when this comes from the same mind,
from the same person. When there is discord in appearance, there is
concord in the soul. For love, indeed, makes us love our friends. Love
sometimes compels us to hurt them. These two are one and the same;
although one has the benefit of love, the other the offense of hate.

(2) How difficult, I ask, or how bitter it is, my dearest friends, when
love is forced to be the cause of hatred. I now am very much afraid
there has happened to me what has often happened to others, namely,
that being solicitous for one I may become irksome to many. When I
wish to hand over to my inseparable friends the young man I am sending to you, my love for him may be the cause of offense to others.[137]
But those who have enough love are not easily offended.

(3) While I am afraid that my recommendation might be less well
received by certain people, I think that their lack of good will is itself
an offense. Indeed, while desiring greatly to please my beloved ones, I
believe my offense annoys those others, and, unless I please them adequately, I will bear the penalty of one who displeases.[138]

(4) On this point, although among yourselves who so wholeheartedly received me in your midst there is no place whatever for fear, still,
in regard to others, you fear for me. My dearest and most beloved
friends, so far am I from being able to displease either your heart or
your head that you are afraid, as I am afraid, that I should displease
somebody else.

---

136. Salv. *Epist.* 1: *MGH AA* 1.1.108–9; translation based on *Writings of Salvian,* 237–40.
137. That is, those whom Salvian seems to have alienated at Lérins.
138. Once again, Salvian is never in the wrong and places any blame on his detractors.

(5) The young man whom I have sent you was, together with his people, captured at Cologne.[139] He at one time had no little fame among his friends. He is well-born and not insignificant in property, and I could perhaps say something more about him, were it not that he is my kinsman. Thus it happens that I say less than I could, lest I seem to speak about myself by speaking further about him. The young man about whom I speak left his mother, an upright and honored widow, at Cologne. She truly is a widow about whom I perhaps can speak in a forthright manner. In addition to her other virtues of chastity and wisdom, she is also noble in her faith, which is always the adornment of all adornments, because without faith there is nothing so adorned that one can adorn it.

(6) This woman, it is rumored, is in such great need and indigence there that she lacks the means either of staying or departing, because she has not enough either to live on or to flee. She is without the wherewithal requisite for livelihood or flight. The only thing left her is that, seeking food as pay for work, she has hired out her hands to the wives of the barbarians.[140] In this way, although by the mercy of God she has been exempt from the chains of captivity, she is a servant through poverty, but she is not reduced to the condition of slavery.

(7) The lady was not wrong in surmising that I possess the good will of some holy people here. Nor do I deny this, lest my denial seem ingratitude. It is clear that, while I do not deny that I possess it, I am quite sure that I do not deserve it, so much so that, although I do possess a measure of their good will, I, nevertheless, am not the cause of it. Whatever good will there is, it has been principally shown me, if I am not mistaken, on account of those who were interested that I should be well received. Consequently, it is perhaps to be feared that, in not acknowledging to them what I have received on their account, I should seem to be denying not so much what is mine but what is theirs. This lady, thinking that it was in my power or more than in my power to help, sent to me this young man whom I am sending to you, in the hope that through my agency and endeavors the good will of my friends would come to the aid of my relatives.[141]

---

139. This seems to mean that he was captured along with everyone else in Cologne, not that he personally was taken as a captive, as happened to the individuals in chapter 3.

140. An example of the economic distress that faced the Roman urban population at this time.

141. Salvian perhaps felt it is necessary to explain why the young man, whom he describes as rather prosperous, abandoned his mother when she was in such dire straits.

(8) Thus, I have done as I was asked to do, but I have done it charily and to few people, lest I should be ungracious in using this favor. I have commended this young man to others, as to you.[142] In the first place, it is not necessary to recommend overmuch a young man who is a relative of mine, no more than it would be necessary to recommend myself. Second, because you reckon me as one of yourselves, you must necessarily consider him who is a part of me somewhat as a part of yourselves. Lastly, my recommendation, being of a different kind, is also of a more excellent character.

(9) To others I have commended this young man in body, to you, in spirit; to others for the benefits of the present life, to you for the hope of eternity; to others on account of short-lived and earthly things, to you, for eternal and heavenly things. And rightly so. Because you are less solicitous for goods of the flesh than of the spirit, I have asked you for more of the latter, because you abound more in it.

(10) Therefore, I ask you, receive this young man as my flesh, and make him, so far as you can, one of your own. Lead and exhort him, teach, train, mold, and regenerate him. May the mercy of Christ our Lord grant that he who is kinsman to me and to the others, because it is more expedient for him, may begin to become kinsman to you, rather than to his own relatives.

(11) Admit him, I beseech you, into those blessed and eternal homes. Receive him into the sacred storehouses. Open to him the treasures of heaven, and so act and proceed that, while you store this young man among your treasures, you make him a part of these very treasures. Powerful is that kindness of the ineffable God that, by adopting him into the fellowship of spiritual goods, you, through him, increase the riches you lavish on him. Indeed, if there is some good natural qualification in him, his hope and salvation should not be of great difficulty to you. Even if he receives no teaching form you, surely the fact that he sees your example is sufficient.
Farewell.

It would seem that there were other factors at play here beyond Salvian's recommendation, or how well Salvian was liked back at Lérins. Salvian was at pains to stress the boy's good family ties and to hint at his ability to pay his own way (regardless of the poverty of his mother).

---

142. Salvian's comments below seem to indicate that these "others" are secular individuals.

Even if the boy's mother had been socially degraded as a result of the barbarian occupation, the family apparently still had hopes that something of the family ambitions could yet be salvaged if the boy could find a place in an influential aristocratic monastery.

Conclusion

The growth of the church and the spread of the Christian ethos created both changes and opportunities. In their conventional manifestations, the latter primarily benefited male aristocrats. But there were ways in which energetic women, too, could find fulfillment, not only in the world of the church, but in other arenas as well. This will be the topic of the next chapter.

CHAPTER 6

Elite Women: Roman Aristocrats and Barbarian Queens

As already seen, the activities of women usually were limited to their family circles and to family matters. Even then, there were restrictions on the extent to which women could exercise choices in two crucial issues: the choice of a mate and the disposition of their property. Some women engaged in the latter through charitable activities. And others, by capitalizing on the stature of their families, were able to play important roles in society and politics. In such cases, they too benefited from the upheaval resulting from the settlement of the barbarians and the growing prominence of the church.

Charitable Activities

The church offered wealthy women various opportunities for self-expression. This was certainly the case in the realm of charitable works. The benevolence of several women was recorded in the one venue where they were expected to proclaim their merits: their epitaphs.

A Model Woman of Marseille

The epitaph of Eugenia of Marseille was written in elegiac couplets inscribed on a marble sarcophagus, decorated with Christ and the apostles, with the hexameters on the left and the pentameters on the right. It cataloged the typical kinds of virtues that were expected of aristocratic women:

6.1[1]   + Noble Eugenia, born of aristocratic blood,
             who lived a life of merits, lies buried here.
          Dying, she departed life with its burdensome body
             so that she would better be able to enter the heavenly home.
          Prudent in spirit, she persevered in the strength of her character,
             Provident, she always embraced praiseworthy activity.
          Rejoicing, she quickly hastened to nourish the starving,
             hungering, O Paradise, for your feasts!
          With her wealth she loosed captives from their undeserved chains,
             and she repatriated those evicted from their homes.
          Her mind was intent on goodness throughout the whole course of
                her life,
             her only concern was to perform upright deeds.
          She slipped away after sixty years; her celebrated offspring,
             grieving with dutiful tears, entombed her here.

Eugenia, by engaging in *opus laudabilis* (praiseworthy activity), fulfilled society's expectation of a respectable aristocratic woman.

A Model Woman of Vienne

Dulcitia, a philanthropist[2] of Vienne, in death advertised her charitable works in an epitaph of the sixth century:

6.2[3]   In this tomb rests in peace,
          a servant of God, of good memory,
          Dulcitia, sanctified by the best character,
          suffused with goodwill, most generous
          in charity. She lived thirty-five
          years, more or less, and died
          in peace nine days before the Kalends of May,

---

1. *CIL* 12:481 = *Anthologia latina,* 2.1:690–91, no. 1447.

2. See E. Clark, "Patrons, Not Priests: Gender and Power in Late Ancient Christianity," *Gender and History* 2 (1990): 259–60, "in the religious sphere . . . women could enter the ranks of benefactors on a footing equal with men and be accorded the same honor."

3. *CIL* 12:2090.

X[. . .] years after the consulate of the consul Basilius,
a distinguished gentleman, during the fourteenth indiction.

The designation *famula dei* (servant of God) suggests that Dulcitia may
have been a religious. The lacuna in the dating formula allows for a
date of either 531 or 546.[4]

Attica's Embellishment

Women of greater means expressed themselves more lavishly, by par-
ticipating in the construction or repair of churches. Attica, the wife of
Magnus Felix, patrician and praetorian prefect of Gaul circa 469,[5]
came from the very peak of the aristocratic pyramid. Her contributions
to work on the church of St. Lawrence-in-Damaso in Rome were recognized in a prominently displayed inscription.[6]

6.3[7]   Whoever seeks mysteries with a mind full of the lord,
               come here: the house of religion lies open.
           These rooms are always devoted to pious awe
               and here God gives ear to our prayers.
           Hasten, therefore, to curb your gleeful passions;
               take care now to approach the sacred portals gladly
           so that you can cast off the sins you have committed
               and avoid whatever evils that noxious error entails.
           Attica, the most distinguished[8] wife of Magnus Felix,
               constructed this monument at her own expense.

Her husband may have received the secular and political honors, but
Attica obtained recognition in her own way.

----

4. The consulate of Basilius was in 508; postconsulates beginning with the Roman
numeral X that also were fourteenth indictions (the relevant cycles began in 517 and 532)
include only those in 531 (XXIIII) and 546 (XXXVIIII).

5. Attica: *PLRE* 2:181–82; Felix: *PLRE* 2:463–64; see Sid.Apoll. *Carm.* 9.6.

6. The reason for her presence in Rome is unknown, although the family did have connections in Italy: see Mathisen, "Resistance and Reconciliation."

7. G. de Rossi, ed., *Inscriptiones Christianae urbis Romae septimo saeculo antiquiores*
(Rome: Libraria Pontificia, 1857–88), 2:151, no. 25.

8. *Clarissima:* Because Attica did not yet have the rank of *inlustris* (illustrious), her phil-
anthropy must have occurred before Felix's high office holding.

The Lady and the Tramp

A woman who engaged in church construction in the mid–fifth century was the wife of Bishop Namatius of Clermont.[9] In his description of her construction activity, Gregory of Tours provided a poignant vignette of her personal life.

6.4[10]   The wife of Namatius built the church of the holy Stephen outside the walls. Because she wished it to be adorned with paintings, she used to hold on her knees a book[11] in which she read tales of ancient deeds and indicated to the painters what subjects should be represented on the walls. One day, as she was sitting reading in the church, it happened that a certain poor man came in to pray. And when he saw her clad in black, for she was advanced in years, he thought that she was one of the paupers, and producing a piece of bread, he put it in her lap and went on his way. She did not despise the gift of this poor man who did not perceive her rank, but took it and thanked him, and put it by, afterward preferring it to her costlier food and receiving a blessing from it every day until it was gone.

Like Eucheria in chapter 1, this woman obviously enjoyed books and literary activity.

A Papal Petition

In other instances, the expectation that women would perform charitable works could result in a bit of pressure upon them to do so. The Gallic noblewoman Firmina received a letter from Pope Gelasius (492–96) as he acted in a fund-raising capacity:

---

9. For another episcopal spouse, note Susanna, the wife of Priscus of Lyon, discussed below. In general, see B. Brennan, "'Episcopae': Bishops' Wives Viewed in Sixth-Century Gaul," *Church History* 54 (1985): 311–23.

10. Greg.Tur. *Hist.* 2.17: translation informed by Dalton, *Gregory,* 59; and Thorpe, *Gregory,* 131–32.

11. Perhaps an illustrated version of the Bible. For another use of biblical illustrations in the construction of a church, see the *Vita Genovefae* (Life of Genovefa), 55: *MGH SRM* 3:238: "quae sunt tradita libris storiarum, pictura referunt" [The things that were reported in the books of histories they made manifest in a picture].

5.5[12]   Gelasius to the illustrious[13] woman Firmina.

It most certainly pertains to the sum total of your reward if the estates that were unfortunately ravaged by barbarians or Romans could be restored by your efforts for the feeding of the needy. So great a multitude of them has congregated in Rome from diverse provinces, which were devastated by the destruction of the wars, that, as God is my witness, we are barely able to satisfy the need. You see, therefore, how much good work you would accomplish if liberated estates, which each soul contributes for its own sake, were to be granted, with your assistance seconding that of God, to the blessed apostle Peter. I beg that you deem it fitting to accept with a welcoming spirit the eulogies of this benediction that I have sent by reason of my affection.

The destruction in question resulted from the war in Italy between Theodoric the Ostrogoth and the patrician Odovacar during the years 489–93. This Firmina probably is to be identified as the *femina inlustris* (illustrious woman) Firmina of Arles. The latter was a relative of Magnus Felix Ennodius, an expatriate Gaul who served as bishop of Pavia circa 514–21, in the very area where the despoiled estates would have been located. Firmina's estate-holding in Italy, rather than in Gaul, would be consistent with family interests in that area, and parallel to the munificence of her probable relative, the wife of Magnus Felix.[14] It is unknown whether she acceded to the papal petition.

Feeding the Fish

In another case, circa the 480s an aristocratic widow of the province of Noricum on the Danube was coerced into providing relief to the poor by the holy man Severinus:

5.6[15]   At the same time, a brutal famine afflicted the city called Faviana, whose residents believed that there would be only one remedy for

---

12. Gelasius, *Epist.* "Ad cumulum vero": *PL* 59:155.

13. She would have received the rank of *inlustris* (illustrious) through her husband, whose identity is unknown and who well may have been deceased.

14. For the relationship between the families of Magnus Felix and Magnus Felix Ennodius, see Mathisen, "Resistance and Reconciliation," 621. See also passage 6.3.

15. Eugippius, *Vita Severini* (Life of Severinus), 3: *PL* 62:1167–96; Mauriz Schuster, *Eugippius. Leben des heiligen Severin* (Vienna, 1946), 26–28 (with German translation).

themselves: if, with religious pleas, they were to invite the man of God[16] from the aforementioned town of Comagenis. Foreseeing that they were coming to him, he was instructed by the Lord to go with them. When he arrived, he began to exhort the townspeople, saying, "You will be able to be freed from such a great evil of famine by the fruits of penitence." After they had profited from such great undertakings, the most blessed Severinus realized, by divine revelation, that a certain widow, Procula by name, had concealed additional foodstuffs. After she had been hauled into the open, he vehemently scolded her: "Why do you, born with the most noble antecedents, show yourself to be a maidservant of cupidity and stand forth as a slave of greed, which, according to the Apostle, is the same as worshiping idols? Behold! While the Lord now mercifully takes counsel on behalf of his servants, you will not have anything to show for your wicked preparations, unless, perhaps, casting into the Danube river the grain that you have callously hoarded, you show to the fish the humanity that you have denied to human beings. For this reason I have come to you rather than to the paupers regarding those items that until now you have thought could be hoarded at a time when Christ is starving." When she had heard this, the woman was terrified by great fear and began freely to distribute to the poor that which she had hoarded.

Some aristocrats, therefore, were not as philanthropic as others, and needed some encouragement before they fulfilled their Christian and civic duty.

Family Advocates

One way in which women could become involved in local politics was by acting on behalf of a male relative. Such endeavors, of course, were part and parcel of the conventional pursuit of family interests, and in this regard would have been a recognized element of traditional social dynamics.

The Ambitions of Alcima and Placidina

In the early sixth century, two blue-blooded Roman women, connected to the families of the Aviti and the Apollinares, enhanced the

---

16. That is, St. Severinus.

status of both themselves and their family. Alcima was the daughter of Papianilla, the daughter of the emperor Eparchius Avitus (455–56), and Sidonius Apollinaris. Placidina was the wife of Alcima's brother Apollinaris.[17] In 515, Bishop Euphrasius of Clermont died, and the two women were determined that Apollinaris, who had fought against the Franks on the losing Visigothic side at the battle of Vouillé in 507, would be the next bishop:

5.7[18]   And when the people chose the sainted Quintianus,[19] who had been expelled from Rodez, Alcima and Placidina, the sister and wife of Apollinaris, visited Bishop Quintianus and said, "Saintly lord, it should be enough for Your Elderliness that you already have been ordained a bishop." They continued, "Will not Your Piety permit your servant Apollinaris to attain the place of this office? Truly, when he has ascended to this eminence, he will do just as you wish. If you incline a kindly ear to our humble petition, you need simply command, and he will obey your every order." He replied, "What can I do, for nothing is assigned to my authority.[20] Indeed, it will suffice if the church will provide daily sustenance for me when I am engaged in prayer." Hearing this, they dispatched Apollinaris to the king. He left and, having offered many gifts, succeeded to the episcopate. But after serving only four months, he withdrew from this world. When this was announced to Theoderic,[21] moreover, he ordered the saintly Quintianus to be installed there.

Another Instant Martyr

Once Apollinaris had become bishop, the two women moved quickly to enhance the family's stature. To this end, like many wealthy women, they sponsored the construction of a church—in this case, for an

---

17. See *PLRE* 2:54 (Alcima), and 889–90 (Placidina). For Apollinaris, see selections 3.8, 3.15–16 above.

18. Greg.Tur. *Hist.* 3.2; for other translations, see Dalton, *Gregory,* 86; and Thorpe, *Gregory,* 162–63.

19. Quintianus was an African exile who had been expelled from Rodez by the Visigoths for scheming to turn the city over to the Franks. He took refuge at Clermont (Greg.Tur. *Hist.* 2.36; see also Greg.Tur. *Vit.pat.* 4), where he became a "bishop without portfolio."

20. This sounds remarkably like the situation faced by Sidonius when the rebellious priests took control of his church (selection 4.3 above).

21. King of the Franks, 511–34.

underappreciated Arvernian martyr. Gregory of Tours discussed some of their methods:

6.8[22]   The martyr Antolianus, moreover, suffered martyrdom in the city of Clermont.[23] Wishing to build a church in his honor, Alcima, the sister of Bishop Apollinaris, and Placidina, his wife, removed the bodies of many saints when they laid the foundations, ignorant of the merits of those whose graves they uncovered. Because, on account of the multitude of other graves, they were unable to bury individually those who had filled the space from antiquity, they covered up the accumulated mound of bones with earth, flinging them into a single trench. And therefore it appeared in a vision to a certain person that this was acceptable neither to God nor to the martyr, and this man saw the blessed Antolianus lamenting with the rest of the saints, and saying, "Woe is me, because on my account many of my brothers have been mistreated; truly, I say that those who have begun this enterprise will be unable to bring it to completion." And that is what happened. Eventually, after the walls had been constructed, they erected over the altar of the building a tower with Parian marble columns and overhanging arches of Heraclean stone,[24] adding to the vault a marvelous picture portrayed with a diversity of colors.

Now, this work was so refined and delicate that for a long time, disrupted by a multitude of cracks, it seemed to hang nearly on the point of ruin. Bishop Avitus, seeing this danger and foreseeing the future collapse of the columns, ordered the beams and shafts, even the tiles, to be removed. When they had been dislodged without any supporting columns to replace them, and after the workers had descended from the scaffolding to have lunch and everyone else had left the basilica, by the will of God the columns, under the immense weight imposed on them, with a resounding crash collapsed over the altar and around the altar, and the interior was filled with a cloud of dust from the pulverized mortar.[25]

---

22. Greg.Tur. *Glor.mart.* 64: for another translation, see *Glory of the Martyrs,* 88–89.

23. Supposedly on 6 February 253. See Greg.Tur. *Hist.* 1.32–33, where Antolianus (along with Limenius, Cassius, and Victorinus) is martyred under Crocus, king of the Alamanni (see Aurelius Victor, *Epitome de caesaribus* [Summary of the Caesars] 41.3). The relics of St. Antolianus were said to have been kept in the church of St. Gallus (see *PL* 71:759).

24. Parian marble came from Parium in Greece; Heraclean stone *(heracleus lapis),* from Heraclea in Lydia, was thought to have magnetic properties.

25. Miraculously, however no one was hurt and the altar was unharmed.

At this time, urban space was at a great premium, and the two women had to build on the site of an old cemetery, probably demolishing an earlier church in the process. They may have been working in such great haste not from any impiety but because they suspected—correctly—that Apollinaris's days were numbered. Perhaps his checkered past had caught up with him. The women would have known that it was necessary to complete the job before another bishop took over, one who was not as committed to their project. Or not committed to it at all. The result, it seems, was a rather slipshod job of construction, even though it did survive a good sixty years before Avitus (ca. 571–600)—whose name suggests that he was another family member—undertook his ill-fated repair attempts.

Choosing the Wrong Side

Nor was this the end of the involvement of these two women in local intrigues. In 527, Placidina's son Arcadius got into trouble:

3.9[26] (9) In addition, Arcadius, one of the Arvernian senators, proposed to Childebert that he ought to make this territory his own. . . .[27] (12) Indeed, Theoderic, arriving in Clermont with his army, pillaged and destroyed the entire region. Meanwhile, Arcadius, who had been the cause of the whole calamity, and through whose foolishness the region now was being laid waste, fled to the city of Bourges, which, at that time, moreover, was in the domain of King Childebert. Furthermore, Placidina, the mother of Arcadius, and Alcima, his father's sister, were apprehended in the city of Cahors.[28] After their property had been confiscated, they were sentenced to exile.

We hear no more of Alcima and Placidina. Their downfall is part of the general decline of the old Roman aristocracy during this period. The family of Sidonius Apollinaris, it seems, was remarkably successful in being able to pick the losers in Gallic conflicts: Sidonius's grandfather had supported the usurper Jovinus (411–13), Sidonius himself had

---

26. Greg.Tur. *Hist.* 3.9, 12; for other translations, see Dalton, *Gregory,* 93–94; and Thorpe, *Gregory,* 171–72.

27. Note the similar proposal of Deoteria in chapter 7.

28. In the early seventh century the sister of Bishop Desiderius of Cahors was named Avita, suggesting that the two women had family connections in this region.

favored the Romans against the Visigoths, his son Apollinaris had fought for the Visigoths against the Franks, and here Arcadius, and his relatives, chose King Childebert over King Theoderic. Arcadius, meanwhile, is last heard of in the service of his patron, Childebert.[29]

Susanna Loses Her Cool

Another woman who assisted the career of her episcopal husband was Susanna, wife of Priscus of Lyon, who had succeeded Gregory of Tours's relative Nicetius in 573. Gregory's portrayal of Priscus suggests that he felt some personal animus toward him, probably because his partisans and practices were different from those of Nicetius. Gregory associated Susanna in the activities of her husband, and one of his primary grievances was that the two allowed the women of Lyon to have greater freedom in the church than Nicetius had permitted them. Gregory also took what seems to be an unseemly pleasure in describing their misfortunes.

6.10[30]   Bishop Priscus, who succeeded Nicetius, began, with his wife Susanna, to persecute and even put to death many of those who had been the close associates of this godly man, not because of any sin that these persons had committed, not because they were guilty of any crime, not because of some theft for which they had been apprehended, but because of the envy that burned within him, for he was jealous of their loyalty to his predecessor. Priscus and his wife did all they could to calumniate the saint. Although it had been a rule long observed by earlier bishops that no woman should go into the rectory,[31] Susanna and her young women used to enter the very cell in which the blessed man had slept. Ultimately, the divine majesty took vengeance on the family of Bishop Priscus for all this. For his wife Susanna was possessed by a demon, and with her hair disheveled, this madwoman was harassed throughout the city, having confessed (so that he might spare her) that God's saint, whom she had denied while she was still sane, was a friend

---

29. As described later in this chapter, passage 6.17.

30. Greg.Tur. *Hist.* 4.36; for translation, see Thorpe, *Gregory,* 231–32; see also Dalton, Gregory, 145–47.

31. *Domus ecclesiae.* The Council of Agde had decreed in A.D. 506, "It is fitting that serving girls, even freed ones, be removed from the pantry and from the seclusion of the church's back room and from the very house in which a cleric lives" (can. 11: *CCL* 148:200).

of Christ. The bishop was seized with a fourth-class fever[32] and began to tremble. After the fever had dissipated, he remained trembling and slow-witted. His son and his whole household also seemed pale and slow-witted, and there was no doubt that they had been smitten by the power of the saintly man.

This is the last one hears of the activities of Susanna and Priscus. In general, one notes in Gregory's discussions of the efforts of these energetic women an underlying air of disapproval. They often came to bad ends: Susanna supposedly went mad, and Alcima and Placidina were dispossessed and exiled.

Barbarian Queens

In Merovingian Gaul, women affiliated with barbarian royal families by either birth or marriage seem to have had rather more freedom to become involved in public activities than their Roman counterparts. Often they did so, nominally at least, on behalf of a male relative; at other times they expressed themselves through activities in the church. The image of the assertive barbarian queen who exercised a positive influence over her stolid husband became a commonplace.

Queen Caretena

One such is the Burgundian queen Caretena, wife of King Gundobad (ca. 473–516). The primary evidence for her existence comes from a verse epitaph, dated to A.D. 506. It comes from the basilica of St. Michael in Lyon, which was originally built by Caretena herself. The epitaph reads:

11[33]   The support of scepters, splendor of the earth, and radiance of the world,
        Caretena wishes her limbs to be embraced in this tomb,
        She whom, as your servant and influential in worldly affairs, you, Christ,
        summon from the realms of this world to your own realm,

---

32. "A typo quartano," also known as the *quartana febris:* the "quartan ague."
33. *CIL* 13:2372 = Ernst Diehl, ed., *Inscriptiones Latinae Christianae veteres* (Berlin: Weidmann, 1925), no. 46 = *MGH AA* 6.2.5 = *Anthologia latina,* 2.2:640–41, no. 1365.

Having obtained, as a just desert, a rich treasure,
which she granted to God for the support of the poor.
For some time her clothing concealed under ruddy purple
a chaste body that chastised adversity;
She concealed her sober fasts with a cheerful demeanor,[34]
and in secret she dedicated her royal limbs to the cross.
Having divided the princely duties with her exalted mate,
she ruled the heights with a shared counsel.
She delighted in inciting her splendid offspring and delightful
grandchildren, enlightened, to the true faith.
Struggling to support her sublime spirit with these endowments,
she did not spurn the heavenly yoke after receiving the diadem;
Once she gained dominion, she yielded to the odoriferous Sabaean
    substance,[35]
she undertook the marvelous work of Solomon,
She personally founded this temple,[36] which resounds throughout
    the world,
and bequeathed lofty lintels to the angelic chorus.
Those prayers that she often offered to the king in her efforts
to set free the accused she now can offer, Christ, to you,
She whom jealous death snatched after her tenth lustrum[37]
has received a better day, even without end.
And now the twice eighth day of September is brought to light
in the year bearing the name of the consul Messala.

Caretena adhered to the ethos of a respectable Roman matron, leading an exemplary life that included chastity, setting free the imprisoned, and church building. She had a daughter and several grandchildren whom she raised as Nicene Christians, in spite of the Arianism of her husband. The epitaph also asserts that in secular life she shared power with the king, but that she ultimately entered the religious life. She died in September 506 after having reached the age of fifty: this would indicate that she had been born circa 456.

---

34. See Sid.Apoll. *Epistulae* 6.12.3, where the wife of King Chilperic praises the fasting of Bishop Patiens of Lyon.

35. I.e., frankincense, from Saba, a place in Arabia.

36. The church of St. Michael.

37. A *lustrum* consisted of five years; hence Caretena lived at least fifty years.

Queen and Bishop

A revealing vignette of Caretena regarding an incident of circa 500 is fortuitously preserved in the *vita* (life) of Marcellus, bishop of Die circa 463–509:

12[38]   Nor, moreover, do I think it fitting to pass over in a sort of silence something that tenacious memory, with its faithful recollection, teaches us was done in the city of Lyon. Therefore, the queen of the Burgundians, Caretena by name, built with marvelous workmanship the basilica of the blessed archangel Michael and requested the presence of many bishops for the purpose of dedicating this most sacred site, among whom was the blessed bishop Marcellus, first among the others on account of her reverence for him.[39] He was well known to the aforementioned queen on account of the fame of his virtues regarding the pursuit of religion, and he was considered to be a special personal patron in Christ. After the rite of consecration had been celebrated, he did not neglect to do something on behalf of his townspeople regarding an immunity from public assessments in the city that he oversaw, for the relief of the citizens in a concession to the city, with the result that through the Christian consort of the king the solicitation of the blessed man came to the ears of King Gundobad. And when, after the plea of his wife, his obdurate spirit was little inclined to granting the favor, the blessed man, arriving in his presence to say farewell, in a familiar exchange, inserted into the ears of the highest power in his own words the pleas that he previously had intimated.[40] At this, when the king acquiesced not at all to these suppliant words, the blessed prelate, trusting to the pity of God, openly stated that he would obtain from his own God that which the king had not yet granted.

And, by the grace of God, the king eventually granted Marcellus's request.

---

38. *Vita Marcelli* (Life of Marcellus), 9: François Dolbeau, "La vie en prose de saint Marcel, évêque de Die. Histoire du texte et édition critique," *Francia* 11 (1983): 124; see also G. Kirner, "Due vite inedite de s. Marcello vescovo di Die," *Studi storici* 9 (1900): 289–327. Cf. selection 4.12 above for another Roman cleric's interview with a Burgundian king.

39. The dedicatory homily, a fragment of which survives, was delivered by Bishop Avitus of Vienne (*PL* 59:314–15).

40. That is, through the medium of the queen.

This tale shows a Roman aristocrat using the good offices of a barbarian queen to attempt to manipulate a barbarian king. In this instance, however, Caratena's influence needed some assistance: Marcellus, according to his hagiographer, had to bring in the heavy artillery.

A Case of Treason

The relationship between Caratena and Gundobad is surprisingly similar to that between another Burgundian king, Chilperic, and his queen, whose name is unknown.[41] Sidonius Apollinaris wrote to his uncle Thaumastus about the positive influence that this queen, whom he nicknamed "Tanaquil" and "Agrippina," had upon Chilperic, whom he styled "Lucumo" and "Germanicus," after Thaumastus's brother Apollinaris had been accused of sedition circa 470:

6.13[42]   Sidonius to his friend Thaumastus, greetings.
 . . . (7) But we have one consolation in our trouble. His Tanaquil restrains our Lucumo. She waits her chance, and rids his ears by a few coaxing words of all the poison with which the whisperers have filled them. You ought to know that we owe it to her interest if up until now the mind of our common patron has not been poisoned against our brothers by these younger Cibyrates;[43] God willing, this never will happen while the present power rules Lyonese Germany,[44] and our present Agrippina exerts her moderating influence on her Germanicus. Farewell.

---

41. It sometimes has been suggested that Caretena was the wife of Chilperic rather than of Gundobad (see *PLRE* 2:260–61), but the just-cited little-known passage from the *vita* of Marcellus makes it clear that this was not the case.

42. Sid.Apoll. *Epist.* 5.7.7; see also 6.12.3. Translation from Dalton, *Sidonius,* 58–59; see also Anderson, *Sidonius,* 2:195.

43. Sidonius is referring to Romans who inform on other Romans to the Germans. Tlepolemos and Hieron, two brothers from Cibyra in Asia Minor, helped the Roman governor Verres plunder Sicily in the years 73–71 B.C.

44. *Lugdunensis Germania:* Sidonius is making a joke here. Lugdunensis Prima was the Roman province in which Lyon lay, but now that part of it was in Burgundian control it had become "Lyonese Germany."

Sidonius here puts barbarian rulers in the context of the heroic Roman past. Tanaquil had great influence over her husband, the Etruscan king of Rome Tarquinius Priscus (ca. 615–571 B.C.), whose original name was Lucumo. She generally was considered to be a role model for assertive women.[45] Agrippina, the stalwart daughter of the emperor Augustus's lieutenant Agrippa, was the wife of Germanicus, the adopted son of the emperor Tiberius, and accompanied him on his military campaigns. The image of the assertive wife was a commonplace for which many precedents could be cited; one recalls the wife of Volusianus, bishop of Tours, discussed in selection 3.27.

Queen Clotilde

No woman is portrayed in the sources as being more aggressive in the pursuit of her family interests than Chlotchildis (Clotilde), the daughter of the Burgundian king Chilperic and the wife of the Frankish king Clovis; she had five children and died in 544.[46] Clotilde was another strong-willed Burgundian. Gregory of Tours, who discussed the independent ways of several barbarian princesses and queens, paid particular attention to Clotilde's active role in politics. He also shows Clotilde in the traditional female role of the primary Christianizing element in the family. Her tale picks up after the Burgundian king Gundobad had killed his brother Chilperic and drowned Chilperic's wife after tying a stone around her neck:

14[47]   (28) Gundobad . . . condemned Chilperic's two daughters to exile; the elder, Crona, entered a convent, and the younger was called Clotilde. Because Clovis frequently sent embassies to Burgundy, the girl Clotilde was observed by his envoys. And when they saw that she was refined and sensible, and they discovered that she was of royal blood,

45. See Ausonius, *Parentalia,* 30, although when Ausonius compared Therasia, the wife of Paulinus of Nola, to Tanaquil (*Epist.* 28.31), the latter indignantly replied that Therasia ought rather be compared to Lucretia (Ausonius, *Epist.* 31.192).

46. Her children included Ingomer (who died as infant), Chlodomer, Childebert, Chlothar, and a daughter Clotilde. For a derivative ninth- or tenth-century *vita,* see *MGH SRM* 2:341–48, and, for translation, McNamara, Halborg, and Whatley, *Sainted Women,* 38–50; see also Godefroid Kurth, *Saint Clotilda,* trans. V. M. Crawford (London: Washbourne, 1913).

47. Greg.Tur. *Hist.* 2.28–31; translation in part from Thorpe, *Gregory,* 140–45; see also Dalton, *Gregory,* 66–70.

they reported all this to King Clovis. He immediately sent an embassy to Gundobad seeking her in marriage. The latter, fearing to refuse, turned her over to Clovis's men, and they, taking the girl, quickly delivered her to the king. When he saw her, Clovis was thoroughly delighted, and he married her, already having a son named Theoderic by a concubine.

(29) Therefore, Clovis's firstborn child by Clotilde was a son. When his mother desired to baptize him, she preached earnestly to her husband, saying, "The gods you worship are worthless, for they cannot support either themselves or others. They are created either from stone, or wood, or metal. The names with which you have endowed them are of men, not of gods, such as Saturn, who is said to have fled in order to avoid being expelled from his kingdom, such as Jupiter himself, the most odious perpetrator of all depravity, debaucher of men, defiler of his relatives, who could not even abstain from sleeping with his own sister, as she herself said, "The sister and wife of Jove."[48] What power have Mars and Mercury? They seem to be endowed with magical skills rather than to have the power of a divine name. But He ought rather to be worshiped who created from nothingness by his word the heavens and earth, and the sea and all things in them, who made the sun shine, adorned the sky with stars, who fills the water with fish, the earth with animals, the air with birds, at whose nod the earth is filled with produce, the trees with fruits, the vines with grapes, by whose hand the human race was created, through whose largess all that very creation serves his own man, whom he created, with obedience and deference."[49] But when the queen said this, the spirit of the king was not moved at all to belief; rather he said, "At the command of our gods all things are created and brought forth. Your god, however, is nowhere manifested, and what is more, he is not even known to have any godlike attributes." Subsequently, the faithful queen brought her son to be baptized, and ordered the church to be adorned with curtains and hangings so that he who could not be influenced by discourse might be inclined to belief through ceremony. After the child, whom they called Ingomer, had been immaculately baptized,[50] he died in the

---

48. Vergil, *Aeneid,* 1.47: the wife of Jupiter (Jove) was his sister Hera. This citation from a classical Roman poet makes the contrast between the as yet unrepentant Frank Clovis and the Burgundian romanophile Clotilde all the more striking.

49. By preaching in this manner, Clotilde assumes the role customarily assigned to the saint in a saint's life.

50. It was not at all uncommon for those on the point of death to be baptized.

same white robes in which he had been reborn. For this reason, the
king was provoked to anger, and he fervently rebuked the queen, saying, "If the boy had been dedicated in the name of my gods, he would
still be alive; but now because he was baptized in the name of your god,
he has ceased to live altogether." To this the queen replied, "I give
thanks to omnipotent God, the creator of all, who judged me not at all
unworthy to have him call to his kingdom the one born from my
womb. My spirit is not touched, moreover, by grief over this incident
because I know that he has been called in his baptismal garments from
this world to be nourished in the sight of God." Afterward she bore
him another son, whom she named at baptism Chlodomer, and when
he became ill, the king said, "Nothing else can happen to him except
for that which happened to his brother: having been baptized in the
name of your Christ he immediately will die." But when the mother
prayed, he recovered with the help of the Lord.

(30) Queen Clotilde continued to pray that her husband might recognize the true God and give up his idol worship, but in no way could
he be moved to this belief. Finally war broke out against the Alamanni,
and in this conflict he was forced by necessity to accept what he had
refused of his own free will. It turned out that when the two armies met
on the battlefield there was great slaughter and the troops of Clovis
were rapidly being annihilated. He raised his eyes to heaven when he
saw this, felt compunction in his heart, and was moved to tears. "Jesus
Christ," he said, "you who Clotilde maintains to be the Son of the living God, you who deign to give help to those in travail and victory to
those who trust in you, in faith I beg the glory of your help. If you will
give me victory over my enemies and if I experience that virtue which
people dedicated in your name say that they have encountered, I will
believe in you and I will be baptized in your name." . . . Even as he said
this, the Alamanni turned their backs and began to run away. And
when the Alamanni saw that their king had been killed, they surrendered themselves to Clovis, saying, "Let not the people perish any
longer, we now are yours." And he, having heartened his people and
departed in peace after the war was concluded, told the queen how he
had merited winning the victory by calling on the name of Christ. This
happened in the fifteenth year of his reign.[51] (31) The queen then
ordered the blessed Remigius, bishop of the city of Reims, to be summoned in secret. She begged him to impart the word of salvation to the

---

51. A.D. 496, if Gregory's date is correct.

king. The bishop asked Clovis to meet him in private and began to urge him to believe in the true God, the maker of heaven and earth, and to abandon the idols, which were of use neither to him nor to others. . . . The king therefore demanded that he be baptized by the bishop. He proceeded to the baptismal font like a new Constantine. . . .[52] Having confessed omnipotent God in the Trinity, the king therefore was baptized in the name of the Father, the Son, and the Holy Spirit and was anointed with the sacred chrism with the sign of the cross of Christ. More than three thousand of his army were baptized, as was his sister Albofleda, but soon after she was gathered to the Lord. . . . Another sister of Clovis, called Lanthechildis, was converted at the same time. She had fallen into the Arian heresy, but she confessed the equality of the Father, the Son, and the Holy Ghost, and received the holy chrism.

If Lanthechildis was an Arian, one wonders whether she might have attempted to convert Clovis to Arianism in the same way that Clotilde advocated for the Nicene faith. Had Clovis become Arian, a way might have been opened for a rapprochement between the Franks and the Visigoths.

After Clovis's death, Clotilde withdrew into the religious life:

6.15[53]   Having done all this, Clovis died in Paris.[54] He was buried in the church of the Holy Apostles, which he and his Queen Clotilde had built. . . . After the death of her husband, Queen Clotilde came to live in Tours. She served as a religious in the church of St. Martin. She lived all the rest of her days in this place, aside from an occasional visit to Paris. She was remarkable for her great modesty and her loving kindness.

Gregory's words demonstrate how proud he was of the repute that Clotilde's residence had brought to his own episcopal city. But, as will be seen, he also was a bit disingenuous about just how "retiring" Clotilde was after the death of her husband

Clovis's four sons, Theodebert, Chlodomer, Childebert, and

---

52. A portentous comparison: Constantine was the first Roman emperor to have been baptized, in A.D. 337.

53. Greg.Tur. *Hist.* 2.43; translation from Thorpe, *Gregory,* 158; see also Dalton, *Gregory,* 81.

54. On 27 November 511.

Chlothar, then divided the kingdom. Clotilde remained in her convent, but did not remove her hands from the reins of power. In 524, she encouraged her sons to avenge the deaths of her mother and father at Burgundian hands:

6[55]   Queen Clotilde arranged a meeting with Chlodomer and her other sons. "My dear children," she said, "do not give me cause to regret the fact that I have brought you up with such care. You must surely resent the wrong that has been done to me. You must do all in your power to avenge the death of my mother and father." When they had listened to her appeal they set out for Burgundy. They marched their troops against Sigismund and his brother Godomar. . . . [The Burgundians were defeated, but Chlodomer was killed.] When her period of mourning was over, Queen Clotilde took Chlodomer's sons into her own household and brought them up. The eldest was Theudovald, the second Gunthar, and the third Chlodovald.

Clotilde's surviving sons then greedily moved to ensure that the sons of the dead Chlodomer would not inherit their share of the kingdom:

7[56]   When Queen Clotilde was living in Paris, Childebert observed that his mother was lavishing all her affection on the sons of Chlodomer, whom I have already mentioned. This made him jealous, for he was afraid that this favor that the queen was showing them might bring them into the line of succession. He sent a secret message to his brother, King Chlothar: "Our mother keeps the children of our brother close by her side and is planning to give them the throne. You must come to Paris without delay. We must take counsel together and make up our minds what is to be done about them. Ought we to cut off their hair and so reduce them to the status of ordinary individuals? Or should we have them killed and then divide our brother's kingdom equally among us?" . . . When they had conferred together, they sent a message to the queen, who was then resident in Paris, "Send the princes to us," they said, "so that they may be raised to the throne." This pleased Clotilde very much, for she knew nothing of their plotting. She

---

55. Greg.Tur. *Hist.* 3.6; translation from Thorpe, *Gregory,* 166–67; see also Dalton, *Gregory,* 88–90.

56. Greg.Tur. *Hist.* 3.18; translation from Thorpe, *Gregory,* 180–82; see also Dalton, *Gregory,* 101–3.

fed the boys and gave them something to drink. "Once I see you succeed him on the throne," she said, "I shall forget that I have lost my son." Off they went, and they were immediately seized and separated from their servants and caretakers, and they were imprisoned in different places, with the servants in one place and the young princes in another. Then Childebert and Chlothar sent to the queen Arcadius, the man about whom I have already told you,[57] with a pair of scissors in one hand and a naked sword in the other. When he came into the queen's presence, he held them out to her. "Your two sons, who are our masters, seek your decision, gracious queen, as to what should be done with the princes. Do you wish them to live with their hair cut short?[58] Or would you prefer to see them killed?" Clotilde was terrified by what he had said, and very angry indeed, especially when she saw the drawn sword and the scissors. Beside herself with bitter grief and in her anguish hardly knowing what she was saying, she answered, "If they are not to ascend the throne, I would rather see them dead than tonsured." Arcadius, insufficiently appreciating her distress and not considering that she might later reflect more fully, quickly returned, announcing and saying, "You can finish the job, for the queen agrees. It is her wish that you should carry out your plan." . . .
[The two boys then were murdered, and the kingdom was divided between Childebert and Chlothar.][59]

Queen Clotilde placed the two small corpses on a bier and followed them in a funeral procession to the church of St. Peter, grieving her heart out as the psalms were sung. There she buried them side by side. One was ten years old and the other only seven. . . .

Queen Clotilde earned the respect of all by her bearing. She gave alms to the poor and spent her nights in prayer. In chastity and virtue she always kept herself pure. She endowed churches, monasteries, and other holy places with the lands necessary for their upkeep; her giving was so generous and so eager that already in her lifetime she was looked upon not as a queen but as the handmaiden of God, whom she served with such zeal. Neither the royal status of her sons nor her

---

57. The grandson of Sidonius Apollinaris and the son of Alcima; discussed above.

58. Long hair was the sign of Frankish royalty; cutting it not only was a rejection of royalty but also, usually, a sign of entry into the church. See John M. Wallace-Hadrill, *The Long-Haired Kings, and Other Studies in Frankish History* (New York: Barnes and Noble, 1962).

59. The third son was able to escape, and became a cleric.

worldly goods nor earthly ambition could bring her into disrepute. In all humility she moved forward to heavenly grace.

Gregory portrayed in Clotilde the kinds of qualities that he saw as acceptable not only for women, but also for saints. One might compare her virtues with those of Caretena above.

Clotilde died on 3 June 544, and Gregory reported:

8[60]   Therefore, Queen Clotilde, full of days and endowed with good works, died in the city of Tours at the time of Bishop Injuriosus. She was borne to Paris with much singing of psalms, and was buried in the sacristy of the basilica of St. Peter next to her sons, Kings Childebert and Chlothar, at the side of King Clovis. For she herself had built this basilica, in which the most blessed Genovefa is buried.

In the passage about Clovis's burial above, this church is called the Church of the Holy Apostles. It later came to be called the Church of St. Genovefa. It should be no surprise that this ambitious queen built a church to house the tomb of the most famous Gallic female saint.[61]

Queen Radegonde

The posterity of Clotilde was ably manifested in the person of Radegonde,[62] who, like Clovis's mother, Basina, was a Thuringian princess. Circa 540, Radegonde married Clotilde's son Chlothar.[63] Subsequently she became a *diaconissa* (deaconess), a rather ambiguous status that apparently—given her marital status—did not require celibacy.[64] She had no children, and circa 550, at about the same time that her husband had her last surviving brother murdered, she retired to her villa at Saix and devoted herself to the religious life.[65] During the

---

60. Greg.Tur. *Hist.* 4.1; for additional translations, see Dalton, *Gregory,* 117; and Thorpe, *Gregory,* 197.

61. For Genovefa, see chapter 7.

62. See René Aigrain, *Sainte Radegonde* (Paris: J. Gabalda, 1924).

63. Chlothar had several other wives as well. On Frankish marital practices, see Jo Ann McNamara and Suzanne F. Wemple, "Marriage and Divorce in the Frankish Kingdom," in *Women in Medieval Society,* ed. Susan M. Stuard (Philadelphia: University of Pennsylvania Press, 1976), 95–124.

64. Venantius Fortunatus, *Vita Radegundis* (Life of Radegonde), 12.

65. Greg.Tur. *Hist.* 3.7.

550s she founded what would become the convent of the Holy Cross at Poitiers, where she settled permanently after the death of Chlothar in 561. Radegonde's activities are richly documented by Gregory of Tours; by her close friend Venantius Fortunatus (later bishop of Poitiers ca. 600–605), who wrote her *vita* after her death in 587; and by one of her nuns,[66] Baudonivia, who added additional material to the *vita* in the early seventh century.

Gregory's account picks up Radegonde's story after the defeat of the Thuringians in 531:

6.19[67] Chlothar, returning home, took with him as his captive Radegonde, daughter of King Bertharius. He married her, although afterward he caused her brother to be slain by wicked men. The queen turned to God and, changing her vestments, built for herself a monastery in Poitiers. By the virtue of her prayers, fastings, charities, and vigils she won so shining a repute that her name was considered to be great among the people.

Gregory subsequently described how, circa 569, Radegonde acquired a most potent relic:

6.20[68] In the time of King Chlothar (511–561), when the blessed Radegonde founded the monastery, she and her community were always submissive and obedient to the earlier bishops. In the time of Sigibert (561–575), moreover, after Maroveus had obtained the see,[69] the blessed Radegonde, moved by her faith and devotion, sent clerics to the east to procure wood of the true cross, and relics of the holy apostles and the other martyrs; they took with them letters from King Sigibert. They set forth and duly returned with the relics. Upon the delivery of these, the queen requested the bishop himself to deposit them in the convent with the chanting of psalms and all due honor. But he disregarded her proposal, mounted his horse, and went off to a

---

66. Terms used for the inhabitants of female monasteries included *monacha* (female monk), a word used by Venantius that soon went out of use; *sanctimonialis* (sanctified woman); and *nonnana* (nun), whose first attested use is by Baudonivia.

67. Greg.Tur. *Hist.* 3.7; translation based on Dalton, *Gregory,* 91; see also Thorpe, *Gregory,* 168–69.

68. Greg.Tur. *Hist.* 9.40; translation from Dalton, *Gregory,* 413–14; see also Thorpe, *Gregory,* 530–31.

69. Of Poitiers.

country estate. The queen then sent a fresh message to King Sigibert, begging him to command one of the bishops to place the relics in the convent with the honor due to them, and in compliance with her vow. The king then enjoined the blessed Euphronius, bishop of Tours, to perform this task. He, coming with his clergy to Poitiers, in the absence of the bishop of that city,[70] brought the holy relics to the monastery with much chanting of psalms, and with the pomp of gleaming tapers and incense.[71] After this event Radegonde on many occasions sought the good grace of the bishop of Poitiers, but she failed, and was forced to go to Arles with the abbess[72] whom she had appointed. There they received the rule of the holy Caesarius and the blessed Caesaria, and on their return put themselves under the protection of the king,[73] because they could find no care for their security in the man who should have been their pastor. The time for the passing of the blessed Radegonde came when this cause of offense was still spreading from day to day. After her death the abbess once more begged her own bishop to take the monastery under his care. At first he was inclined to refuse, but afterward, on the advice of those about him, he promised to become their father, as it was meet that he should, and whenever need was, to take up their defense. He therefore went to King Childebert and obtained a diploma granting him the regular control of this convent, such as he had over the rest of his diocese. But I believe there remained in his heart some resentment.

Gregory's concluding comments give some insight into just why Maroveus had proved so recalcitrant. Radegonde's convent, even though located not only within his diocese but also in his own episcopal city, was not under his episcopal jurisdiction. In his view, the installation of a piece of the true cross in Radegonde's possession would

---

70. That is, Maroveus.

71. This would be an example of what has come to be known as the ceremony of *adventus* (arrival), on which see Sabine MacCormack, "Change and Continuity in Late Antiquity: The Ceremony of Adventus," *Historia* 21 (1972): 721–52.

72. Named Agnes (see the following passage). One might wonder, however, whether Radegonde, who had vowed never to leave the convent, actually undertook such an arduous journey.

73. The rule of Caesarius restricted a bishop's authority over a convent, as would have the placement of the convent under the king's control: both would have alienated the bishop of Poitiers. For the monastery for women at Arles and its rule, see William E. Klingshirn, *Caesarius of Arles: The Making of a Christian Community in Late Antique Gaul* (Cambridge: Cambridge University Press, 1994).

have weakened his own authority yet further, and the intervention of the bishop of Tours likewise would have exacerbated his resentment. Only after Radegonde's death was he able to have his authority over the convent ratified.

Given the hard feelings that existed between Radegonde and Maroveus, it should be no surprise that she was all the more determined to ensure that her convent would be preserved after her death in the manner in which she had established it.[74] To that end, she authored, in her own hand, a letter addressed to bishops in general.[75] It was quoted in full by Gregory of Tours:

6.21[76]　Copy of the letter: Radegonde the Sinner[77] to all the bishops, sanctified lords and fathers in Christ and most worthy of an apostolic seat.

The first steps of a meet project can only move strongly to fulfillment when the matter is brought to the ears of our common fathers, the physicians and the shepherds of the fold, and commended likewise to their hearts. For the active sympathy proceeding from their love, the sage counsel proceeding from their power, the support proceeding from their prayers all unite to give it furtherance.

Because in time past, delivered from the chains of secular life by the providence and inspiration of the divine mercy, I turned of my own will to the rule of religion under Christ's guidance, and with ardent mind also considered how I might help forward others, that with the approval of the Lord my desires might become profitable to the rest, I established at Poitiers a monastery for nuns, founded and enriched by the most excellent lord King Chlothar. After its foundation, I myself endowed this monastery with the gift of all the property that the royal munificence had bestowed upon me. Moreover, I appointed for this community gathered together under Christ's protection the rule according to which the holy Caesaria lived, and which the care of the blessed Caesarius, bishop of Arles, had compiled to suit her needs from

---

74. Radegonde's model, Caesarius of Arles, did the same in his extant will.

75. For letters by later medieval women, see Karen Cherewatuk and Ulrike Wiethaus, *Dear Sister: Medieval Women and the Epistolary Genre* (Philadelphia: University of Pennsylvania Press, 1993).

76. Greg.Tur. *Hist.* 9.42: translation from Dalton, *Gregory,* 418–21; see also Thorpe, *Gregory,* 534–38.

77. The manuscripts read either *peccatrix* (the sinner) or *pictavus* (of Poitiers). Radegonde, however, was not a native of Poitiers, and it would have been unusual to refer to her as such.

the institutions of the holy fathers. With the approval of the most blessed bishops of Poitiers[78] and the other sees, and by the choice of our own community, I appointed as abbess the lady Agnes, my sister, whom I have loved and brought up from her earliest youth; and I submitted myself in regular obedience to her authority next to that of God. And following the apostolic example, I myself and my sisters, when we entered the monastery, made over by deed all our substance in earthly possessions, reserving nothing for ourselves, from fear of that which befell Ananias and Sapphira.[79] But because the moments and times of man's lot are uncertain, and the world runs to its end,[80] and there be those who rather seek the fulfillment of their own than the divine will, I remit to you, apostolic fathers, in my lifetime, and with all due devotion, this page containing my prayer to you, in the name of Christ.

And because I cannot in person throw myself at your feet, I make prostration vicariously through this letter, and by the Father, Son, and Holy Spirit, and by the tremendous Day of Judgment, I adjure you, as if you stood before me, to protect us from any tyrant, and secure to us the favor of our rightful King. And if haply after my death anyone, whether the bishop of the city,[81] or a royal officer, or any other person shall, as I trust shall never befall, either by suggestion of wicked men or by action of law, seek to trouble the sisterhood or to break the rule, or appoint any other abbess than my sister Agnes, whom the most blessed Germanus in the presence of his brethren consecrated with his benediction; or if the community itself, which I may not think possible, shall murmur and seek change; or if any person, even the bishop of the city, shall seek to claim, by new privileges over and above those enjoyed by his predecessors or any other persons in my lifetime, either power in the monastery or over its property; or if any shall essay against the rule to go forth thence; or if any prince or bishops or other powerful person, or any of the sisters, shall with sacrilegious intent diminish or appropriate the property that the most excellent lord

---

78. In contrast, of course, with the disapproval of Maroveus, which was left unmentioned.

79. See Acts 5:1–11. After selling their land, they held back part of the proceeds, and God struck them dead.

80. A common apocalyptic or millenarianist point of view that the end of the world was at hand.

81. A suggestion that Maroveus might be inclined to countermand Radegonde's wishes.

Chlothar or the most excellent kings his sons bestowed upon me, and I, by his injunction and permission, transferred to the monastery to have and hold, of which transmission I obtained confirmation by letters of the most excellent lords the kings Charibert, Guntram, Chilperic, and Sigibert under their oath and signature, or the gifts that others have given for the good of their souls or the sisters have bestowed out of their own possessions; may they through my prayer and the will of Christ in such wise be confronted with God's wrath, and that of yourselves and your successors, that as robbers and despoilers of the poor they may be shut out from your grace. Let nothing, in the face of your resistance, ever avail to diminish or to change in anything either our rule or the possessions of the monastery. . . . Let it not happen that this our abbess, so many times herein named, shall be harassed or molested, or that anything pertaining to our monastery shall be hereafter diminished, or in any wise changed. . . .

And I pray you, holy bishops, and our most excellent lords and kings, and the whole Christian people, by the Catholic faith in which you are baptized, when God shall ordain that I pass from the light of this world, let my poor body be buried in that basilica, be it at the time completed or unfinished, which I have begun to build in honor of the holy Mary, the mother of the Lord, and wherein many of our sisters are already laid to rest . . .

And I beseech with many tears that this my petition, signed by my own hand, be preserved in the archives of the cathedral church.[82] . . . And when you shall have kept the trust that I leave you as befits your high estate, you shall be partakers in His merits whose apostolic charge you fulfil, and worthily renew His example.

Accounts of several of these events also were articulately recounted by Baudonivia in her narrative of Radegonde's life, and it is interesting to compare and contrast the two versions.[83] The following excerpts describe Radegonde's withdrawal to her convent, Chlothar's attempt to reclaim her as his wife, and her acquisition of a fragment of the true cross.

---

82. Radegunda's letter actually fared better by being incorporated into Gregory's history.

83. For these lives, see Sabine Gaebe, "Radegundis: Sancta, Regina, Ancilla. Zum Heligkeitsideal der Radegundisviten von Fortunat und Baudonivia," *Francia* 16 (1989): 1–30.

84 Baudonivia, the most humble of all, to Abbess Dedimia[85] and the entire glorious congregation of Lady Radegonde, saintly ladies, endowed with the grace of merits:

You impose upon me a task that is no less difficult to accomplish than "it is to touch the sky with my finger,"[86] that is, that I presume to say something about the life of the saintly lady Radegonde, whom you knew best . . . For I, acknowledge this in myself, that I am weak and have little eloquence of comprehension, "because however much it is worthwhile for the learned to speak out it is in the same measure worthwhile for the witless to keep silent,"[87] . . . I will not repeat what Bishop Fortunatus, an apostolic man, wrote about the life of the blessed woman, but I will [discuss] what he omitted to avoid prolixity, just as he himself explained in his book when he said, "Let this small amount suffice regarding the virtues of this blessed woman lest excessiveness cause offense, nor should it be reckoned too brief when her eminence can be recognized from a few things."[88] Therefore, with the inspiration of the divine power, which the blessed Radegonde struggled to satisfy in this world and with which she reigns in the afterworld, I attempt to describe in unpolished and rustic speech some of the things she did and to include a few of her many miracles . . .

(5) . . . The aforementioned Radegonde, her spirit intent on Christ, through the ordination of the exalted King Chlothar established a monastery for herself at Poitiers with the inspiration and assistance of God. Bishop Pientius, an apostolic man, and Duke Austrapius[89] quickly constructed the building with royal ordination. The saintly queen, rejoicing and rejecting the false blandishments of the world, entered into this monastery, where she acquired the ornaments of perfection and a great congregation of girls for Christ, the immortal bridegroom. When an abbess had been chosen, and also appointed, she

---

84. Baudonivia, *De vita sanctae Radegundis, eiusdem virtutes* (On the life of St. Radegonde, her virtues): *MGH SRM* 2:378–95; for additional translations, see McNamara, Halborg, and Whatley, *Sainted Women*, 86–90, 96–99; and Joan M. Petersen, *Handmaids of the Lord: Contemporary Descriptions of Feminine Asceticism in the First Six Christian Centuries* (Kalamazoo, Mich.: Cistercian Publications, 1996).

85. One of the successors of Agnes as abbess of the convent.

86. Venantius Fortunatus, *Vita Hilarii Pictaviensis* (Life of Hilary of Poitiers), 1.

87. Venantius Fortunatus, *Vita Marcelli* (Life of Marcellus), 1.

88. Venantius Fortunatus, *Vita Radegundis* (Life of Radegonde), 39.

89. Subsequently, Austrapius became a priest and was designated to be Pientius's successor, but a certain Pascentius obtained the see instead (Greg.Tur. *Hist.* 4.18).

handed over to her all of her property, having set aside her own authority and keeping nothing for herself by her own right, so that, unencumbered, she might hasten in the footsteps of Christ and gain as much more for herself in heaven by however much she renounced more in this world. Indeed, her saintly life soon began to ignite in a life of humility, the richness of charity, the luminescence of chastity, and the sumptuousness of fasting; and she devoted herself to her celestial bridegroom with such total love that, embracing God with a pure heart, she felt that Christ was living within her.

(6) But, envious of good people, the enemy of humankind, whose will she shuddered to do even while she lived in this world, did not cease persecuting her, seeing that she then learned through messengers what she always feared: the exalted king[90] had come to Tours along with his son, the most exalted Sigibert, as if for devotional purposes, so that he might more easily approach Poitiers in order to receive his queen.[91]

(7) When she learned this, the blessed Radegonde wrote prayerful letters with divine attestation to Germanus,[92] bishop of the city of Paris, an apostolic man, who then was with the king. She sent them secretly through her agent Proculus[93] with gifts and blessings. And when this man, full of God, read her words, weeping and with divine attestation he prostrated himself at the feet of the king in front of the tomb of Saint Martin, seeing that it had been intimated to him in the letters that the king should not go to Poitiers. Understanding that this was a petition of the blessed queen, the king was so full of grief and motivated by penitence, that, rejecting his wicked counsellors and declaring that he, unworthy, did not deserve to have such a queen any longer, he also prostrated himself before the portals of Saint Martin at the feet of Germanus, the apostolic man, and begged that Germanus seek forgiveness from the blessed Radegonde on his behalf, in order that she might pardon him because he had sinned against her because of wicked counsellors. Whence, divine vengeance vindicated itself upon them: just like Arius, who, competing against the Catholic faith, lost all his entrails in the privy,[94] thus it turned out regarding those who acted against the blessed queen. Then the king, fearing the judgment of God because when she had lived with him his queen had obeyed the will of

---

90. I.e. Chlothar.
91. That is, to reclaim her as his wife.
92. Bishop of Paris A.D. 555–76; his life also was written by Fortunatus.
93. Otherwise unknown.
94. A similar fate befell the priest who had troubled Sidonius Apollinaris; see chapter 3.

God rather than his own, asked Germanus quickly to visit her. Thus, the lord Germanus, an apostolic man, going to Poitiers and having entered the monastery, in the oratory dedicated to the name of the lady Mary prostrated himself at the feet of the saintly queen, imploring forgiveness on behalf of the king. Truly rejoicing that she had been snatched from the maw of the world, she kindly indulged him and adapted herself to the service of God. She was freed, now, to follow Christ, whom she always had loved, wherever He might go, and she hastened to Him with a devoted spirit. Intent on such matters, she therefore made herself a guard of her own body as if it were a prison by remaining wakeful throughout the night during an extra service of vigils. And although she was forgiving to others she became a judge for herself, she was conscientious toward others but severe to herself in abstinence, generous to all but sparing toward herself, with the result that it did not suffice for her to be weeping with fasting unless she also triumphed over her own body. . . .

(16) After gathering the relics of the saints, if it had been possible she would have asked the Lord Himself, in His seat of majesty, to live here visibly. Although her carnal eye could not see Him, her spiritual mind, attentive with sedulous prayers, regarded Him. But because the Lord "withholds no good thing from those who walk in innocence"[95] and from whomever seeks Him with a whole heart and with a whole spirit and with a whole mind, just as this blessed woman did, the divine clemency showed itself to be kindly disposed and put the idea in the mind of her in whose breast it abode day and night, that, just like the blessed Helena,[96] she, imbued with wisdom, full of the fear of God, and glorious with good works, should pay tribute to the wood where the ransom of the world was hung for our salvation so that He might snatch us from the power of the devil. Thus it was that when it was found, Helena clapped with both hands and, with her knee bent to the ground, worshipped the Lord at the spot where she recognized that the divine cross itself had been lifted up for the raising of the dead, saying, "In truth, you are the Christ, the Son of God, who came into the world and redeemed your captive people, whom you created, with your precious blood." What she did in her eastern country the blessed Radegonde did in Gaul. And because as long as she lived in the world she wished to do nothing without counsel, she sent letters to the most exalted lord King Sigibert,

95. Ps. 84:11.
96. The mother of the emperor Constantine (306–37); she subsequently was believed to have discovered the true cross, hence the comparison with Radegonde in this context.

under whose authority this country was governed, in order that he might permit her, for the salvation of the entire country and the stability of his kingdom, to petition wood of the Lord's cross from the emperor. He kindly offered assent to the petition of the saintly queen. Full of devotion and aroused by desire, she, who had made herself a pauper for the sake of God, did not send gifts to the emperor. But, relying on prayer, she sent her own messengers in the company of the saints, whom she ceaselessly invoked. And she obtained what her prayers had requested, that she would rejoice to have, residing in one place, the blessed wood of the cross of the Lord, decorated with gold and gems, and many relics of the saints that the east possessed. At the petition of the saintly woman the emperor sent envoys with gospels decorated with gold and gems. But when the wood, where the salvation of the world had hung, arrived at the city of Poitiers along with the congregation of saints, and the bishop of that place[97] together with the entire population devotedly would have wished to receive it, the enemy of the human race[98] brought it about through his minions that they rejected the ransom of the world and did not want to receive it in the city—in a manner causing the blessed Radegonde to suffer tribulations claiming one thing in place of something else, in the Jewish manner,[99] which it is not our business to discuss. They themselves would see; the Lord knows those who are his. But she, with a blazing soul and a fighting spirit, wrote again to the most kindly king that they did not desire to receive salvation into the city. In the interval during which her messengers would return from the lord king, she entrusted the cross of the Lord and the guarantees of the saints, accompanied by the chanting of priests, to his own monastery at Tours that he had founded there for his own salvation. The holy cross suffered no lesser injury on account of envy than did the Lord, who, called by a faithful courier and summoned before governors and judges, patiently suffered all sorts of wickedness so that what He had created would not perish. In what great torment did her entire congregation, with daily grieving and weeping, place itself, in fastings, in vigils, and in the gushing of tears, until such time that the Lord observed the humility of his servant, and placed the idea in the heart of the king that he should provide judgment and justice in the midst of the people. Thus committed, the king sent his faithful ser-

---

97. Maroveus, who steadfastly opposed Radegonde's attempts to expand her influence at his expense.

98. That is, Satan.

99. That it, the Jews of Palestine who supposedly had opposed Helena's attempts to recover the cross.

vant, Count Justin,[100] an illustrious man, to Euphronius, bishop of the city of Tours, an apostolic man, ordering him to place the most glorious cross of the Lord and the relics of the saints in the monastery of the lady Radegonde with fitting honor, which was in fact done. The blessed woman exulted in joy with her entire company and bequeathed this gift from heaven, wonderful and given perfected to her congregation that she had assembled in the service of the Lord, knowing in her spirit that after her death they would have too little joy. Although this best provider and good governess rejoiced that, in company with the King of heaven, whence she would be able to continue to support them, she would never abandon her flock, she also bestowed upon them the ransom of the world from the guarantee of Christ, which they had sought from a distant land, for the honor of the place and the salvation of the women in her monastery. There, with the aid of the virtue of God and the assistance of the power of heaven, blind eyes receive the light, deaf ears are opened, mute tongues return to their duty, the lame walk, and demons are put to flight. What more? Whoever, afflicted by any sort of infirmity, comes in faith returns healed by the virtue of the holy cross. Who can say what a wondrous sort of gift the blessed woman bequeathed to the city? Whence, whoever lives in faith blesses her name. Indeed, with divine attestation she commended her monastery to the most exalted lord kings and the most serene lady, Queen Brunhilde,[101] whom she loved with dear affection, and to the sacrosanct churches and their bishops.

The receipt at Poitiers of the fragment of the true cross—which still survives there—was a most portentous event, so much so that it was commemorated by Radegonde's confidant Venantius Fortunatus in a poem, "Vexilla regis prodeunt" (The king's advancing banners wave), written in four-line iambic tetrameter couplets, that continues to be part of the western Christian liturgy:

3[102]   The King's advancing banners wave!
      The Cross gleams out its mystery
      where He that made the body gave

---

100. Otherwise unknown, but presumably the count of Tours.

101. Daughter of Athanagild, king of the Visigoths in Spain, and wife of King Sigibert.

102. Venantius Fortunatus, "Vexilla regis prodeunt": F. J. E. Raby, ed., *The Oxford Book of Medieval Latin Verse* (Oxford: Oxford University Press, 1959); for translation, see Lindsay, *Song of a Falling World,* 271–72; see also A. Fremantle, ed., *A Treasury of Early Christianity* (New York: Viking, 1953), 497–98.

His body to the gallows-tree.
With jagged nails His flesh is torn.
  Offering broken feet and hands
  as sign that our redemption's born,
  the sacrifice perfected stands.
The lance has pierced Him in the side,
  the cruel edge has entered in.
  Our wounds of guilt are cleansed, the tide
  of blood and water laves our sin.
This truth was anciently foretold.
  Now David's prophecy proves good,
  that cited to all the world: Behold!
  God ruled us from a throne of wood.
O beautiful and radiant tree!
  draped with His kingly crimson-dye,
  He chose the wood that worthily
  might lift such holy flesh on high.
O blessed! in your arms was laid
  the ransom of the ages, Christ.
  He bore us out of Hell. You weighed
  in scales of death those limbs unpriced.
Around your wood sweet odors pour.
  Your nectarous sap is death's defeat.
  Glad in the fertile fruit you bore,
  you love the triumph you complete.
Altar and victim, hail to you!
  O glorious was His abject pain.
  Life from death His victory drew,
  and life in death he made our gain.

Conclusion

In different kinds of traditional contexts there were opportunities for women to express themselves, enhance their status, and receive personal satisfaction. Ecclesiastical activities in particular gave women a genuine opportunity for self-expression. Women carried out charitable activities, founded churches and convents, and in some cases, like Clotilde and Radegonde, became saints. The next chapter will show that there also were other ways in which women and members of other disadvantaged or disenfranchised groups could express their individuality.

CHAPTER 7

Inappropriate Activities: Leadership, Necromancy, and Rebellion

It has been seen that the late antique social environment granted its most conspicuous benefits to male aristocrats, be they Romans or barbarians. As new opportunities, such as ecclesiastical office, became available, these too soon were appropriated by the male aristocratic establishment. So what was a slave, a pauper, or a woman who desired a greater degree of self-expression to do?

There were a number of what one might call "inappropriate activities" by means of which otherwise unprivileged individuals voiced their opinions or pursued their ambitions. Such persons were often women, whose opportunities for self-expression and fulfilment generally were limited regardless of their wealth, social status, or ethnicity. Aristocratic women, for example, who but for their gender would have had the normal options available to the aristocratic elite, sometimes engaged in undertakings that their male counterparts considered objectionable. Other kinds of unprivileged individuals did likewise.

Genovefa Saves Paris

On some occasions, ambitious and assertive women overstepped the bounds of normally acceptable behavior and assumed roles that generally were reserved for aristocratic men. Opportunities sometimes were furnished by political disruptions. In 451, during the invasion of Gaul by Attila and the Huns, the men of Paris panicked and were on the verge of abandoning the city. The holy woman Genovefa then organized the women of the city:

7.1[1]   ... (12) When the news got out that the king of the Huns, Attila, overcome by savagery, had begun to devastate the province of Gaul, the
citizens of Paris, as a result stricken with terror, attempted to convey
the moveable property and money of their assets to other safer cities.
Genovefa, assembling their wives, urged them to persevere in fasts and
prayers and vigils as much as possible so that, like Judith and Esther,
they might be able to escape the menacing catastrophe. Therefore,
agreeing with Genovefa and engaging in vigils for several days in the
baptistery, along with fasting and prayers, just as Genovefa had urged,
they abode in God. In the same way she also urged their husbands not
to remove their property from Paris, for she foretold that the ferocious
people would devastate those cities that they believed would be safer
whereas Paris would be saved, unharmed by enemies under the protection of Christ, just as it happened.

The observances that Genovefa initiated sound very similar to the
"Rogations" subsequently established by Bishop Mamertus of Vienne
in the 460s, which comprised prayers, fasts, and processions, and
became very popular both in and out of Gaul.[2] One wonders whether
he had heard of Genovefa's initiative, which certainly had the desired
result, for the Huns did indeed turn aside, and Paris was saved.

Deoteria Takes Charge

Nor was Genovefa the only Gallic woman who exercised local leadership in the face of invasion. Gregory of Tours told how Deoteria took
charge after the Frankish prince Theodebert, the son of King
Theoderic I (511–34), demanded the surrender of the fortress of
Cabrières, near Béziers, in the early 530s.

7.2[3]   (22) There was living there at this time a married woman full of energy
and resource whose name was Deoteria. Her husband had gone off to

---

1. *Vita Genovefae* (Life of Genovefa), 12: *MGH SRM* 3:219; for additional translation,
see McNamara, Halborg, and Whatley, *Sainted Women,* 23, which uses the seventeenth-
century text in the *Acta sanctorum* (Acts of the saints) *January* 1.204–38, which has some
variations from the *MGH* text.
    2. Described in Sid.Apoll. *Epist.* 7.1. Mamertus's Rogations were held about a month
after Easter.
    3. Greg.Tur. *Hist.* 3.22–23, 26–27: for translation, see Thorpe, *Gregory,* 183–85; see also
Dalton, *Gregory,* 103–5.

Béziers. She sent messengers to Theodebert to say, "No one can resist you, noble prince. We accept you as our ruler. Come to our town and do with it what you will." Theodebert marched to the fort and entered it. And seeing the people subdued, he did them no harm. Deoteria went to meet him. He found her attractive, fell in love with her, and made love to her in his own bed.

(23) . . . While this was going on, Theodebert learned that his father was gravely ill, and he knew that if he did not hurry home to him and find him still living, he would be disinherited by his uncles and would not be able to return there. So, at this news, putting aside everything else, he proceeded there, leaving Deoteria and her daughter[4] at Clermont. And a few days after he had departed, Theoderic [511–34] died, in the twenty-third year of his reign. Then Childebert [511–58] and Chlothar [511–61][5] arose against Theodebert [534–48], wishing to seize his kingdom. But he appeased them with gifts, and, defended by his retainers, he established himself in his kingdom. Later, sending to Clermont, he summoned Deoteria thence and married her.[6] [Subsequently, however, Deoteria began to fear for her position and saw her own daughter as a potential rival.]

(26) Deoteria, seeing her daughter[7] quite matured and fearing that the king would desire her and take her, placed her in a carriage drawn by untamed bulls and pitched her from a bridge. She died in the same river. This happened in the city of Verdun. [Theodebert then encountered criticism from the Franks.]

(27) Because this was now the seventh year after he had been betrothed to Visigard,[8] and he did not wish to marry her because of Deoteria, all the Franks were quite outraged against him because he had abandoned his betrothed.[9] He became apprehensive, and divorcing Deoteria, by whom he had a small son named Theodebald, he married Visegard. He remained married to her but a short time, and after her death he married another; he did not in fact marry Deoteria again.

---

4. Presumably by her first husband. Thorpe (*Gregory,* 184) assumes a daughter by Theodebert, but subsequent discussion makes this quite impossible.

5. Theodebert's two uncles.

6. It is unknown what happened to her husband.

7. Clearly, not the child of Theodebert.

8. The daughter of Wacho, king of the Lombards, suggesting that Theodebert's reluctance to marry her also caused serious diplomatic difficulties.

9. One is reminded of the case of Aunegilda in chapter 3.

In this case, Deoteria's desires eventually were thwarted by Theodebert's perceived need to adhere to the requirements of both society and politics. There is no word of her ultimate fate—although unlike many others in her position, she does seem to have lived to tell the tale.

It is impossible to know whether other strong-willed women provided leadership similar to that of Genovefa and Deoteria. Very likely they did—for they would have had just as much reason to protect their interests as their male counterparts. But any others lacked a devoted hagiographer, or a voluble historian, to provide a record of their deeds.

Ecclesiastical Expression

In the church, women did have the opportunity to indulge in philanthropic activities. In other areas, however, they were brought up short. For example, women were excluded from everyday liturgical activities. In two pronouncements, for example, the *Statuta ecclesiae antiqua* (Ancient statutes of the church), an anonymous tract compiled in southern Gaul in the late fifth century, stated, "Let not a woman, no matter how learned and holy, presume to instruct men in an assembly," and "Let not a woman presume to baptize."[10]

Women as Clerics

But such attitudes did not stop women from attempting to participate in liturgical rites. In the early sixth century, three bishops from the province of Lugdunensis III—Licinius of Tours, Melanius of Rennes, and Eustochius of Angers[11]—attempted to restrain two priests who encouraged the participation of women in the liturgy.

7.3[12]   The bishops Licinius, Melanius, and Eustochius to the priests Lovocatus and Catihernus, their most blessed lords and brothers in Christ.

---

10. "Mulier, quamvis docta et sancta, viros in conventu docere non praesumat"; "mulier baptizare non praesumat": *Statuta ecclesiae antiqua* 37, 41: *CCL* 148:172–73.

11. All three attended the Council of Orléans in 511, which gives an approximate date to this incident.

12. Licinius of Tours, Melanius of Rennes, and Eustochius of Angers, *Epist.* "Viri venerabilis": Louis Duchesne, "Lovocat et Catihern, prêtres bretons de temps de saint Mélaine," *Revue de Bretagne et de Vendée* 7 (1885): 5–18 (with French translation); A. Jülicher, "Ein gallischen Bischofsschreiben des 6. Jahrhunderts als Zeuge für die Verfassung der Montanistenkirche," *Zeitschrift für Kirchengeschichte* 16 (1896): 664–71.

We have learned through the report of that venerable man the priest Speratus that, bearing certain altars, you do not cease from making a circuit of the dwellings in the territories of different cities, and that you presume to celebrate masses there with women, whom you call *conhospitae*[13] and whom you admit to the divine sacrifice to such an extent that while you distribute the eucharist they hold the chalices in your presence and presume to administer the blood of Christ to the people. The novelty and unheard-of superstition[14] of this action grieves us to no small extent because such a horrible sect, which demonstrably never has existed in Gaul, seems to be emerging in our times. The oriental fathers called it Pepodianism on account of the fact that Pepodius was the originator of this schism. Because these people presumed to have women as their associates in the divine sacrifice, the fathers prescribed that whoever wished to cling to this error was to be rendered separated from ecclesiastical communion. Therefore, we believe that Your Charity ought to be admonished, in the first place, in the love of Christ, for the sake of ecclesiastical unity and the integrity of the Catholic faith, that when the pages of these letters come to you, an immediate cessation from the aforementioned practices shall have followed, that is, from the aforementioned altars—which we have no doubt were consecrated, as is fitting, by priests—and from those women, whom you call *conhospitae,* which appellation is not spoken or heard without a certain shivering of the spirit because it disgraces the clergy and such a detestable name strikes shame and horror into blessed religion.

Therefore, according to the statutes of the Fathers, we prescribe to Your Charity not only that little women[15] of this sort should not pollute the divine sacraments on account of this illicit ministration, but also that, with the exception of a mother, maternal aunt, sister, or granddaughter,[16] if anyone should wish to have anyone under the roof of his little cell for cohabitation, by canonical sentence let him be restrained from the threshold of the sacrosanct church. It is fitting, therefore, dearest brothers, that you exhibit a most rapid emendation,

---

13. Literally, "guests together"; subsequent discussion suggests the bishops thought they were cohabiting with the priests. Jülicher reads *cenhospitae,* "guests at the meal."

14. *Superstitio,* a word traditionally used to refer to pagan practices.

15. *Mulierculae:* a demeaning and insulting reference.

16. The same relatives are named in the canons of the "Second Council of Arles" (*CCL* 148:114) of ca. A.D. 500. Canon 18 of the Council of Agde of 506 (*CCL* 148:200), however, named mothers, sisters, daughters, and granddaughters; and note the discussion of Susanna in the previous chapter.

if it is true as it has been reported to us with regard to the aforementioned business, because for the sake of the health of souls and of the edification of the people it is expedient to rectify quickly practices so perverted from the ecclesiastical order, lest the pertinacity of this obstinacy lead you to greater confusion, and lest we have to come to you with the apostolic rod—should you refuse charity and be surrendered to Satan in the ruin of the flesh—so that your spirit might be saved. To be surrendered to Satan is this: when someone has been separated from the ecclesiastical flock on account of his own sin, let him have no doubt that he shall be devoured by both demons and rapacious wolves. Likewise, we also recall the advice of the Evangelist, where he says, "If our members scandalize us," that is, whoever of the Catholic Church enters heresy, "it is therefore more useful that this single member, which defiles the whole church, be excised rather then that the whole church be brought down into ruin."[17]

Let these few words, which we have said from many, be sufficient. Give much effort to the communion of charity, and take care to set out with the most eager devotion upon the royal road[18] from which you have strayed a little, so that you both may gain profit from obedience and we may rejoice that you are to be saved through our petition.

The Celtic-looking names and the itinerant nature of their ministrations have led to suggestions that the priests were Britons, part of the refugee population from Britain.[19]

Women as Priests

A little more can be said about the Pepuzites, whose practices Lovocatus and Catihernus were supposedly following. In a fifth-century catalog of heresies they were said to have alloted greater rights to women:

7.4[20]   The twenty-seventh heresy is that of the Pepuzites; they get their name from a certain place that Epiphanius[21] says is a deserted city. They,

---

17. Matt. 5:29–30.

18. *Viam regiam.* Cf. Faust. *De gratia* (On grace), prologue, "omissa via regia" (having departed from the royal road) (referring to the heresiarch Pelagius).

19. See Duchesne, "Lovocat et Catihern," 9.

20. *Praedestinatus* (The predestined one), 27: *PL* 53:596–97; the Italian writer Arnobius Junior has been proposed as the author.

21. Epiphanius of Salamis in Cyprus, who wrote *On the Heresies.*

however, thinking that it is something holy, call it Jerusalem. Among them they give so much leadership to women that they even honor them with the priesthood. They also say that there are two churches in this same city of Pepuza, of Quintilla and Priscilla.

The Fate of the Priscillianists

The women involved in these activities were operating, albeit irregularly, on the fringes of the established church. Others went one step further and adopted practices that were viewed as even more unacceptable. In the mid-380s, a number of Spanish and Gallic women enthusiastically embraced the reforms of Priscillian of Avila, which offered them a greater degree of participation than was available in the traditional church.[22] Representatives of the established social order, of course, attempted to impugn Priscillian's reputation, as seen in this passage from the *Chronicle* of Sulpicius Severus.

7.5[23] Priscillian was able to remain wakeful very much and to bear hunger and thirst, not at all desirous of possessions, and most sparing in their use. But he also was excessively vain and conceited more than was fitting on account of his knowledge of pagan learning; in fact, it is thought that beginning in his youth he had practiced magic arts. When he ventured upon his destructive doctrine, he enticed many nobles and even more of the common people by his persuasive authority and his flattering manner. At this point, women, desirous of new things, flowing with faith and with a nature curious about everything, flocked to him in swarms, for, affecting an air of humility in speech and dress, he inspired dignity in himself and reverence from everyone. . . . [He and his followers then travelled to Gaul.]

At Bordeaux, they were expelled by Delphinus,[24] but they nevertheless lingered for a while on the estate of Euchrotia[25] and infected several persons with their errors. They then resumed the journey they had undertaken with a completely shameful and disgraceful throng,

---

22. For Priscillian, see Henry Chadwick, *Priscillian of Avila: The Occult and the Charismatic in the Early Church* (Oxford: Clarendon, 1976).

23. Sulpicius Severus, *Chronicon* (Chronicle), 2.46–48: *CSEL* 1:99–101.

24. Bishop of Bordeaux.

25. The wife of the rhetorician Attius Tiro Delphidius of Bordeaux, who served under the usurper Magnentius (350–53) but was subsequently pardoned. He died before Euchrotia's involvement with Priscillian. See *PLRE* 1:246.

accompanied by their wives and even by other women, among whom were Euchrotia and her daughter Procula, regarding whom it was reported that, having become pregnant through fornication with the men of Priscillian, she aborted her fetus using herbs. . . . [They then were arrested, brought to Trier, and tried before the praetorian prefect Evodius.]

Priscillian was heard and convicted of a double charge: of practicing magic, and he did not deny that he studied obscene teachings, and that he organized nocturnal meetings of lewd women and that he was accustomed to pray in the nude. Evodius pronounced him guilty and remanded him into custody. When he appealed to the emperor, the trial records were forwarded to the palace, and the monarch determined that Priscillian and his comrades ought to suffer capital punishment. . . . Latronianus[26] and Euchrotia also were executed.

Under imperial rule, such practices, and the use of magic and divination in particular, were seen as extremely subversive and were savagely repressed. But this use of state authority to execute the losers in Christian disputes over jurisdiction and teaching became a cause celèbre and brought the emperor Maximus (383–88) into much disrepute. After the decline of Roman authority, however, the authorities often exhibited greater forbearance toward such individuals, even toward the practice of sorcery.

The Supernatural

Nor was Priscillian the only person who was said to have used magical arts during this period. Far from it. In fact, the practice of sorcery was rampant during Late Antiquity.[27] Recourse to the supernatural seems to have served several important roles. For one thing, it furnished an opportunity for self-fulfilment to those whose aspirations might have

---

26. Not otherwise mentioned, but presumably a supporter of Priscillian, perhaps somehow connected to Euchrotia. There is no indication of the fate of Procula: *PLRE* 1:246 suggests that she was executed too.

27. See, in general, Peter Brown, "Sorcery, Demons, and the Rise of Christianity from Late Antiquity into the Middle Ages," in *Witchcraft Confessions and Accusations,* ed. M. Douglas (London: Tavistock, 1970), 17–45; V. I. J. Flint, *The Rise of Magic in Early Medieval Europe* (Princeton: Princeton University Press, 1991); and F. Graf, *La magie dans l'Antiquité Greco-Romaine* (Paris: Belles lettres, 1994).

been thwarted in other regards. Furthermore, it provided a socially acceptable means of expressing controversial opinions. It allowed the boundaries of convention momentarily to be crossed. Perhaps the extraordinary nature of supernatural manifestations made them acceptable because, not being part of the normal social order, they were not, in some sense, in violation of it.

The pervasive fascination with the supernatural crossed lines of class, gender, and economic status.[28] Which is not to say, however, that all who dabbled in it were perceived or treated equally. Individuals from the privileged classes who engaged in such activities often went on to become bishops or saints. Supernatural manifestations involving them were described as miracles and were lauded in the literary sources.[29] Less savory persons who engaged in similar activities were described as *mathematici* (fortune-tellers), *magi* (magicians), *harioli* (diviners), and so on, and generally encountered not only opprobrium and disdain, but also a touch of trepidation.

Two Con-Men and Their Mark

An illustration of how such persons were perceived is found in the *Querolus,* where the gullible protagonist (Querolus) encounters in the street two henchmen (Sardanapallus and the Sycophant) of the magician Mandrogerus. The two con-men begin the scene by pretending not to know that they are being overheard.

7.6[30]   *Sard. [Whispering]* Hey! There he is. *[Loudly enough for Querolus to hear]* I wish, by Hercules, to meet that fellow I just saw. I've known magicians and soothsayers, but I certainly don't know one like him. He knows how to decipher a man, not like some tricksters usually do.

Quer. [At first talking to himself] Hey! What kind of diviner are they discussing?

Sard. But what I just saw is something new. When he spots you, first

---

28. Even bishops like Sidonius Apollinaris could claim to have some knowledge of practices such as astrology; see his *Epist.* 8.11.9.

29. No bishop, or saint, worth his or her salt was not endowed with the ability to deal with the supernatural; see e.g., the *Life of Germanus of Auxerre,* 11, for an encounter with a ghost.

30. *Querolus* 2.2 (47–64), ed. Peiper, 25–26; ed. Jacquemard–Le Saos, 30–42.

he tells you your name, then he expounds on your parents, your servants, and your entire family, as if he knows what you've done for your whole life and what you're going to do later: he explains it all.

Quer. This sounds good, by Hercules; I don't know who this is, but this story isn't to be passed up.

Sycoph. I ask you, if you have no objection, should we go to meet that magician on some sort of pretext?

Sard. Oh, stupid and silly me for not having consulted him immediately!

Sycoph. I would think, by Hercules, that you knew, in fact, that there is no time for it.

Quer. Why don't I find out everything? *[To them]* Greetings, friends.

Sycoph. Greetings to you who offered greetings to us.

Quer. What are you up to, something secret?

Sard. Secret from the public, not secret from discreet men.[31]

Quer. I heard you mention something about a magician.

Sard. That's right. Our discussion was about someone who divines everything. But, whoever he is, I don't know.

Quer. Is there such a person?

Sard. Yes, indeed. Sycophant, as I said, I ask you, on your own behalf and that of your friends, if you will humor me, to go there along with me.

Sycoph. I already said that I'd go freely and moreso, if I had the time now.

Sard. Stay awhile.

Quer. I ask you, friend, not to leave so quickly. I too would like to know for myself who he was, the one you were just discussing.

Sycoph. By Hercules, I don't know; I have other business. My relatives and friends are already expecting me at home.

Sard. By God, it's hard to persuade this man. Neither your relatives nor your friends are expecting you now. Stay awhile.

Quer. I ask you, friends, if my company isn't annoying to you, I'd like to consult him along with you.

Sard. I fear, by Hercules, that he'll make it difficult for us if he sees too many people.

---

31. The consulting of soothsayers, of course, was illegal.

Sycoph. That's fine, by Pollux. There! If you please, you were seeking a comrade; now you have one. Don't bother me.

Quer. I ask you, friend, if that's how it seems to him, let him go: we'll
go together.

Sard. But we need him, because he's seen that man and he knows
him well.

Quer. *[To the Sycophant]* It's only fair that you render us this service, for the plan requires it to be so.

Sycoph. Not at all, by Hercules, *he* knows him better and *he* is more
friendly with him.

Quer. But I now ask your trust: who is this man, or where does he
come from?

Sycoph. As far as I know, he's called Mandrogerus—this I know.

Quer. *[Shivering with delight]* Oh! A charming name, by Hercules, I
already think that this concerns magicians.

Sycoph. He speaks first of past events. If you know them all, then
he'll discuss the future.

Quer. By Hercules, you describe a great magician. And you don't
want to consult him?

Sycoph. I certainly do, but at the moment I just don't have the
time.[32]

Eventually, all three did go off to consult Mandrogerus.

Specific examples of magicians and soothsayers are often mentioned
by Gregory of Tours. The lesser social status of these individuals is
demonstrated, among other things, by Gregory's frequent failure even
to give their names. And in nearly every case the individual is a woman.

Demonical Possession

Sometimes the supernatural was manifested as some form of mental illness. Affected persons typically were described as being possessed by
demons. Their activities could be used not only as literary foils to
demonstrate the power of a holy person or saint, but also, it seems, as
a mechanism for the expression of controversial opinions and public
sentiment.

In one case, circa 585, Magnericus, bishop of Trier, went to the

---

32. See the companion volume for additional text.

church of St. Maximinus at Trier to pray for Bishop Theodorus of Marseille, who had been detained by King Childebert:

7.7[33]   He prayed and wept for a long time. . . . As he did so a woman who was possessed by the spirit of error began to shout at him. "You wicked man, grown old in sinfulness," she said. "You who petition the Lord for our enemy Theodorus, surely you realize that no day passes without our begging that this man who unceasingly fans the flames that consume us should be exiled from Gaul. All the same, you go on praying for him! You would be wiser to concentrate on the affairs of your own church and to ensure that the poor lack nothing, instead of using up all your energy in praying for Theodorus." Then she added, "This is a sorry day for us, for we are powerless to destroy him." And although we ought not to put credence in anything that devils say, nevertheless the sort of man that he was is clear from what the lamenting demon said about him.

In this case, the woman's outburst provided an outlet for an aspect of public opinion for which there was no institutionalized method of expression.

A Death in the Ecclesiastical Family

Another case of possession occurred at the death of the abbot Aredius of Limoges in 591:

7.8[34]   On the sixth day of his illness, a certain woman, who had long been possessed of an unclean spirit of which the saint had been unable to cure her, and whose hands were bound behind her back, began to shout, "Run, citizens! Leap for joy, you people! Go out to meet the saints and martyrs who are gathering together for the passing of St. Aredius! Here is Julian of Brioude, and here Privatus of Mende. Martin has come from Tours, and Martial from Aredius' own city.[35] Here

---

33. Greg.Tur. *Hist.* 8.12; translation from Thorpe, *Gregory,* 443; see also Dalton, *Gregory,* 337.

34. Greg.Tur. *Hist.* 10.29; translation from Thorpe, *Gregory,* 591–92; see also Dalton, *Gregory,* 468.

35. All of these were famous Gallic saints. St. Martial was the first bishop of Limoges, supposedly in the mid–third century.

come Saturninus of Toulouse, Dionysius of Paris, and all the others now in heaven to whom you are wont to pray as God's saints and martyrs." Her master had her tied up, but he was unable to hold her. She broke her bonds and hurried off to the monastery, shouting as she went. Only a short time later the saintly man breathed his last, there being considerable evidence that he was taken up by angels. During his funeral, just as the grave was closing over him, Aredius cleansed this woman from the curse of the devil who infested her, together with another woman possessed by an even more evil spirit.

In her madness, the woman served as a cheerleader for Aredius by publicly promoting his eligibility to be included among the ranks of Gaul's most distinguished saints.

Supernatural Intervention

On other occasions, prophecies were uttered without being directly attributed to diabolical or demoniacal possession. For example, after the death of Bishop Venerandus of Clermont in the early fifth century, a controversy arose—as was often the case—over the choice of a new bishop:

7.9[36]   After his death, the most shameful argument arose among the local inhabitants concerning the election of a bishop to replace him. Different factions were formed, some of which wanted this man and others that, and there was great dissension among the people. One Sunday when the electing bishops were sitting in conclave, a woman wearing a veil over her head to mark the fact that she was a true servant of God came boldly in and said: "Listen to me, priests of the Lord! You must realize that it is true that not one of those whom they have put forward for the bishopric finds favor in the sight of God. This very day the Lord in person will choose Himself a bishop. Do not inflame the people or allow any more argument among them, but be patient for a little while, for the Lord will now send us the man who is to rule over our church." As they sat wondering at her words, there came in a man called Rusti-

36. Greg. Tur. *Hist.* 2.13: translation from Thorpe, *Gregory,* 129–30; see also Dalton, *Gregory,* 57.

cus,[37] a priest of the diocese of Clermont. He was the very man who had been pointed out to the woman in a vision. As soon as she set eyes on him she cried, "That is the man whom the Lord elects! That is the man whom He has chosen to be your bishop! That is the man whom you must consecrate." As she spoke the entire population forgot all its previous disagreement and shouted that this was the correct and proper choice. To the great joy of the populace, he was set on the episcopal throne and accepted as bishop.

This prophecy seems to have been a one-time occurrence: there is no indication that the woman was in the habit of doing such things. Her outburst occurred at a crucial point, and resolved a crisis that could not be settled by other means.

The Paris Fire

On another occasion, in 585, a woman prophesied that Paris would be stricken with a great conflagration.

7.10[38]   There was at this time a woman resident in the city of Paris who made the following pronouncement to the townsfolk: "You must know that the whole of this town is about to be destroyed by a firestorm. You had better evacuate it." They mostly laughed at her, saying that she had had her fortune told, or that she had dreamed it, or that she had been possessed by the noontide demon.[39] "None of what you say is true," she answered. "What I tell you is what is really going to happen. I saw in a vision a man coming out of St. Vincent's church, radiant with light, holding a wax candle in his hand and setting fire to the merchants' houses one after another." Finally, on the third night after the woman said these things, as twilight set in, one of the citizens lit a lamp and went into a storehouse to fetch oil and other things that he needed there, but he left his lamp behind, next to a cask of oil. His house was the first one next to the gate that gives access at midday. Having caught fire from this light, the house was incinerated, and others began to

---

37. The Rustici were one of the most distinguished families of late antique Gaul, as already seen in chapter 1.

38. Greg.Tur. *Hist.* 8.33: for translation, see Thorpe, *Gregory,* 465–66; see also Dalton, *Gregory,* 356–57.

39. For the "daemonium meridianum," see the *Life of Eutropius,* selection 5.2 above.

catch fire from it. Then, when the fire spread upon those imprisoned in the jail, the blessed Germanus[40] appeared to them and, shattering the beam and chains by which they were held captive and having opened the door to the jail, he permitted those who had been imprisoned to depart unharmed. They exited and betook themselves to the basilica of St. Vincent, in which the grave of the blessed bishop[41] is situated, Therefore, as the wind blew the flames here and there through the whole city, and the conflagration dominated with all of its force, it began to approach the other gate, where the oratory of the blessed Martin was located, which at one time had been built because he had cured the leprosy of a blighted man by means of a kiss.

The fire eventually ran its course, and as for the woman who had made the prophecy, nothing more of her was said.

Bishop as Necromancer

Some women made something of a career out of their fortune-telling. They were thought of as latter-day manifestations of the Pythia, who had been the priestess of Apollo at Delphi, with the ability to foretell the future.[42] Even members of the Christian ecclesiastical establishment, such as Gregory of Tours, accorded such persons an accepted, if irregular, place in society. An incident in which Gregory himself not only participated but even indulged in a little bit of necromancy of his own occurred at a dinner of the Frankish prince Merovech circa 570. Gregory began with an innocent sort of fortune-telling, the *sortes biblicae* (biblical lottery), in which one randomly opened the Bible and read the first verse one saw. This custom, based upon the pagan *sortes vergilianae* (Vergilian lottery), which used Vergil's *Aeneid* in the same way, had been forbidden by several Gallic church councils.[43]

11[44] One day, I was invited to a banquet of his. As we sat side by side, he begged me to read some passages to him for the instruction of his soul.

---

40. St. Germanus of Paris, not St. Germanus of Auxerre.

41. That is, St. Germanus of Paris.

42. Her name was derived from that of Pytho, the serpent slain at Delphi by Apollo.

43. E.g. the Council of Vannes of ca. 461/491 (can. 16: *CCL* 148:156), and the Council of Agde of 506 (can. 42: *CCL* 148:210–11).

44. Greg.Tur. *Hist.* 5.14: translation from Thorpe, *Gregory,* 269–72; see also Dalton, *Gregory,* 179–84.

I opened the book of Solomon and read the first verse I found. It contained these words, "The eye that mocketh at his father, the ravens of the valley shall pick it out."[45] Merovech did not see the point of this, but it is my opinion that the verse was chosen by the Lord.

Then Guntram[46] sent one of his lads to a certain woman, already known to him in the time of King Charibert, who had the spirit of the Pythia and could tell him the things to come. He also used to claim that she had foretold for him the very time, not only the year but even the hour, when King Charibert was to die.[47] She sent back to him these proclamations through his servants: "It is foreordained that King Chilperic will die this year, and that King Merovech will obtain the entire kingdom, with his brothers excluded. You, indeed, will hold the dukedom of his entire kingdom for five years. But in the sixth year you will obtain the favor of the episcopate,[48] with the approval of the people, in a city that is located north of the Loire, on the right bank. Then, as an old man and full of days, you will depart from this world." And when the returning servants announced this to their master, he was immediately aroused by vanity, as if he already sat on the throne in the church of Tours, and he reported these words to me. Mocking his credulity, I said, "Such things must be requested only from God, for the things that the Devil promises ought not to be believed." As he departed in confusion, I also greatly ridiculed a man who thought that such things were to be believed. Subsequently, on a certain night, after vigils had been performed in the basilica of the holy bishop,[49] while I was lying in my bed asleep, I saw an angel flying through the air. And when it passed over the holy basilica, it said in a great voice, "Woe, woe! God has stricken Chilperic and all his sons, nor will any who came from his loins rule his kingdom in the future." He had at that time—daughters excepted—four sons from various wives. But when this dream was fulfilled in the future, I clearly realized that the things the soothsayers promised were false.

---

45. Prov. 30:17.

46. Guntram Boso, a *dux* (duke) of King Sigibert.

47. The use of necromancy to learn a person's time of death was very common. Roman legislation made it illegal to do so for the emperors.

48. The woman clearly was familiar with the common practice of high secular officials being able to secure episcopal sees.

49. That is, in the basilica of St. Martin.

Gregory, apparently, was not going to play second fiddle to a wise woman when it came to sorcery, whatever name it went by. Necromancy and prophecy were acceptable, it seems, as long as they were carried out in a Christian guise.

Putting Sorcery to Work

Gregory also told of another woman who made a career out of her prophetic propensities and circa 585 came into conflict with a bishop—with predictable results.

12[50] At this time there was a woman who had the spirit of the Pythia. She gained much profit for her masters by her prowess in divination. She so won their favor that they set her free and let her live as she wished. If anyone had been the victim of a robbery or any other disaster, she would immediately announce where the thief had fled, to whom he had handed over his ill-gotten gains, or what else he had done with them. Every day she acquired more and more gold and silver, and she would walk about so loaded with jewelry that she was looked upon by the common people as a sort of goddess. When this reached the ears of Agericus, bishop of Verdun, he sent to have her arrested. She was seized and brought before him, and, in accordance with what we read in the Acts of the Apostles [Acts 16:16], he realized that she was possessed by an unclean spirit that had the spirit of the Pythia. When Agericus had pronounced over her the power of exorcism and had anointed her forehead with holy oil, the Devil cried out and revealed his identity to the bishop. However, Agericus was unsuccessful in freeing the woman of this devil, and she was allowed to depart. She realized that she could no longer live in that neighborhood, so she made her way to Queen Fredegund and sought refuge with her.

This case shows how a woman of servile origin was able, as a result of her magical skills, not only to gain her freedom, but also to become quite well-to-do to boot. She provides an analogue to Andarchius, discussed in chapter 3.

---

50. Greg.Tur. *Hist.* 7.44: translation from Thorpe, *Gregory,* 426–27; see also Dalton, *Gregory,* 320.

Hatching a Plot

Another wise woman was of sufficient status and reputation that Gregory even deigned to give her name: Septimima, the nurse of the children of King Childebert. Her story involves Faileuba, the wife of King Childebert II; Queen Brunhilde (Childebert's mother); and Droctulfus, Septimima's paramour and coconspirator. While Faileuba was recovering from the loss of a newborn child in 589, she learned about a conspiracy, which she reported to Childebert:

7.13[51]   Her words, moreover, were to this effect, that Septimima, nurse to the royal children, was to persuade the king to banish his mother, desert his wife, and marry another woman. In this way the conspirators hoped to do with the king what they wished and to obtain from him what they asked. If the king refused to agree to what Septimima was to press upon him, he was to be killed by witchcraft. His sons were to be trained to succeed him, and in the meantime the conspirators would take over the government, the young princes' mother and grandmother being banished all the same. The informers said that those privy to the plot were Sunnegysilis, the count of the stables, the referendary Gallomagnus, and Droctulfus, who had been deputed to help Septimima in bringing up the royal children. Septimima and Droctulfus were taken into custody. They were immediately put to the torture by being stretched upon the rack, whereupon Septimima confessed that she had killed her husband by witchcraft because she was in love with Droctulfus, and that he had joined with her in fornication. . . . Septimima and Droctulfus were severely beaten and her face was disfigured with red-hot irons . . . and she was packed off to the country estate of Marlenheim to turn the mill and grind the grain.

Septimima's scheme to become a power behind the throne, therefore, came to nought. At least, however, she was allowed to live, something that probably would not have happened in Roman times.[52]

---

51. Greg.Tur. *Hist.* 9.38: for translation, see Thorpe, *Gregory,* 524–26; see also Dalton, *Gregory,* 408–9.

52. See, e.g., Ammianus Marcellinus 26.3.3 for a chariotteer who was executed for apprenticing his son to a sorcerer.

Sorceress as Saint

Only rarely did a sorceress "make good." One who did was St. Genovefa of Paris, who lived in the mid–fifth century and had the good fortune to have an account of her life composed in the first half of the sixth century by a devoted hagiographer. The great bulk of her *vita* consists of miracles that she performed. Many were of the typical sort: curing the sick (including the paralyzed, blind, and deaf), casting out demons, and raising the dead.[53] She also was able to create wine and oil ex nihilo, to light candles, and to cause doors to open of their own accord.[54]

But other miracles were somewhat sinister in nature, and by a detractor could have been associated with sorcery. She had the ablity not only—like the sorceresses mentioned by Gregory—to predict the future,[55] but also to read minds. The latter power seems to have caused some concern. Even her dutiful biographer had a little trouble explaining it:

4[56] (10) And to many living in this world she clearly revealed their secret thoughts, which, on account of disdainful people, it is better to pass by in silence rather than to point out to the envious, who have a great penchant for slander. For when they resent good people, they reveal their own superstitious mentality . . .

In spite of his promise, Genovefa's hagiographer could not resist mentioning one instance of mind reading, when Genovefa pointed out a false virgin of Bourges by "revealing the place and the time and very man who had violated her body."[57] Other occult activities of Genovefa included the abilities to summon and subdue sea monsters, and to control the weather.[58]

---

53. Sick: *Vita Genovefae*, 36–38; paralyzed: 24, 28, 32, 35, 38; blind: 5, 23, 36 (bis), 48; deaf: 41, 48; demons: 29, 38, 44–46, 51; dead: 31, 42.

54. Wine and oil: *Vita Genovefae*, 19, 51. Candles: 20–22. Doors: 25, 27.

55. *Vita Genovefae*, 16.

56. *Vita Genovefae*, 10: *MGH SRM* 3:218; for another translation, see McNamara, Halborg, and Whatley, *Sainted Women*, 22.

57. *Vita Genovefae*, 29.

58. Sea monsters: *Vita Genovefae*, 34; weather: 49–50, on which cf. the sorcerer of Orange, selection 5.2 above.

Genovefa also had a disturbing tendency to cause those who provoked her to become ill or disabled: on three different occasions she
blinded them—one was her own mother (in this case, she did relent and
lift the curse twenty-one months later).[59] In another instance, she used
her power on behalf of a less-privileged individual at Orléans:

(43)[60] And it happened that in the same city she interceded with a certain man on behalf of a blameworthy servant. And it is said that after
he, obdurate with pride and cunning, in no way pardoned the servant
she addressed him with these words: "If you consider me despicable as
a suppliant, my Lord Jesus Christ does not despise me, because he is
clement in forgiveness." And when that man returned home, he soon
was inflamed with such a fever that, gasping and burning, he was
unable to rest during the entire night. Moreover, the next day at first
light, with his mouth open and dribbling saliva like an *urus,* which in
ordinary speech means an ox, having thrown himself at Genovefa's
feet, he even prayed that pardon, which the day before he had refused
to his servant, be given to him. Truly, with the blessed Genovefa sign-
ing him, all fever and illness departed from him, and the master, thus
whole in spirit and body, likewise granted pardon to his servant.

Such intercession, of course, was typical of the activities of male holy
men. When a woman presumed to try to do the same, she initially was
disregarded. Only by summoning divine retribution was she able to
prevail.

In 451, early in her career, Genovefa encountered some popular
hostility: "The citizens of Paris rampaged against her, saying that she
appeared as a false prophet in her own times. . . . The citizens therefore
conspired to punish Genovefa by pelting her with stones or drowning
her in a vast pool."[61] She only was rescued by the timely arrival of a
cleric from Auxerre, who read to the crowd some *eulogiae* (fine words)
about her that had been left by St. Germanus of Auxerre.

---

59. *Vita Genovefae,* 5, 23, 33. In the Salic Law, the penalty for such "bewitching" was 63
solidi (*Lex Salica* 19.2).

60. *Vita Genovefae,* 43: *MGH SRM* 3:233; for translation, see McNamara, Halborg, and
Whatley, *Sainted Women,* 33.

61. "Insurrexerunt in eam cives Parisiorum, dicentes, pseudoprophetam suis temporibus
aparuisse . . . tractantibus ergo civibus ut Genovefam aut lapidibus obrutam aut vasto gur-
gite mersam punirent" (*Vita Genovefae,* 12–13).

What, one might ask, caused the resentment toward Genovefa? Part of the explanation may lie in the kinds of undertakings she engaged in. Along with doing things that were permitted to women, such as church building,[62] she also participated in activities that were customarily reserved for men. Her organization of the defense of Paris in 451 against the Huns already has been discussed, as has been her assumption of the role of mediator. Furthermore, she took responsibility for freeing captives, and for relieving a famine that occurred in Paris during a siege by the Franks, perhaps in the 470s.[63] All of these were typical male endeavors, and the subsequent failure to give Genovefa her due resulted in her biographer's plaintive assertion that her deeds were just as meritorious as those of Martin of Tours and Anianus of Orléans: "Moreover, does not Genovefa deserve to be honored, who likewise averted the aforementioned army from afar by her prayers, so that Paris was not surrounded?"[64]

How, then, was Genovefa able to go on to sainthood when so many like her were condemned as witches—a fate that Genovefa herself seems only narrowly to have averted? Her rehabilitation owes much, it seems, to her association with St. Germanus of Auxerre. That, perhaps, plus the fact that she seems to have been an aristocrat herself. Nor did it hurt to have an earnest hagiographer who was willing to make her case for her.

Attacking the Ecclesiastical Establishment

In many areas of endeavor, opportunities for advancement, recognition, and self-fulfilment were available only to aristocratic men. This certainly was the case in politics, in the church, and, usually, in the literary world. Nonaristocrats of either sex who desired similar fulfilment had to adopt unorthodox methods. Sometimes, as seen in the cases of Amantius and even Andarchius, these activities fell—barely—within the bounds of social acceptability. In the case of Genovefa, too, the social safety valves only barely functioned.

---

62. She built a church of St. Dionysius: *Vita Genovefae,* 13ff.

63. Captives: *Vita Genovefae* 25, 55 (posthumously). Famine: 34–40. For the role of aristocratic men in famine relief, see Mathisen, "Nature or Nurture."

64. "Porro Genovefa nonne dignum est honorari, quae idem orationibus suis praedictum exercitum, ne Parisius circumdaret, procul abegit?": *Vita Genovefae,* 14.

The Pseudo-Christ

But some extraordinary individuals went too far. There are examples of blatant opposition to the established social order. Sometimes, the ecclesiastical establishment was challenged at its very foundations. One case involved a particularly egregious invocation of the supernatural. In A.D. 590, a Gallic opportunist claimed to be Christ himself. Gregory of Tours put some interesting twists on the tale, portraying him as something of an early-day televangelist cum Robin Hood.

7.15[65]　And in Gaul, the plague that I have often mentioned attacked the province of Marseille, and a savage famine afflicted Angers, Nantes, and Le Mans. In fact, this was the beginning of the sorrows, according to that which the Lord says in the Gospels, "There will be pestilence, famine, and earthquakes in various places, and false Christs and false prophets will rise up, and they will present signs and prodigies in the sky to the extent that they will lead the chosen into error,"[66] just as has happened at the present time.

At the time of the plague a man from Bourges entered a forest in order to chop some wood. There, he was attacked by a swarm of flies sent by the Devil, and he became insane for two years, whence one is given to understand that this wickedness was a discharge from the Devil. Subsequently, after passing through the neighboring cities, he arrived in the province of Arles, and there, clothed in animal skins, he prayed as if he were a religious. In order to fool him, the adverse side gave him the power to prophesy. Then, so that he might proceed to greater iniquity, he left his place and, abandoning the aforementioned province, entered the territory of Javols, presenting himself as a great man and not afraid to profess himself to be Christ. He traveled with a certain woman whom he passed off as his sister, and whom he had called Mary. A multitude of people flocked to him with their sick, whom he cured with his touch. His followers gave him gold, silver, and clothing, which he, in order to mislead them more easily, doled out to the poor. Prostrating himself on the ground, pouring out prayers with the aforementioned woman, and arising, he again ordered those stand-

---

65. Greg.Tur. *Hist.* 10.25; translation informed by Dalton, *Gregory,* 461–63; and Thorpe, *Gregory,* 584–86.

66. Matt. 24:7; Mark 13:22.

ing about to worship him. He even foretold the future; he foresaw illness for some, afflictions for others, and future salvation only for a few. All this he did by devilish arts and by tricks that I cannot explain. A great number of people were deceived by him, not only the uneducated, but even priests in orders. More than three thousand people followed him wherever he went.

Then he began to rob and despoil those he met on the road, giving to the poor and needy all he took. He made death threats against bishops and townspeople if they refused to worship him. Entering the territory of St-Paulien, he proceeded to a place called Anicium[67] and halted with his whole band near the neighboring churches, disposing his men like an army, as if to attack Aurelius, at that time bishop of the diocese. He then sent before him, as messengers to anounce his arrival, naked men, who leapt and performed antics as they went. The bishop, astounded at these doings, sent to him stout fellows[68] to ask of him the meaning of these proceedings. One, who was foremost among them, first bowed down as if to kiss his knees, thus impeding his movements, and commanded him to be seized and stripped. He then in a trice drew his sword and cut him to pieces.

So fell and died this Christ, who should rather be called Antichrist, and all his following were dispersed. The woman Mary was put to the torture, and she disclosed all his visionary schemes and his tricks. The men whose wits, by his devilish cunning, he had deranged so that they believed in him, never wholly recovered their senses, but ever professed him to be Christ, and this Mary to be partaker in his divinity. And throughout all the land of Gaul there arose many, attracting to themselves by such deceptions weak women, who in a frenzy proclaimed them to be saints; and so they magnified themselves among the people. I myself saw many of them, whom by sharp reproof I strove to recall from their errors.

Gregory not only understood that such phenomena seemed to be engendered by times of community stress, but also recognized how prevalent that they were.

---

67. Le Puy.
68. Cf. the henchmen of Bishop Cautinus of Clermont who imprisoned the priest Anastasius in selection 2.7 above.

The Nuns' Revolt

By far the most spectacular example of assertiveness by women during Late Antiquity is the revolt of the nuns of Poitiers in 589–90. The primary players included the nun Clotilde, a putative daughter of King Charibert and namesake of the wife of Clovis; Basina, a daughter of King Chilperic and therefore a cousin of Clotilde; the prioress Justina, niece of Gregory of Tours; and Leobovera, abbess of the convent of the Holy Cross. Gregory became personally involved himself and provided a lengthy account of the incident.

7.16[69] (39) In the monastery at Poitiers there arose a great scandal. The Devil seduced the heart of Clotilde, who boasted herself to be the daughter of King Charibert. Relying upon her kinship with the royal house, she bound the nuns by oath to join in bringing charges against the abbess Leobovera, who should then be expelled from the monastery, while she herself should be chosen superior in her place. She then left the convent with forty or more nuns, including her cousin Basina, daughter of Chilperic, saying, "I am going to my royal kinsfolk, to make known to them the insults put upon us, how we are humiliated in this place as though we were not kings' daughters but the offspring of low serving-women."[70] Rash and unhappy woman, not remembering how conspicuous for humility was the blessed Radegonde, foundress of that monastery.

She now went forth from this house and came to Tours, and giving me greeting, said, "I beseech you, holy bishop, deign to take under your protection and to maintain these virgins, reduced to great humiliation by the abbess of Poitiers, while I myself go to our royal kinsmen to make plain to them all that we suffer, and then come again." I answered them, "If the abbess is in fault, or has in anything transgressed any of the canons, let me go to my brother, Bishop Maroveus, and together let us convict her of offense, then, when the matter is arranged, go back into the monastery, lest that which the holy Radegonde accumulated through perpetual fasts and prayers and with constant charity be wantonly dispersed." But she replied, "Not so, but we

---

69. Greg.Tur. *Hist.* 9.39–43; translation from Dalton, *Gregory,* 409–21; see also Thorpe, *Gregory,* 526–39.

70. Note that Clotilde's opportunity to act in this manner was predicated upon her royal birth. Others of lesser status would not have had such an opportunity.

will seek the kings." Then I said, "Why do you resist the voice of reason? Why do you refuse to heed my episcopal admonition? I fear that the assembled bishops of the churches may remove you from communion."[71] . . . Clotilde said, "No more delay will detain us here before we go to the kings, whom we know to be our kinsfolk." They had come from Poitiers on foot, nor did they have the benefit of a single horse. They therefore were breathless and without resources. Not even on the road had anyone offerred them any food or nourishment. They in fact arrived in our city on the first day of the month; there were in fact great rainstorms, and the roads were a quagmire as a result of the immense excess of water.

(40) They also disparaged their bishop, saying that it was through his deceit that they had been driven to forsake the monastery. . . . With the other nuns left at Tours and entrusted to the care of her cousin,[72] Clotilde went on to King Guntram.[73] Having been received by him and honored with gifts, she returned to Tours. . . . She awaited the bishops, who had been ordered by the king to come and adjudicate their quarrel with the abbess. Many of them, however, had been enticed by evil men, and had been joined in matrimony even before she returned from the king. And while they were awaiting the arrival of the bishops, they felt that none would come. So they returned to Poitiers and fortified themselves inside the basilica of St. Hilary. They allied themselves with thieves, murderers, adulterers, and those guilty of all sorts of crimes, preparing themselves for battle and saying, "We are queens, nor will we enter our monastery until the abbess has been thrown out." [Gundegiselus, bishop of Bordeaux, and other bishops, including Maroveus of Poitiers, gather in the city and attempt to restore order.]

(41) But when they obstinately resisted, and after the bishops, in accordance with the letter cited above, sentenced them to excommunication, the crowd of the aforementioned ruffians assaulted them in the very basilica of St. Hilary with such carnage that the bishops were thrown onto the pavement and were scarcely able to get up, and, in

----

71. Bishops could threaten to excommunicate those who challenged them. In this instance, Gregory himself did not have the authority to do so because these were not his own parishoners.

72. That is, Basina.

73. Her presumed uncle Guntram, however, had no authority to act inasmuch as Poitiers lay in the territory of her cousin Childebert II. But subsequent events show that Clotilde would receive no backing from Childebert, so perhaps she hoped at least for moral support from Guntram.

addition, the deacons and other clerics left the basilica covered in blood, their heads broken. Such a great terror pervaded them, at the instigation of the Devil I do believe, that they left the holy place without even saying goodbye to each other, and each departed by any road upon which he could skulk off. . . . After this, Clotilde selected overseers and occupied the estates of the monastery, and whomever she was able to capture at the monastery she subjugated to servitude, assailing them with blows and slaughter, threatening that, if she were able to enter the monastery, she would expel the abbess by throwing her from the wall to the ground. When this was reported to King Childebert, he immediately issued a direct order to Count Macco to correct this situation with all his effort.

Macco was count of Poitiers and seems to have been doing nothing to get the situation under control. Nor did he do anything now, and there followed a fruitless exchange of letters, following which King Childebert again intervened:

(43)[74] . . . Then King Childebert, because he was suffering persistent aggravations from each side, that is to say from the monastery and from the woman who had departed from it, deputed the priest Theutharius[75] to resolve the quarrels that they were carrying on among themselves. When Clotilde and the other women were summoned to a hearing, they replied, "We cannot come because we have been suspended from communion. If we merit being reconciled, then we will no longer postpone coming to a hearing." Hearing this, Theutharius returned to the bishops.[76] And after he had reported to them regarding this matter, he was unable to obtain any resolution regarding their communion, and he therefore returned to the city of Poitiers. But the nuns now one after another had departed, some to their parents, others to their own homes, some to those monasteries where they had been previously, for living together they could not bear the harsh winter on account of a shortage of wood. Even so, a few remained with Clotilde and Basina. In fact, there was great discord even among them because each wished to favor herself over the other.

---

74. Greg.Tur. *Hist.* 9.43; for translations, see Dalton, *Gregory,* 422; and Thorpe, *Gregory,* 538–39.

75. Apparently a cleric of Poitiers.

76. Bishops meeting with Childebert, not those chased out of Poitiers.

The Revolt Continues

But this was not the end of the revolt, for in the following year Clotilde, still unrepentant, again took the offensive.

7[77]   Meanwhile, the scandal sprung from the seed of the devil's sowing in the monastery of Poitiers grew daily in ranker wickedness. Clotilde, set upon rebellion, had gathered around her, as I said above, a band of murderers, evil-doers, adulterers, fugitives from justice, and men guilty of every crime,[78] whom she now ordered to break by night into the monastery, and drag the abbess out by force. . . . The men made their way in, lit a candle, and went to and fro through the building with weapons in their hands, seeking her, until they came into an oratory and found her prostrate on the floor before the shrine of the Holy Cross. Then one, fiercer than the rest, who had come to do the vile deed of cleaving the abbess with the sword, was stabbed by a companion's dagger, I think not without the aid of the divine providence. . . . Now the whole band came on with lances and drawn swords. They slashed the nuns' robes, and nearly cut their hands; they then seized the lady provost,[79] mistaking her for the abbess in the darkness, and after tearing off her veil and letting down her hair, dragged her forth. . . . In the meantime, men were being slain at the tomb of St. Radegonde, and some persons were cut down in a tumult before the very shrine of the blessed Cross. As day followed day, the madness was continuously increased by the arrogance of Clotilde. The murders and other assaults of which I have spoken were continually committed by these turbulent ruffians, and her insolence swelled so high that she even looked down upon her cousin Basina from her superior height, until the latter began to repent.

Ultimately, King Childebert again ordered Count Macco to intervene. This time he took aggressive action. Clotilde's cutthroats were overpowered: "Some were tied to posts and beaten, others had their hair

---

77. Greg.Tur. *Hist.* 10.15; translation based on Dalton, *Gregory,* 446–49; see also Thorpe, *Gregory,* 567–71.

78. If this catalog sounded good once (as above), for Gregory it must have sounded even better twice.

79. Justina, the niece of Gregory of Tours.

shorn, others their hands cut off, and still others lost their ears and noses."[80] Clotilde then was brought before an episcopal hearing:

Then,[81] when the bishops who were there had been seated on a tribunal, Clotilde came before them. She showered abuse and accusations upon the abbess, asserting that she had a man in the monastery clothed in female garb and supposed to be a woman, where he was most plainly of the male sex, and that this person had regularly attended the abbess. "There he stands yonder," she said, pointing at him with her finger. There, in truth, he stood, in the face of all present, wearing woman's clothes, as I have said. He now declared that he was unable to do a man's work, and for that reason had assumed this garb. As for the abbess, he only knew her by name and had never seen her or exchanged a word with her, inasmuch as he lived at a distance of more than forty miles from Poitiers.[82]

Clotilde, failing in her attempt to convict the abbess on this charge, went on, "What sort of holiness can this abbess claim, she who makes men eunuchs and keeps them about her in the custom of the imperial palace?".[83] When the abbess was questioned, she responded that she know nothing of this matter. Then, when Clotilde produced the name of a eunuch servant, the physician Reovalis came forward, saying, "That servant, when he was a child, had a malady of the groin and began to be considered to be incurable. His mother approached St. Radegonde so that she might order that some attention would be given to him. And having summoned me, Radegonde asked me if I could help in any way. Then I, just as I had once seen the physicians do in the city of Constantinople, excised his testicles and restored the boy, healthy, to his distressed mother. I attest that the abbess knows nothing of this business." But when she was unable to prove the abbess in no way culpable in this matter, Clotilde began to make other wild accusations.

---

80. Ibid.

81. Ibid. This is a very long chapter.

82. So what, one wonders, was he doing there?

83. The palaces of the Roman emperors, especially those in the East, were manned by squads of eunuchs under the authority of the *Praepositus sacri cubiculi* (chief of the sacred bedchamber); see, e.g., Keith Hopkins, "Eunuchs in Politics in the Later Roman Empire," *Proceedings of the Cambridge Philosophical Society* 189 (1963): 62–80; and Dirk Schlinkert, "Der Hofeunuch in der Spätantike," *Hermes* 122 (1994), 342–59.

Eventually, Leobovera was able to discredit all the accusations against her. Clotilde and her companions then were called to task for their own offenses. They were excommunicated, and the abbess was restored to her convent.

This incident generated a great deal of interest and discussion in Gregory's time—Gregory gave it more press than any other event he discussed. Of course, the fact that it involved women of noble birth (or who at least claimed noble birth) who were challenging the authority of bishops would have especially piqued the interest of Gregory's aristocratic audience.

The Murder of Lampridius

As for the less privileged, any attempts they may have made at rebellion received scant attention. Of course, there always had been bandits and brigands of one kind or other, and in this category one might put the Vargi, the Bacaudae, and the followers of Coroticus. But cases of the use of violence against the establishment are hard to find. A rare example comes from Sidonius Apollinaris, who reports that circa 480 the orator Lampridius of Bordeaux was murdered by his slaves, after, it seems, the latter had made the mistake of consulting astrologers about the manner of his death:

8[84]   Sidonius to his friend Lupus, greetings.
         . . . (3) It is only recently that the news reached me of the murder of Lampridius the rhetor, whose death would have caused great anguish for my love for him even if main force had not snatched him from human affairs. . . . (9) Unfortunately he had the indefensible, I might say the fatal, fault of superstition. He was curious as to the manner of his death and consulted those African astrologers whose nature is as fiery as their native climate. They considered the position of the stars when he was born, and told him his climacteric year, month, and day. . . . (10) Death enmeshed our reckless inquirer into the future exactly when and how it had been foretold; all his efforts to evade it were in vain. (11) He was strangled by his own slaves in his own house. Choked and throttled, he

---

84. Sid.Apoll. *Epist.* 8.11.3–13; translation from Dalton, *Sidonius,* 2.159–65; see also Anderson, *Sidonius,* 2.455–75.

died the death of Scipio of Numantia, if not quite that of Lentulus, Jugurtha, and Sejanus.[85] The one relieving feature in the cruel business was the discovery of crime and criminal as soon as the day broke. The first sight of the body was enough to show a fool or a blind man that death had come by violence. (12) The livid hue, the protruding eyes, the distorted features with their look of mingled fury and anguish, all were so many proofs of what had happened. The floor was wet about his lips, because the scoundrels had turned him with his face to the ground when the deed was done, as if to suggest that life had left him with a sudden hemorrhage. The source, inciter, and ringleader of the conspiracy was first captured; next his accomplices were seized and separately confined until the terror of torture drew the truth from their unwilling breasts. (13) Would that we could say that our friend had not deserved his end by his rash and ill-advised resort to vain advisers. But I fear that he who presumes to probe forbidden secrets sets himself beyond the pale of the Catholic faith. He deserves the lot of all who put unlawful questions and receive replies that point to doom. His death was avenged, it is true, but only the survivors gain by that, for the execution of a murderer cannot mend the mischief; it only affords a certain satisfaction of revenge. . . . Farewell.

In this instance, the authorities prevailed, and the culprits were punished for their crime—as was Lampridius himself, for inquiring into matters that best were left alone.

More specifically, Paulinus of Pella related how, circa 414, Bazas was beset both by barbarian attack and by "a servile faction mixed with the insane fury of a few young, and even freeborn, men, which was armed in particular for the slaughter of the nobility."[86] Paulinus himself barely escaped assassination.[87] Such activities, of course, would have been savagely and instantly suppressed by the aristocratic establishment.

---

85. Scipio Aemilianus, who captured Numantia in 133 B.C., was discovered dead of unspecified causes in 129 B.C. The other three were strangled for crimes against the state, Lentulus Sura in 63 B.C. for his support of Catiline, the Numidian king Jugurtha in 104 B.C. for revolting against Rome, and Sejanus in A.D. 31 for offending Tiberius.

86. "Factio servilis paucorum mixta furori / insano iuvenum [nequam] licet ingenuorum, / armata in caedem specialem nobilitatis": Paulinus of Pella, *Eucharisticos* (Thanksgiving), 334–36.

87. "Instantemque mihi specialem percussorem / me ignorante alio iussisti [sc. deus] ultore perire": Paulinus of Pella, *Eucharisticos,* 339–40.

Conclusion

To outward appearances, the male aristocratic world of Late Antiquity was a closed shop—women and the less privileged need not apply for membership. But closer investigation suggests that, in some venues at least, opportunities for self-expression were available to nonelite individuals. And if they were not available, sometimes these persons were not averse to taking matters into their own hands.

Epilogue: Having the Last Word

This volume will conclude with some "last words," those of Remigius, bishop of Reims circa 480–533, in his last will and testament.[1] Remigius is a known person: he baptized the Frankish king Clovis in the late 490s,[2] he corresponded with Sidonius Apollinaris and others, and his *vita* (life) was composed in the ninth century by Bishop Hincmar of Reims.[3] His will provides several windows into the world that lay between the Roman and barbarian periods. It demonstrates the extent to which privileged Romans could attempt to influence events even after they were gone. It shows how Roman legal traditions continued in the face of social, political, and economic change. It illustrates the preeminent role played by the Christian church not only in social but also in economic matters. And it provides valuable insights into the nomenclature, occupations, and family situations of less privileged members of society.

E.1[4] In the name of the Father and the Son and the Holy Spirit, glory to God. <Christogram> Amen.

---

1. For the will, see A. H. M. Jones, P. Grierson, and J. Crook, "The Authenticity of the 'Testamentum s. Remigii,'" *Revue belge de philologie et d'histoire* 35 (1957): 356–73; for Remigius, see K. Schäferdiek, "Remigius van Rheims, Kirchenmann einer Umbruchzeit," *Zeitschrift für Kirchengeschichte* 94 (1983): 256–78. For Merovingian wills, see Ulrich Nonn, "Merowingische Testamente. Studien zum Fortleben einer römischer Urkundenform im Frankenreich," *Archiv für Diplomatik* 18 (1972): 1–129: other extant wills include those of Caesarius of Arles (A.D. 540), Domnulus of Le Mans (early sixth century), Annemundus of Lyon (A.D. 655), and Queen Radegonde (late sixth century) (*HF* 9.42).

2. See chapter 5.

3. *MGH SRM* 3:250–349; for discussion, see Baudouin De Gaiffier d'Hestroy, "La vie de s. Remi par Hincmar," *Analecta bollandiana* 96 (1978): 271–79.

4. *Testamentum Remigii* (Will of Remigius): *MGH SRM* 3:336–47; *PL* 65:969–74.

I, Remigius, bishop, in possession of the episcopate of the city[5] of Reims,[6] create my testament by praetorian law[7] and command that this shall be valid in place of codicils:[8] will any legality seem to be missing?

Whenever I, Bishop Remigius, have passed from this light, you be my heir, blessed and venerable Catholic church of the city[9] of Reims, and you, nephew, Bishop Lupus, whom I always have cherished with a special love, and you, my grandson,[10] the priest Agricola, who have pleased me with your dutifulness since your childhood, in all my property that comes to my lot before I die, except for that which I bestow, bequeath, and order to be given individually, or which I desire each of you, personally, to have.

You, my blessed heir the church of Reims, shall possess the tenant farmers I have in the territory of Portus,[11] whether those from my paternal and maternal property, or those whom I purchased along with my brother, Bishop Principius[12] of blessed memory, or those whom I received as gifts: Dagaredus, Profuturus, Prudentius, Tennaicus, Maurilio, Baudoleifus, Provinciolus, and the women Niviatena, Lauta, and Suffronia. You also will take under your control the slave Amorinus, and you will claim for yourself by the authority of this testament the fields I possess in the land of Portus, along with the meadows, pastures, and forests. I leave to my successor,[13] the future bishop, the white paschal robe, two coverlets with doves, [and] three veils, which are for the services on feast days in the dining room, the living quarters, and the kitchen. I have divided between you, my heir,

---

5. Remigius uses the word *civitas,* a Roman administrative center.

6. In the following translation, modern place-names are used for Roman places whose modern equivalents are certain (e.g. Reims, Laon); for other places, the Latin names are given.

7. *Iure praetoria:* the rulings issued by the urban praetor at Rome during the Republican and early Imperial period; they were codified by Salvius Julianus during the reign of the emperor Hadrian (117–38). The more usual formula is *iure civili aut praetorio* (by civil or praetorian law); see Jones, Grierson, and Cook, "Authenticity of the Testamentum," 358. Such phrases had little real meaning at this period, but were traditional and made documents look more authoritative.

8. Remigius did, however, add a codicil to his will.

9. Here the word is simply *urbs,* any urban center.

10. *Nepos,* a word that also can mean "nephew" here must mean "grandson," given that Lupus was designated "fili fratris mei," that is, "son of my brother," or "nephew."

11. Identified as modern Château-Porcien, on the Aisne River north of Reims.

12. Bishop of Soissons.

13. That is, at Reims.

and your diocese,[14] the church of Laon,[15] the eighteen-pound silver vase, after patens and chalices have been made, as I wished with God's favor, for the sacrosanct ministry. For you, my heir the aforementioned church, I order the other silver vase, which the lord king Clovis of illustrious memory, whom I received from the sacred font of baptism,[16] thought it fitting to bestow upon me so that I might make out of it whatever I wanted, to be fabricated into an incence burner and an engraved chalice. I will do this myself, if I live long enough; if I close my final day beforehand, you, Bishop Lupus my nephew, mindful of your position, will effect the aforementioned designs. To my fellow priests and deacons who are at Reims, I dispense twenty-five solidi to be divided equally in common. In a like manner, they will possess the vine nursery located above my vineyard on the Suippe River,[17] along with the vinemaster Melanius, whom I assign in place of the church servant Albovichus, so that Albovichus might enjoy the fullest liberty.[18] To the subdeacons I order to be given two solidi, to the readers two solidi, to the doorkeepers and juniors two solidi. Let there be granted to the paupers enrolled in the *matricula,*[19] who beg for alms before the doors of the church, two solidi, whence they might refresh themselves. At Vacculiacum,[20] I command that Frunimius, Dagaleifus, Dagaredus, Ductio, Baudovicus, Uddulfus, and Vinofeista are to be free. Let Tenneredus, who was born of a free mother,[21] make use of free status.

You, truly, Bishop Lupus, son of my brother, will take under your control Nifastes and his mother Muta, and also the vineyard that the vinekeeper Aeneas cultivates. I command that Aeneas and Monulfus, his younger son, enjoy freedom. You will assign to your jurisdiction Mellovicus the swineherd and Pascasiola, his wife, [and] Vernivianus

---

14. *Diocesim:* ultimately, the word *dioecesis* meant an episcopal see, but in Remigius's time and earlier it referred to a parish.

15. *Lugdunensem,* i.e., *Lugdunum Clavatum,* modern Laon. Originally a parish of Reims, it became an episcopal see perhaps in the sixth century.

16. Clovis was baptized at Reims by Remigius in the late 490s. This phrase has caused scholars who believed (wrongly) that Clovis had been baptized at Tours to declare Remigius's will a forgery.

17. Latin *Subnis,* north of Reims, a tributary of the Aisne.

18. That is, Melanius was to replace Albovichus, who was allowed a life of leisure, probably in retirement.

19. The official list of paupers who were supported by the church.

20. Location unknown.

21. He would have taken his legal status from his father, who must have been a slave.

along with his children, with the exception of Widragasius, to whom I grant freedom. I command that my slave at Cesurnicum[22] is yours. You will take under your control the part of the fields that my brother, Bishop Principius, held, along with the forests, meadows, and pastures. I bequeath [to you] my slave Viteredus, whom Mellovicus owned. I consign to your jurisdiction and control Teneursolus, Capalinus, and his wife Teudorosera; in addition, let Teudonivia also be free by my command. You shall retain Edoveifa, who is married to your man, and her family. I order the wife of Aregildus and her family to be free. You will claim for yourself my part of the meadow that I have next to you at Laon, located at the foot of the mountains, and the little meadows that I held, which are at Jovia.[23]

To you, moreover, my grandson the priest Agricola, who lived your childhood within my domestic walls, I hand over and consign the slave Merumvastis and his wife Meratena and their son Marcovicus, by name; his brother Medovicus I order to be free. I bequeath to you Amantius and his wife Daero; I order their daugher Dasovinda to be free. I assign to your portion the slave Alaric, whose wife, whom I redeemed and set free, I commend to be protected as freeborn. You will take under your control Bebrimodus and his wife Mora; their son Monacharius will be rewarded with the favor of freedom. You will claim under your control Mellaricus and his wife Placidia; let Medaridus, their son, be freed. I give to you the vineyard that Mellaricus made at Laon. I bequeath to you likewise the slave Brittobaude and also Gibericus, [and] the vineyard that Bebrimodus made, so that my offering[24] might be made on the sacred altars on the feast days and on every Sunday, and so that annual banquets might be provided for the priests and deacons of Reims.

And to my grandson[25] Praetextatus I delegate Moderatus, Tottio, Marcovicus, the slave Innocentius, whom I received from my tenant[26] Profuturus, four spoons from among the larger ones, the vinegar-cruet, the lamp that the tribune Frieredus gave me, the silver-figured staff, a vinegar holder for his little son Parovius, and three spoons[27]

---

22. Identified as modern Cerny-en-Laonnois.
23. Location unknown.
24. *Oblatio:* that is, the wine from the vineyard.
25. Remigius now makes bequests to other members of his family.
26. *Originarius:* a form of *colonus,* or tenant farmer.
27. Presumably from among the smaller ones.

and the cape whose fringes I bought. To Remigia[28] I consign the three spoons that are engraved with my name,[29] and the tablecloth with the same name, which I consider to be ceremonial, and I also give her the vase, regarding which I spoke to Gundobad.[30] And to my blessed daughter[31] the deaconess Hilaria I delegate a slave girl, Noca by name; and I give the vine footage that is joined to the vineyard that Cattusio made; and I consign [to her] my portion of Talpusiacum[32] for the sake of the prayers that she ceaselessly dispenses for me. To Aëtius, my grandson, I transmit the part of Cesurnicum that came to me by lot of division, with all the jurisdiction that I held and possessed; also the lad Ambrosius to his jurisdiction and control. I order the tenant farmer Vitalis to be free, and his family to belong to my grandson Agathimerus, to whom I give the vineyard that I placed and established with my own labor at Vindonissa,[33] under this condition, so that an offering might be made from his division on all the feast days and Sundays at the sacred altars in commemoration of me, and so that, Lord willing, annual banquets might be provided for the priests and deacons at Laon.

I give to the church of Laon eighteen solidi that the priests and deacons may distribute among themselves in an equal division. Let the church of Laon claim for itself my portion of Setia[34] in its original state. I commend to Your Sanctity, my nephew Bishop Lupus, those whom I command to be free: Catussio and his wife Auliatena, Nonnio, who made my vineyard, Sunnoveifa, who was born of good parents and whom I redeemed as a captive,[35] and her son Leoberedus; [also] Mellaridus and Mellatena, the cook Vasans, Caesaria, Dagarasera and Baudorosera, [their] grandson Leo, and Marcoleifus, son of Totno: all of these, my nephew Bishop Lupus, you will protect as free by sacerdotal authority. To you, moreover, my heir church, I give Flavianus and his wife Sparagildis; I establish that their little daughter

---

28. Perhaps a granddaughter.

29. Tableware engraved with the name of its owner was common during Late Antiquity.

30. Not, apparently, the Burgundian king of the same name, but rather some family retainer who could attest which vase was meant.

31. A daughter by religion rather than by blood, although surely a relative of some degree, perhaps a granddaughter.

32. Location unknown.

33. Identified as Vendresse-et-Troyon.

34. Or *Secia;* location unknown.

35. Even a well-born person who was redeemed became the dependent of the redeemer if he or she no longer had the wherewithal to reimburse their benefactor.

Flavarasera is free. The priests and deacons of Reims will possess Foedamia, the wife of Melanius, and their little daughter.[36] I command that the tenant farmer Cispiciolus is free and that his family belong to my grandson Aëtius; the farmhouse at Passiacum[37] comes to both, that is, to Aëtius and Agathimerus. I hand over the boy Leudocarius to Profuturus; I order Leudovera to be given to Profutura. To the sub-deacons, readers, doorkeepers, and juniors of Laon I leave four solidi. To the paupers enrolled in the *matricula* a solidus is given for their refreshment.

For the commemoration of my name I delegate to the church of Soissons eight solidi; to the church of Châlons-sur-Marne six solidi; to Mosomagum[38] five solidi; to Vongensis,[39] the field next to the gristmill that is located there; to the church of Catarigum[40] four solidi, and the same shall be granted to Portus for the commemoration of my name. For the familial devotion of the archdeacon Ursus, I give to this house-hold the fine homespun cape and the other fuller one, two light cloaks, the rug that I have on the bed, and the better tunic that I will leave at the time of my passing. You, my heirs the bishop Lupus and the priest Agricola, may divide my pigs equally among yourselves. Frieredus, for whom I provided fourteen solidi so he would not be killed, may have two remitted; let him give twelve for the construction of a chapel in the basilica of a chapel of the lord martyrs Timothy and Apollinaris.

Thus I do, thus I bequeath, thus I witness this. All others are not heirs; these are all. Moreover, evil trickery in this my testament is absent and will be absent; each letter or character found in it has been made in my presence, while it was being reviewed and emended by me.

Done at Reims on the day and consulate written above,[41] with the signatories present and accounted for.

---

36. Whose name Remigius apparently had forgotten. Remigius now lists the inhabitants of Setia who are not left to the church of Laon. If Melanius is the vinemaster mentioned above who was left to the church of Reims, then Remigius was very thoughtful to ensure that his wife and daughter did not end up under a different jurisdiction.

37. Identified as Paissy.

38. *Mosomagensi,* in the territory of Reims, identified as Mouzon; perhaps the same as *Momociacum,* said by Gregory of Tours to have had a bishop (*Glor.conf.* 52).

39. Identified as Voncq.

40. Identified as modern Charleville-Mézières.

41. There are, however, no "day and consul cited above." Either the date has dropped out, or the writer of the will was following a standard formula and did not notice the incon-sistency. Note too that instead of the previously standard *consulibus,* one now has simply *con-sule:* by this time, with the name of the eastern consul often not widely known in the west, it had become common to date by only a single consul.

<Christogram>[42] I, Bishop Remigius, have reviewed, signed, and sub-scribed to my testament, and in the name of the Father and the Son and the Holy Spirit, with God's assistance, I have completed it.
<The remaining text probably appeared on the outside of the will, after it had been bound up, to ensure that it had not been tampered with.>
I, Pappolus, distinguished gentleman, was present and subscribed.
I, Rusticolus, distinguished gentleman, was present and subscribed.
I, Eulodius, distinguished gentleman, was present and subscribed.
I, Eutropius, distinguished gentleman, was present and subscribed.
I, Dauveus, distinguished gentleman, was present and subscribed.
After the testament was composed, or rather signed, it occurred to my senses that I should depute to the basilica of the lord martyrs Timothy and Apollinaris the silver missorium of six pounds there, so that from it the future site of my remains might be provided.

---

42. Signatures were often prefaced by the chi-rho sign, or Christogram.

Appendixes

Roman Emperors

Legitimate emperors are shown in **bold.**

Diocletian (284–305)
Constantius I (305–6)
Constantine I (306–37)

Western Portion of Empire

Constantine II (337–40)
Constans (337–50)
Magnentius (350–53) (usurper in Gaul and West)
Julian (361–63) (East and West)
Valentinian I (364–75)
Gratian (367–83)
Valentinian II (375–92)
Theodosius I (379–95) (East and West)
Magnus Maximus (383–88) (usurper in Britain, Gaul, and Spain)
Eugenius (392–94) (usurper in Italy)
Honorius (395–423)
Marcus and Gratian (406) (usurpers in Britain)
Constantine III (407–11) (usurper in Britain and Gaul)
Priscus Attalus (409–10, 414–15) (usurper in Italy and Gaul)
Maximus (409–11) (usurper in Spain)
Jovinus (411–13) (usurper in Gaul)
Constantius III (420)
Maximus (420–22) (usurper in Spain)
Johannes (423–25) (usurper in Italy)
Valentinian III (425–55)

Petronius Maximus (455)
Eparchius Avitus (455–56)
Majorian (457–61)
Libius Severus (461–65)
Anthemius (467–72)
Olybrius (472)
Glycerius (473–74)
Julius Nepos (474–80)
Romulus (475–76) (usurper in Italy)

Eastern Portion of Empire

Constantius II (337–61)
Julian (361–63) (East and West)
Jovian (363–64)
Valens (364–78)
Procopius (365–66) (usurper in Constantinople)
Theodosius I (379–95) (East and West)
Arcadius (383–408)
Theodosius II (402–50)
Marcian (450–57)
Leo I (457–74)
Zeno (474–91)
Anastasius (491–518)
Justin I (518–27)
Justinian I (527–65)
Justin II (565–78)
Tiberius II Constantine (578–82)
Maurice Tiberius (582–602)
Phocas (602–10)

Selected Bishops of Rome (Popes)

Sylvester (314–35)
Mark (336)
Julius (337–52)
Liberius (352–66)
Damasus (366–84)
Siricius (384–99)
Anastasius (399–401)
Innocent (401–17)
Zosimus (417–18)
Boniface (418–22)
Celestine (422–32)
Sixtus (432–40)
Leo (440–61)
Hilarus (461–68)
Simplicius (468–83)
Felix (483–92)
Gelasius (492–96)
Anastasius (496–98)
Symmachus (498–514)
Hormisdas (514–23)
John (523–26)
Felix (526–30)
Boniface (530–32)
. . .
Gregory (590–604)

Barbarian Rulers

In most instances, the names of barbarian rulers are not Latinized, as they often appear in the sources, hence *Euric* rather than *Euricus*. Moreover, the most common renditions of names also are used, hence *Euric* rather than *Evoricus,* or *Clovis* rather than *Chlodovechus*.

Burgundians (in Gaul)

Gundahar (411–37)
Gundioc (455–73)
Chilperic I (–455–)
Chilperic II (ca. 458–ca. 480)
Godegisel (ca. 473–500)
Gundobad (ca. 473–516)
Sigismund (516–23)
Gundemar (523–32)
End of Burgundian Kingdom

Franks (in Gaul)[1]

Faramund (?–ca. 436)
Chlogio (ca. 436–56)
Childeric (ca. 456–81)
Clovis (481–511)
Theoderic I, son of Clovis (511–34)
Chlodomer, son of Clovis (511–24)
Childebert, son of Clovis (511–58)

---

1. From Edward James, *The Franks* (Oxford: B. Blackwell, 1988), 171.

Chlothar I, son of Clovis (511–61)
Theodebert, son of Theoderic I (534–48)
Theodebald, son of Theodebert (548–55)
Chilperic I, son of Chlothar I (561–84)
Charibert, son of Chlothar I (561–67)
Guntram, son of Chlothar I (561–92)
Sigibert I, son of Chlothar I (561–75)
Childebert II, son of Sigibert (575–95)
Brunhilda, regent, wife of Sigibert (575–95)
Chlothar II, son of Chilperic I (584–629)
Fredegund, regent, wife of Chilperic I (584–97)
Theodebert II, son of Childebert II (595–612)
Theoderic II, son of Childebert II (595–613)

Italy

Odovacar (476–91)
End of Italian Kingdom

Ostrogoths (in Italy)[2]

Theoderic I (490–526)
Athalaric (526–34)
Amalasuintha, regent, wife of Theoderic (534–35)
Theodahad (534–36)
Witigis (536–40)
Hildebald (540–41)
Eraric (541)
Totila (541–52)
Teias (552)
End of Ostrogothic Kingdom

Vandals (in Spain and North Africa)[3]

Godigisel (406)
Gunderic (406–28)

2. From T. Burns, *A History of the Ostrogoths* (Bloomington: Indiana University Press, 1984), 95.
3. See *PLRE.*

Gaiseric (428–77)
Huneric (477–84)
Gunthamund (484–96)
Thrasamund (496–523)
Hilderic (523–31)
Gelimer (531–34)
End of Vandal Kingdom

Visigoths (in Gaul and Spain)[4]

Alaric (ca. 391–410)
Athaulf (410–15)
Sigeric (415)
Wallia (415–18)
Theoderic I (418–51)
Thorismund (451–53)
Theoderic II (453–66)
Euric (466–84)
Alaric II (484–507)
End of Visigothic Kingdom of Toulouse in Gaul
Gesalic (507–11)[5]
Amalaric (511–31)
Theoderic the Ostrogoth, regent for Amalaric (511–26)
Theoderic/Theudis (531–48)
Theodisclus (548–49)
Agila I (549–54)
Athanagild (revolted in 550) (551–68)
Liuva I (568–73)
Leovigild, brother of Liuva (569–86)
Reccared I (586–601)

Suevi (in Spain)[6]

Hermeric pre-419–438 (441)
Rechila (438–48)

---

4. The first section from *PLRE,* vol. 2.
5. The remainder from R. Collins, *Early Medieval Spain* (New York: St. Martin's, 1983), 299.
6. From Richard Burgess, University of Ottawa, private communication.

Rechiarius (448–56)
Maldras (warlord, 457–60)
Aioulfus (usurper, 457)
Framtane (warlord, 457–58)
Rechimund (Remismund?) (warlord, 459–64; king, 464–?)
Frumarius (warlord, 460–64)
Remismund (465–)[7]
Chararic (550s?)
Ariamir (558/9–)
Theodemir (–569/570)
Miro (570–83)
Eboric (583–84)
Audeca (584–85)
End of Suevic Kingdom

7. The remainder from Collins, *Early Medieval Spain,* 299.

APPENDIX 4

Glossary

adscripticius	"Enrolled person"; a type of *colonus*
advocatus	A legal specialist, often in the civil service
agens in rebus	An imperial agent
Arvernia	The territory of the city of Clermont
augustus	Senior emperor
auricularius	Royal official
caesar	Junior emperor
censualis	Official who kept property and tax records
clarissima femina	"Most distinguished woman"
colonus	Tenant farmer, usually tied to the soil
comes	"Comrade" (of the emperor), generally in the sense of "count," usually a high-ranking military officer
comes civitatis	"Count of the city," a city administrator
comes domesticorum	Also *comes domesticorum et protectorum:* "count of the domestics (and protectors)," commander of imperial bodyguards
comes rei militaris	"Count of military affairs," a general of field army units
comes rei privatae	"Count of the private purse," an imperial finance minister
comes sacrarum largitionum	"Count of the sacred largesses," an imperial finance minister

comitatenses	The imperial field army
comitatus	The imperial court
consiliaris	Royal counselor
consistorium	The emperor's advisory council
consul ordinarius	"Ordinary consul": Two were appointed yearly and gave names to the year.
consul suffectus	"Replacement consul" appointed later in the year; did not give name to the year
consularis	"Consular," provincial governor of intermediate rank
consulate	The period during which a consul was in office
corrector	Governor of a province in Italy
cura palatii	"Caretaker of the palace," an imperial official
curialis	Member of a local senate, a town councillor
cursus honorum	"Course of offices," the standard career path in secular or ecclesiastical service
decurio	Decurion: a member of a local senate, a town councillor
delator	"Betrayer": an informer
diocese	Large administrative unit consisting of several provinces
domesticus	Member of the imperial bodyguard or a royal court
dux	"Duke," a general of local militia
honestiores	Persons of privileged status
honoratus	A person with any claim to rank or status
humiliores	Persons of less privileged status
Ides	The fifteenth day of the month in March, May, July, and October; otherwise the thirteenth
indiction	A fifteen-year cycle, at the end of which the taxes were reassessed

inquilinus	Cottager, less privileged than a *colonus* on the social scale
iudex	"Judge"; usually a provincial governor
Kalends	The first day of the month
lacuna	A missing section of a text
legatus	An imperial or royal legate or ambassador
magister equitum	"Master of horse," imperial generalissimo second in seniority
magister militum	"Master of soldiers," an imperial generalissimo
magister militum per Gallias	"Master of soldiers in Gaul," imperial generalissimo third in seniority
magister officium	"Master of offices," akin to a prime minister
magister peditum	"Master of foot," imperial generalissimo first in seniority
magister utriusque militiae	"Master of both services," an imperial generalissimo commanding both cavalry and infantry
maior domus	"Mayor of the palace," a royal court official
militia	Any kind of secular or military service
municeps, municipalis	Member of a town council
Nones	The seventh day of the month in March, May, July, and October; otherwise the fifth
notarius	An imperial factotum, or a scribe
officialis	A secular official
originarius	"Native inhabitant," a *colonus* tied to the land
otium	"Leisure," along with *militia,* the goal of a Roman aristocrat
palatinus	A court official
patricius	Patrician, the highest nonimperial rank
plebeian	A free, humble person
potens	A person with *potentia*
potentia	Personal authority

praefectus praetorio	"Praetorian prefect," overseer of several dioceses
praefectus sacri cubiculi	"Prefect of the sacred bedchamber," a eunuch
praefectus urbi	"Prefect of the city," the administrator of Rome or Constantinople
praepositus	An overseer
praeses	Lowest-ranking governor of a province
prefecture	Very large administrative unit consisting of two or more dioceses
primicerius notariorum	"Chief of the notaries," an imperial official
proconsul	Highest-ranking provincial governor
protector	Member of the imperial bodyguard
protector et domesticus	Member of the imperial bodyguard
province	Smallest imperial administrative unit
puer	Often used to refer not to a child but to an individual in some kind of dependent position; "lad"
quaestor sacri palatii	"Quaestor of the sacred palace," the imperial "attorney general"
rationalis	Accountant
referendarius	Royal court official
res privata	Imperial property belonging to the emperor
sacrae largitiones	The imperial treasury
saecularis	A secular official, or more generally, person living in the secular world
scholasticus	A scribe, or, more generally, educated person
senator	A person with a claim to Roman aristocratic status
spatharius	"Sword-bearer" (of a barbarian king)
togatus	"Wearer of a toga"; a bureaucrat
tribunus (et notarius)	An imperial factotum
tributarius	Dependent person whose tax assessment falls upon the property owner

vicarius	"Vicar," administrator in charge of a diocese
v.c. = vir clarissimus	"Most distinguished gentleman," the lowest senatorial rank
v.i. = vir inlustris	"Illustrious gentleman," a high senatorial rank
v.s. = vir spectabilis	"Respectable gentleman," an intermediate senatorial rank

APPENDIX 5

Sources Quoted

Bibliography

Language and Literature

Auerbach, Erich. *Literary Language and Its Public in Late Antiquity and the Middle Ages.* Trans. Ralph Manheim. New York: Pantheon Books, 1965.

Baldwin, Barry. "Literature and Society in the Later Roman Empire." In *Literary and Artistic Patronage in Ancient Rome,* ed. Barbara K. Gold, 67–83. Austin: University of Texas Press, 1982.

Balme, M. G., and M. S. Warman. *Aestimanda: Practical Criticism of Latin and Greek Poetry and Prose.* London: Oxford University Press, 1965. Greek and Latin selections illustrating different stylistic and rhetorical usages.

Bergmann, Wilhelm. *Studien zu einer kritischen Sichtung der südgallischen Predigtliteratur des 5. und 6. Jahrhunderts.* Leipzig: Dieterich'sche Verlag, 1898; rpt. Aalen: Scientia Verlag, 1972.

Cameron, Averil. *Christianity and the Rhetoric of Empire: The Development of Christian Discourse.* Berkeley and Los Angeles: University of California Press, 1991.

Corsaro, Francesco. *Querolus: Studio introduttivo e commentario.* Bologna: R. Patron, 1965.

Courcelle, Pierre. *Les lettres grecques en Occident, de Macrobe à Cassiodore.* 2d ed. Paris: E. de Boccard, 1948. Translated by Harry E. Wedeck as *Late Latin Writers and Their Greek Sources* (Cambridge: Harvard University Press, 1969).

Cristiani, Léon. *Saint Eucher de Lyon: Du mépris du monde.* Paris: Nouvelles éditions latines, 1950.

Curtius, Ernst R. *Europäische Literatur und lateinisches Mittelalter.* 6th ed. Bern: Francke, 1967.

Dekkers, Eligius, and Aemilius Gaar, eds. *Clavis patrum latinorum, qua in novum corpus christianorum edendum optimas quasque scriptorum recensiones a Tertulliano ad Bedam.* 2d ed. Turnhout: Brepols, 1961.

Delehaye, Hippolyte. *Les passions des martyrs et les genres littéraires.* 2d ed. Brussels: Société des Bollandistes, 1966.

Duckett, Eleanor S. *Latin Writers of the Fifth Century.* New York: H. Holt, 1930; rpt. New York: Archon, 1969.

Duval, Paul-Marie. *La Gaule jusqu'au milieu du Ve siècle.* Paris: Editions A. et J. Picard, 1971.

Glover, Terrot R. *Life and Letters in the Fourth Century.* New York: G. E. Stechert, 1968.

Haadsma, R. A., and J. Nuchelmans. *Précis de latin vulgaire.* Oxford: J. B. Wolters, 1966. Discussion of aspects of vulgar Latin followed by selected passages through the seventh century with word usage notes.

Heinzelmann, Martin. "Neue Aspekte der biographischen und hagiographischen Literatur in der lateinischen Welt (1.–6. Jh)." *Francia* 1 (1973): 27–44.

Herrmann, L. "Querolus (Le Grognon)." *Latomus* 96 (1968): 67–167.

Janson, Tore. *Latin Prose Prefaces: Studies in Literary Conventions.* Studia Latina Stockholmensia 13. Stockholm: Ivar Haegström, 1964.

Kenney, E. J. *The Classical Text: Aspects of Editing in the Age of the Printed Book.* Berkeley and Los Angeles: University of California Press, 1974.

Laistner, Max L. W. *Thought and Letters in Western Europe, A.D. 500 to 900.* London: Methuen, 1931.

Lana, Italo. *Analisi del Querolus.* Turin: G. Giappichelli, 1979.

Lockwood, Dean F. "The Plot of the Querolus and the Folk-Tales of Disguised Treasure." *Transactions of the American Philological Association* 44 (1913): 215–32.

Loyen, Andre. *Sidoine Apollinaire et l'esprit précieux en Gaule aux derniers jours de l'empire.* Paris: Les Belles Lettres, 1943.

Manitius, Max. *Geschichte der lateinischen Literatur des Mittelalters.* Vol. 1: *Von Justinian bis zur mitte des zehnten Jahrhunderts.* Munich: C. H. Beck, 1911.

Mathisen, Ralph W. "The *Codex Sangallensis* 190 and the Transmission of the Classical Tradition." *International Journal of the Classical Tradition* 5 (1998): 163–94.

———. "Epistolography, Literary Circles, and Family Ties in Late Roman Gaul." *Transactions of the American Philological Society* 111 (1981): 95–109.

———. "The Theme of Literary Decline in Late Roman Gaul." *Classical Philology* 83 (1988): 45–52.

McKitterick, Rosamund, *The Carolingians and the Written Word.* Cambridge: Cambridge University Press, 1989.

Noble, Thomas F. X., and Thomas Head, eds. *Soldiers of Christ: Saints and Saints Lives from Late Antiquity and the Early Middle Ages.* University Park: Pennsylvania State University Press, 1995.

Peter, Hermann W. G. *Der Brief in der römischen Literatur.* Leipzig, 1901; rpt. Hildesheim: Olms, 1965.

Raby, Frederic J. E. *A History of Secular Latin Poetry in the Middle Ages.* Oxford: Clarendon, 1934.

Reynolds, L. D., and N. G. Wilson. *Scribes and Scholars: A Guide to the Transmission of Greek and Latin Literature.* Oxford: Clarendon, 1968.

Roberts, Michael. *The Jeweled Style: Poetry and Poetics in Late Antiquity.* Ithaca, N.Y.: Cornell University Press, 1989.

Rohlfs, G. *Sermo vulgaris latinus.* Tübingen: Max Niemeyer, 1969. Collection of passages with brief notes, through the seventh century.

Rusch, William G. *The Later Latin Fathers.* London: Duckworth, 1977.

Schanz, Martin. *Geschichte der römischen Litteratur bis zum Gesetzgebungswerk des Kaisers Justinians.* Part 4: *Die römische Litteratur von Constantin bis zum Gesetzgebungswerk Justinians.* 2d half: *Die Litteratur des fünften und sechsten Jahrhunderts.* Munich, 1920.

Smith, Thomas A. *De gratia: Faustus of Riez's Treatise on Grace and Its Place in the History of Theology.* Notre Dame, Ind.: University of Notre Dame Press, 1990.

Thompson, James Westfall. *The Literacy of the Laity in the Middle Ages.* Berkeley: University of California Press, 1939; rpt. New York: B. Franklin, 1960.

Wes, Marinus. "Gesellschaft und Literatur in der Spätantike." *Ancient Society* 18 (1987): 173–202.

Wright, Frederick Adam, and T. A. Sinclair. *A History of Later Latin Literature: From the Middle of the Fourth to the End of the Seventeenth Century.* New York: Macmillan, 1931; rpt. London: Dawson, 1969.

History and Society

Amory, Patrick. *People and Identity in Ostrogothic Italy, 489–554.* Cambridge: Cambridge University Press, 1997.

Arjava, Antti. *Women and Law in Late Antiquity.* Oxford: Clarendon, 1996.

Arnheim, M. T. W. *The Senatorial Aristocracy in the Later Roman Empire.* Oxford: Clarendon, 1972.

Arnold, Carl Franklin. *Caesarius von Arelate und die gallische Kirche von seiner Zeit.* Leipzig: J. C. Hinrichs, 1894; rpt. Leipzig: Zentralantiquariat der DDR, 1972.

Arsac, P. "La dignité sénatoriale au Bas-Empire." *Revue historique de droit français et étranger* 47 (1969): 198–243.

Balsdon, J. P. V. D. "Auctoritas, Dignitas, Otium." *Classical Quarterly* 10 (1960): 43–50.

Barnes, Timothy D. "Who Were the Nobility of the Roman Empire?" *Phoenix* 28 (1974): 444–49.

Barnish, Samuel J. "Transformation and Survival in the Western Senatorial Aristocracy, c. A.D. 400–700." *Papers of the British School at Rome* 56 (1988): 120–55.

Beck, Henry G. J. *The Pastoral Care of Souls in South-east France during the Sixth Century.* Analecta Gregoriana 51. Rome: Gregorian University, 1950.

Bosl, Karl. "On Social Mobility in Medieval Society: Service, Freedom, and Freedom of Movement as Means of Social Ascent." In *Early Medieval Society,* ed. S. L. Thrupp, 87–102. New York: Appleton-Century-Crofts, 1967.

Bowersock, G. W., Peter R. L. Brown, and Oleg Grabar, eds. *Late Antiquity: A Guide to the Postclassical World.* Cambridge, Mass.: Harvard University Press, 1999.

Brennan, Brian. "Senators and Social Mobility in Sixth-Century Gaul." *Journal of Medieval History* 11 (1985): 145–61.

Brown, Peter R. L. *Power and Persuasion in Late Antiquity: Towards a Christian Empire.* Madison: University of Wisconsin Press, 1992.

———. "The Rise and Function of the Holy Man in Late Antiquity." *Journal of Roman Studies* 61 (1971): 80–101.

———. *Society and the Holy in Late Antiquity.* Berkeley and Los Angeles: University of California Press, 1982.

———. *The World of Late Antiquity.* New York: Harcourt Brace Jovanovich, 1974.

Burns, T. S. *Barbarians within the Gates of Rome: A Study of Roman Military Policy and the Barbarians, ca. 375–425 B.C.* Bloomington: Indiana University Press, 1994.

Bury, John B. *History of the Later Roman Empire from the Death of Theodosius I to the Death of Justinian (A.D. 395 to A.D. 565).* 2d ed. London: Macmillan, 1923.

Cameron, Averil. *The Later Roman Empire.* Cambridge: Harvard University Press, 1993.

Charanis, Peter. "On the Social Structure of the Later Roman Empire." *Byzantion* 17 (1944–45): 39–57.

Curchin, Leonard. "Social Relations in Central Spain: Patrons, Freedmen, and Slaves in the Lives of a Roman Provincial Hinterland." *Ancient Society* 18 (1987): 75–89.

Dauge, Yves Albert. *Le barbare. Recherches sur la conception romaine de la barbarie et de la civilisation.* Collection Latomus 176. Brussels: Latomus, 1981.

Demougeot, Emilienne. "Le *conubium* dans les lois barbares du VIe siècle." *Recueil de memoires et travaux* 12 (1983): 69–82.

Dill, Samuel. *Roman Society in Gaul in the Merovingian Age.* London: Macmillan, 1926; rpt. New York: Barnes and Noble, 1970.

———. *Roman Society in the Last Century of the Western Empire.* 2d ed. London: Macmillan, 1921; rpt. New York: Meridian, 1958.

Duthoy, Robert. "Le profil social des patrons municipaux en Italie sous le haut-empire." *Ancient Society* 15–17 (1984–86): 121–54.

Fowden, Garth. *Empire to Commonwealth: Consequences of Monotheism in Late Antiquity.* Princeton: Princeton University Press, 1995.

———. "The Pagan Holy Man in Late Antique Society." *Journal of Hellenic Studies* 102 (1982): 33–59.

Gage, J. *Les classes sociales dans l'Empire romain.* Paris: Payot, 1964.

Gardner, Jane F. "Proofs of Status in the Roman World." *Proceedings of the Classical Association* 84 (1987): 15–16.

Garnsey, P. *Social Status and Legal Privilege in the Roman Empire.* Oxford: Clarendon, 1970.

Geary, Patrick. *Before France and Germany: The Creation and Transformation of the Merovingian World.* New York: Oxford University Press, 1988.

Genicot, Leopold. "The Nobility in Medieval *Francia:* Continuity, Break, or Evolution." In *Lordship and Community,* ed. F. L. Cheyette. New York: Holt-Rinehart-Winston, 1968.

Giardina, A., ed. *Societá romana e impero tardoantica.* Rome: Laterza, 1986.

Haarhoff, Theodore J. *Schools of Gaul: A Study of Pagan and Christian Education in the Last Century of the Western Empire.* London: Oxford University Press, 1920.

Harries, Jill. *Sidonius Apollinaris and the Fall of Rome, A.D. 407–485.* Oxford: Clarendon, 1994.

Heinzelmann, Martin. *Bischofsherrschaft in Gallien: Zur Kontinuität römischer Führungsschichten von 4. bis 7. Jahrhundert.* Munich: Artemis, 1976.

———. "Gallische Prosopographie 260–527." *Francia* 10 (1982): 531–718.

———. "Prosopographie et recherche de continuité historique: L'exemple des Ve-VIIe siècles." *Mélanges de l'Ecole Française de Rome. Moyen Age* 100 (1988): 227–39.

Hen, Yitzhak. *Culture and Religion in Merovingian Gaul, A.D. 481–751.* Leiden: Brill, 1995.

Hirschfeld, Otto. "Die Rangtitel der römischen Kaiserzeit." *Sitzungsberichte der königlichen-preussischen Akademie der Wissenschaft* (Berlin) 25 (1901): 579ff.

Hohlfelder, Robert L., ed. *City, Town, and Countryside in the Early Byzantine Era.* New York: Columbia University Press, 1982.

Hopkins, M. K. "Elite Mobility in the Roman Empire." *Past and Present* 32 (1965): 12–26.

———. "Social Mobility in the Later Roman Empire: The Evidence of Ausonius." *Classical Quarterly* 11 (1961): 239–49.

James, Edward. *The Origins of France: From Clovis to the Capetians, 500–1000.* New York: St. Martin's, 1982.

Jones, Arnold H. M. *The Later Roman Empire, A.D. 284–640: A Social, Economic, and Administrative Survey.* Norman: University of Oklahoma Press, 1964.

Keenan, J. G. "The Names Flavius and Aurelius as Status Designations in Later Roman Egypt." *Zeitschrift für Papyrologie und Epigraphik* 11 (1973): 33–63; 13 (1974): 263ff.

Kellett, Frederick W. *Pope Gregory the Great and His Relations with Gaul.* Cambridge: Cambridge University Press, 1889.

King, P. D. *Law and Society in the Visigothic Kingdom.* Cambridge: Cambridge University Press, 1972.

Koch, P. *Die byzantinischen Beamtentitel von 400 bis 700.* Jena, 1903.

Langgärtner, Georg. *Die Gallienpolitik der Päpste im 5. und 6. Jahrhunderts. Eine Studie über den apostolische Vikariat von Arles.* Bonn: Peter Hanstein, 1964.

Larsen, Jakob A. O. "The Position of Provincial Assemblies in the Government and Society of the Late Roman Empire." *Classical Philology* 29 (1934): 209–20.

Lee, A. D. *Information and Frontiers: Roman Foreign Relations in Late Antiquity.* Cambridge: Cambridge University Press, 1993.

Löhken, H. *Ordines dignitatum: Untersuchungen zur formalen Konstituierung der spätantiken Führungsschicht.* Cologne: Bohlau, 1982.

Lütkenhaus, W. *Constantius III: Studien zu seiner Tätigkeit und Stellung im Westreich 411–421.* Bonn: Habelt, 1998.

MacMullen, Ramsay. "Social Mobility and the Theodosian Code." *Journal of Roman Studies* 54 (1964): 49–53.

Martindale, John R. *The Prosopography of the Later Roman Empire.* Vol. 2: *A.D. 395–527* Cambridge: Cambridge University Press, 1980.

Mathisen, Ralph W. "Crossing the Supernatural Frontier in Western Late Antiquity." In *Shifting Frontiers in Late Antiquity,* ed. Ralph W. Mathisen and H. Sivan, 309–20. Aldershot: Ashgate, 1996.

———. "The Ecclesiastical Aristocracy of Fifth-Century Gaul: A Regional Analysis of Family Structure." Ph.D. diss., University of Wisconsin, 1979.

———. *Ecclesiastical Factionalism and Religious Controversy in Fifth-Century Gaul.* Washington, D.C.: Catholic University of America Press, 1989.

———. "Emigrants, Exiles, and Survivors: Aristocratic Options in Visigothic Aquitania." *Phoenix* 38 (1984): 159–70.

———. "Emperors, Consuls, and Patricians: Some Problems of Personal Preference and Precedence." *Byzantinische Forschungen* 17 (1991): 173–90.

———. "Nature or Nurture: The Gallic Famine of circa A.D. 470." *Ancient World* 24 (1993): 91–105.

———. *Roman Aristocrats in Barbarian Gaul: Strategies for Survival in an Age of Transition.* Austin: University of Texas Press, 1993.

———. *Studies in the History, Literature, and Society of Late Antiquity.* Amsterdam: Adolf Hakkert, 1991.

Mathisen, Ralph W., and H. Sivan, eds. *Shifting Frontiers in Late Antiquity.* Aldershot: Ashgate, 1996.

Matthews, John F. *Western Aristocracies and Imperial Court, A.D. 364–425.* Oxford: Clarendon, 1975.

Morris, John. *The Age of Arthur: A History of the British Isles from 350 to 650.* New York: Scribner, 1973.

Murray, A. C. *Germanic Kinship Structure: Studies in Law and Society in Antiquity and the Early Middle Ages.* Toronto: Pontifical Institute of Medieval Studies, 1983.

Nicols, John. "Prefects, Patronage, and the Administration of Justice." *Zeitschrift für Papyrologie und Epigraphik* 72 (1988): 201–17.

Oost, Stewart I. *Galla Placidia Augusta: A Biographical Essay.* Chicago: University of Chicago Press, 1968.

Ostrogorsky, George. "Observations on the Aristocracy in Byzantium." *Dumbarton Oaks Papers* 25 (1971): 1–32.

Picard, G. C. "Observations sur la condition des populations rurales dans l'empire romain, en Gaule et en Afrique." *Aufstieg und Niedergang der römischen Welt* 2.3 (1975): 98–111.

Pietri, Charles. "Aristocratie et société cléricale dans l'Italie chrétienne au temps d'Odoacre et de Théoderic." *Mélanges des Ecole Française de Rome et de Athènes* 93 (1981): 417–67.

Pohl, Walter, and Helmut Reimitz, eds. *Strategies of Distinction: The Construction of Ethnic Communities, 300–800.* Leiden: Brill, 1998.

Pricoco, Salvatore. *L'isola dei santi. Il cenobio di Lerino e le origini dei monachesimo gallico* Rome: Edizioni dell'Ateneo et Bizzarri, 1978.

Prinz, Friedrich. *Frühes Mönchtum im Frankenreich. Kultur und Gesellschaft in*

Gallien, den Rheinlanden und Bayern am Beispiel der monastische Entwicklung (4.–8. Jahrhundert). Munich: Oldenbourg, 1965.

Ramage, E. S. *Urbanitas: Ancient Sophistication and Refinement*. Norman: University of Oklahoma Press, 1973.

Randers-Pehrson, Justine Davis. *Barbarians and Romans: The Birth Struggle of Europe, A.D. 400–700*. Norman: University of Oklahoma Press, 1983.

Reinhold, Meyer. "Usurpation of Status and Status Symbols in the Roman Empire." *Historia* 20 (1971): 275–302.

Reuter, Timothy, ed. *The Medieval Nobility: Studies on the Ruling Classes of France and Germany from the Sixth to the Twelfth Century*. Amsterdam: North Holland, 1979.

Reydellet, M. *La royauté dans la littérature latine de Sidoine Apollinaire à Isidore de Séville*. Rome: Ecole française de Rome, 1981.

Riché, Pierre. *Education et culture dans l'Occident barbare, VIe–VIIIe siécles*. Paris: Editions du Seuil, 1962. Trans. John Contreni as *Education and Culture in the Barbarian West, Sixth through Eighth Centuries* (Columbia: University of South Carolina Press, 1976).

Rouche, Michel. *L'Aquitaine des Wisigoths aux Arabes, 418–781: Naissance d'une région* Paris: Touzot, 1979.

Rousseau, Philip. *Ascetics, Authority, and the Church in the Age of Jerome and Cassian*. Oxford: Clarendon, 1978.

Seeck, Otto. *Geschichte des Untergangs der antiken Welt*. Vol. 6. Stuttgart: J. B. Metzler, 1920; rpt. 1966.

———. *Regesten der Kaiser und Päpste für die Jahre 311 bis 476 n. Chr. Vorarbeit zu einer Prosopographie der christlichen Kaiserzeit*. Stuttgart: J. B. Metzler, 1919.

Selle-Hosbach, Karin. *Prosopographie merowingischer Amtsträger in der Zeit von 511 bis 613*. Bonn: Selle-Hosbach, 1974.

Shanzer, Danuta. "Dating the Baptism of Clovis: The Bishop of Vienne vs the Bishop of Tours." *Early Medieval Europe* 7 (1998): 29–57.

Sprandel, Rolf. "Struktur und Geschichte des merowingischen Adels." *Historische Zeitschrift* 193 (1961): 33–71.

Stein, Ernst. *Geschichte des spätrömischen Reiches vom römischen zum byzantinischen Staate (284–476 n. Chr.)*. Vienna: L. W. Seidel und Sohn, 1928. Trans. Jean-Rémy Palanque as *Histoire du Bas-Empire*, vol. 1: *De l'état romaine à l'état byzantine (284–476)* (Paris: Desclée de Brouwer, 1959; rpt. Amsterdam: A. M. Hakkert, 1968).

Stephenson, Carl. "The Common Man in Early Medieval Europe." *American Historical Review* 51 (1946): 419–38.

Stroheker, Karl F. *Der senatorische Adel im spätantiken Gallien*. Tübingen: Alma Mater, 1948; rpt. Darmstadt: Wissenschaftlichen Buchgesellschaft, 1970.

Sundwall, Johannes. *Abhandlungen zur Geschichte des ausgehenden Römertums*. Helsinki: Centraltryckeri och Bokbinderi Aktiebolag, 1919; rpt. New York: Arno Press, 1975.

———. *Weströmische Studien*. Berlin: Mayer and Müller, 1915.

Thompson, Edward A. *Romans and Barbarians: The Decline of the Western Empire.* Madison: University of Wisconsin Press, 1982.

———. *Saint Germanus of Auxerre and the End of Roman Britain.* Woodbridge: Boydell Press, 1984.

Van Dam, Raymond. *Leadership and Community in Late Antique Gaul.* Berkeley and Los Angeles: University of California Press, 1985.

Wallace-Hadrill, John M. *The Long-Haired Kings, and Other Studies in Frankish History.* New York: Barnes and Noble, 1962.

Webster, Leslie, and Michelle Brown, eds. *The Transformation of the Roman World, A.D. 400–900.* Berkeley and Los Angeles: University of California Press, 1997.

Whittaker, C. R. *Frontiers of the Roman Empire: A Social and Economic Study.* Baltimore: Johns Hopkins University Press, 1994.

Wickham, Chris J. *Early Medieval Italy: Central Power and Local Society, 400–1000.* Totowa, N.J.: Barnes and Noble, 1981.

Corpora of Inscriptions

Allmer, A., and P. Dissard, eds. *Musée de Lyon: Inscriptions antiques.* 4 vols. Lyon, 1888–94.

Dessau, H., ed., *Inscriptiones latinae selectae.* 2d ed. 5 vols. Berlin: Weidmann, 1954–55.

Diehl, E., ed. *Inscriptiones latinae christianae veteres.* Berlin, 1925–31.

Espérandieu, E., ed. *Inscriptions latines de Gaule (Narbonnaise).* Paris, 1929.

Gauthier, N., ed. *Recueil des inscriptions chrétiennes de la Gaule.* Vol. 1: *Prémière Belgique.* Paris: Centre national de la recherche scientifique, 1975.

Hirschfeld, O., ed. *Corpus inscriptionum latinarum.* Vol. 12: *Inscriptiones Galliae Narbonensis latinae.* Berlin, 1888.

Hirschfeld, O., C. Zangenmeister, A. von Domaszewski, O. Bohn, and E. Stein, eds. *Corpus inscriptionum latinarum.* Vol. 13: *Inscriptiones Trium Galliarum et Germaniarum latinae.* Berlin, 1899–1943.

Le Blant, E., ed. *Inscriptions chrétiennes de la Gaule antérieures au VIIIe siècle.* Paris, 1856–65.

Wieullemier, P., ed. *Inscriptions latines des Trois Gaules, Gallia.* Supp. 17. Paris: Centre national de la recherche scientifique, 1963.

Sources in Translation

Adelson, Howard L., ed. *Medieval Commerce.* Princeton: Van Nostrand, 1962.

Ambrose. *Letters.* Trans. Mary Melchior Beyenka. New York: Fathers of the Church, 1954.

Ammianus Marcellinus. *Ammianus Marcellinus.* Trans. John C. Rolfe. 3 vols. London: Loeb, 1963.

———. *The Roman History of Ammianus Marcellinus.* Trans. C. D. Yonge. London: Bohn, 1887.

Augustine. *Commentary on the Lord's Sermon on the Mount with Seventeen Related Sermons.* Trans. Denis J. Kavanagh. New York: Fathers of the Church, 1951.

———. *Concerning the City of God against the Pagans.* Trans. David Knowler. London: Penguin, 1972.

———. *Confessions.* Trans. R. S. Pine-Coffin. London: Penguin, 1961.

———. *The Happy Life, Answer to Skeptics, Divine Providence and the Problem of Evil, Soliloquies.* Trans. Ludwig Schopp et al. New York: Cima, 1948.

———. *Letters.* Trans. Wilfrid Parsons. New York: Fathers of the Church, 1951–89.

———. *On Christian Doctrine.* Trans. D. W. Robertson. New York: Bobbs-Merrill, 1958.

———. *On Free Choice of the Will.* Trans. Anna S. Benjamin and L. H. Hackstaff. New York: Bobbs-Merrill, 1964.

———. *Treatises on Various Subjects: The Christian Life, Against Lying, Continence, Patience, The Excellence of Widowhood, The Work of Monks, The Usefulness of Fasting, The Eight Questions of Dulcitius.* Trans. Mary Sarah Muldowney et al. New York: Fathers of the Church, 1952.

Ausonius. *Ausonius: With an English Translation.* Trans. Hugh G. Evelyn White. 2 vols. London: Loeb, 1919.

Bachrach, Bernard S., trans. *Liber historiae Francorum.* Lawrence: Coronado Press, 1973.

Brentano, Robert, ed. *The Early Middle Ages, 500–1000.* New York: Free Press, 1964.

Brittain, F., ed. *Penguin Book of Latin Verse.* London: Penguin, 1962.

Caesarius of Arles. *Caesarius of Arles: Life, Testament, Letters.* Trans. W. Klingshirn. Liverpool: Liverpool University Press, 1994.

———. *The Rule for Nuns of Caesarius of Arles: A Translation with a Critical Introduction.* Trans. C. McCarthy. Washington, D.C.: Catholic University of America Press, 1960.

———. *Sermons.* Trans. Mary Magdeleine Mueller. Vols. 1–2. New York: Fathers of the Church, 1956.

Cantor, Norman F., ed. *The Medieval Reader.* New York: Harper-Collins, 1994.

Cassian, John. *The Works of John Cassian.* Trans. Edgar C. S. Gibson. New York, 1894.

Cassiodorus. *An Introduction to Divine and Human Readings.* Trans. L. W. Jones. New York: Columbia University Press, 1946.

———. *The Letters of Cassiodorus, Being a Condensed Translation of the Variae Epistolae of Magnus Aurelius Cassiodorus Senator.* Trans. Thomas Hodgkin. London: H. Frowde, 1886.

———. *The Variae of Magnus Aurelius Cassiodorus Senator.* Trans. S. J. B. Barnish. Liverpool: Liverpool University Press, 1992.

Claudian. *Claudian's Panegyric on the Fourth Consulate of Honorius.* Trans. William Barr. Liverpool: Liverpool University Press, 1981.

Drew, Katherine F., trans. *The Burgundian Code: Book of Constitutions or Law of*

Gundobad. Additional Enactments. Philadelphia: University of Pennsylvania Press, 1949.

———. *The Laws of the Salian Franks.* Philadelphia: University of Pennsylvania Press, 1991.

———. *The Lombard Laws.* Philadelphia: University of Pennsylvania Press, 1973.

Ennodius. *The Life of Saint Epiphanius by Ennodius.* Trans. G. M. Cook. Washington, D.C.: Catholic University, 1942.

Eugippius. *The Life of S. Severinus by Eugippius.* Trans. George W. Robinson. Cambridge, Mass.: Harvard University Press, 1914.

———. *Leben des heiligen Severin.* Trans. Ludwig Bieler. Washington, D.C.: Catholic University of America Press, 1965.

Eusebius of Caesarea. *Eusebius' Praeparatio Evangelica: Selections from Gaisford's Text.* Trans. J. Edwin de Hirsch-Devine. Lampeter, 1904.

———. *The History of the Church from Christ to Constantine.* Trans. G. A. Williamson. New York: Penguin, 1989.

Fairley, W., trans. *Notitia Dignitatum or Register of Dignitaries.* In *Translations and Reprints from the Original Sources of European History,* vol. 6, no. 4. Philadelphia: University of Pennsylvania Press, 1900.

Fredegarius. *The Fourth Book of the Chronicle of Fredegar with Its Continuations.* Trans. J. M. Wallace-Hadrill. London: Greenwood, 1960.

Fremantle, Anne, ed. *A Treasury of Early Christianity.* New York: Viking, 1953.

Geary, Patrick J., ed. *Readings in Medieval History.* Peterborough, Ont.: Broadview, 1989.

Gennadius. *Jerome and Gennadius, Lives of Illustrious Men.* Trans. E. C. Richardson. New York, 1892.

Gordon, Colin D. *The Age of Attila: Fifth-Century Byzantium and the Barbarians.* Ann Arbor: University of Michigan Press, 1966.

Gregory of Tours. *Glory of the Confessors.* Trans. Raymond Van Dam. Liverpool: Liverpool University Press, 1988.

———. *Glory of the Martyrs.* Trans. Raymond Van Dam. Liverpool: Liverpool University Press, 1988.

———. *The History of the Franks.* Trans. Lewis Thorpe. London: Penguin, 1974.

———. *The History of the Franks by Gregory of Tours.* Trans. O. M. Dalton. Vol. 2. Oxford: Clarendon, 1927.

———. *History of the Franks by Gregory, Bishop of Tours: Selections, Translated with Notes.* Trans. Ernest Brehaut. New York: Norton, 1969.

———. *Life of the Fathers.* Trans. Edward James. Liverpool: Liverpool University Press, 1985.

Henderson, E. F. *Select Historical Documents of the Middle Ages.* London: Bell, 1892.

Hillgarth, J. N., ed. *The Conversion of Western Europe, 350–750.* Englewood Cliffs, N.J.: Prentice-Hall, 1969.

Hoare, F. R., trans. *The Western Fathers: Being the Lives of Martin of Tours, Ambrose, Augustine of Hippo, Honoratus of Arles, and Germanus of Auxerre.* Trans. F. R. Hoare. New York: Sheed and Ward, 1954.

John the Lydian. *On the Magistracies of the Roman Constitution.* Trans. T. F. Carney. Lawrence: Coronado, 1971.

Jordanes. *The Origin and Deeds of the Goths.* Trans. C. C. Mierow. Princeton: Princeton University Press, 1915.

Justinian. *The Digest of Roman Law: Theft, Rapine, Damage, and Insult.* Trans. C. F. Kolbert. London: Penguin, 1979.

Leo the Great. *The Letters and Sermons of Leo the Great.* Trans. C. Feltoe. New York, 1895.

Maas, Michael. *Readings in Late Antiquity: A Sourcebook.* London: Routledge, 2000.

Mathisen, Ralph W. *Ruricius of Limoges and Friends: A Collection of Letters from Visigothic Aquitania.* Liverpool: University of Liverpool Press, 1999.

McDermott, William C., ed. *Monks, Bishops, and Pagans: Christian Culture in Gaul and Italy, 500–700. Sources in Translation Including the World of Gregory of Tours.* Philadelphia: University of Pennsylvania Press, 1975.

McHugh, Michael P., trans. *The Carmen de Providentia Dei Attributed to Prosper of Aquitaine.* Washington, D.C.: Catholic University of America Press, 1964.

McNamara, Jo Ann, John E. Halborg, and E. Gordon Whatley, trans. *Sainted Women of the Dark Ages.* Durham, N.C.: Duke University Press, 1992.

Mendell, C. W., ed. *Latin Poetry Before and After.* Hamden, Conn.: Archon, 1970.

Murray, Alexander C. *From Roman to Merovingian Gaul: A Reader.* Peterborough, Ont.: Broadview, 2000.

Nestorius. *The Bazaar of Heracleides.* Trans. G. R. Driver. Oxford: Clarendon, 1925.

Nixon, C. E. V., and Barbara Saylor Rodgers, trans. *In Praise of Later Roman Emperors.* Berkeley: University of California Press, 1994.

Orientius of Auch. *The Commonitorium of Orientius.* Trans. M. D. Tobin, Washington, D.C.: Catholic University, 1945.

Paul the Deacon. *History of the Langobards.* Trans. W. D. Foulke. New York: Longmans-Green, 1907.

Paulinus of Nola. *The Letters of St. Paulinus of Nola.* Trans. P. G. Walsh. 2 vols. Westminster, Md.: Newmann, 1966–67.

Peter Chrysologus. *Selected Sermons* (with Saint Valerian, *Homilies*). Trans. George F. Ganss. New York: Fathers of the Church, 1953.

Pharr, Clyde, trans. *The Theodosian Code and Novels and the Sirmondian Constitutions.* Princeton: Princeton University Press, 1952.

Pomerius, Julianus. *The Vita Contemplativa of Julianus Pomerius.* Trans. Mary Josephine Suelzer. Westminster, 1947.

Procopius. *Procopius. History of the Wars.* Trans. H. B. Dewing. London: Loeb, 1914.

Rivers, Theodore J., trans. *Laws of the Alamans and Bavarians.* Philadelphia: University of Pennsylvania Press, 1977.

———. *Laws of the Salian and Ripuarian Franks.* New York: AMS, 1986.

Salvian of Marseille. *On the Government of God.* Trans. Eva M. Sanford. New York: Columbia University Press, 1930.

————. *The Writings of Salvian, the Presbyter.* Trans. Jeremiah F. O'Sullivan. New York: Cima, 1947.

Sidonius Apollinaris. *The Letters of Sidonius.* Trans. O. M. Dalton. 2 vols. Oxford: Clarendon, 1915.

————. *Poems and Letters.* Trans. W. B. Anderson. 2 vols. London: Loeb, 1936, 1965.

Stevenson, J., ed. *Creeds, Councils, and Controversies: Documents Illustrative of the History of the Church, A.D. 337–461.* New York: Seabury, 1966.

Sulpicius Severus. *The Works of Sulpicius Severus.* Trans. Alexander Roberts. New York, 1894.

Thatcher, Oliver J., and Edgar H. McNeal, eds. *A Source Book for Medieval History.* New York: Scribner, 1905.

Theophanes. *The Chronicle of Theophanes: An English Translation of "anni mundi 6095–6305" (A.D. 602–813).* Trans. Harry Turtledove. Philadelphia: University of Pennsylvania Press, 1982.

Tyconius. *The Book of Rules of Tyconius.* Trans. F. C. Burkitt. Cambridge: Cambridge University Press, 1894.

Venantius Fortunatus. *Venantius Fortunatus: Personal and Political Poems.* Trans. Judith George. Liverpool: Liverpool University Press, 1995.

Vincentius of Lérins. *The Commonitory of Vincent of Lérins.* Trans. C. A. Heurtley. New York: Cima, 1894.

E. Walford, trans. *The Greek Ecclesiastical Historians of the First Six Centuries of the Christian Era.* 6 vols. London: Bagster, 1843–46. Eusebius, vols. 1–2, Socrates Scholasticus, vol. 3, Sozomen, vol. 4, Theodoret, vol. 5, Evagrius, vol. 6.

Walsh, Gerald G., et al., trans. *Niceta of Remesiana, Writings. Sulpicius Severus, Writings. Vincent of Lerins, Commonitories. Prosper of Aquitaine, Grace and Free Will.* Washington, D.C.: Catholic University of America Press, 1949.

Zachariah. *The Syriac Chronicle Known as That of Zachariah of Mytilene.* Trans. F. J. Hamilton and E. W. Brooks. London: Methuen, 1899.

Zosimus. *The History of Count Zosimus.* Trans. J. Davis, W. Green, and T. Chaplin. London: Methuen, 1814.

————. *The New History.* Trans. Ronald T. Ridley. Sydney: Australian Association for Byzantine Studies, 1982.

Index